CALL HIM GEORGE

GEORGE LEWIS

Call Him George

Jay Allison Stuart

LONDON : PETER DAVIES

FIRST PUBLISHED 1961

Printed in Great Britain for Peter Davies Limited by Novello and Company Limited London W 1

This book is dedicated, with gratitude and affection, to those three wise men with understanding hearts:

William Russell, Alfred Lion, and David Stuart.

They know why.

preface

ONE spring night in 1959 an earnest, intense young man came to me during the intermission of a George Lewis concert in Denmark. His English was excellent, though slowed a bit by nervousness. He was a most determined Dane. He had long been wanting the answers to certain questions about George Lewis and now he meant to have them. As he questioned me I noticed that he used the first person plural—"we"—and I realized suddenly that he was a spokesman for thousands of people we had seen during the preceding weeks in Great Britain and Europe, hundreds of whom had besieged both George and me for answers to these same questions. And for an equal number in George Lewis's own country who seek him out relentlessly on every engagement to ask questions which have by now become notable for their similarity.

At the end of the questioning the young man thanked me, and then said: "You cannot realize how much it means to us to know about this man. We love him very much, and it is not only as a great musician that we love him, but as a man. We know that much that has been written about him is wrong and mistaken, but it is all we have to go by. We wish we knew him better."

His words sparked the fire beneath the biography of George Lewis that I had been "going to write" for many years. During those years material for the book was being gathered in strange and out of the way places, written on any surface that would take the imprint of pen or pencil or, on more than one occasion, lipstick. My notes had accumulated until they threatened to make a tent-dweller of me. My "reference library" was a succession of boxes, growing progressively larger as the years went on. There

were no books in that library, only bits and pieces and oddments of paper: the backs of envelopes; hastily purchased notebooks, purse size; scraps of programmes; menus; a "reserved" sign from the table of a Chicago night club on which, in cramped handwriting, I attempted to capture some of the wisdom and the memories of Baby Dodds; an airplane ticket envelope from which I would eventually decipher the story told to me by an aged Negro in San Francisco, about the first time he heard George Lewis in New Orleans many years before. There are notes in my "library" on envelopes and stationery from hotels in New York, San Francisco, Los Angeles, Cincinnati, Chicago, London, Manchester, Odense, Stockholm, Malmo, Berlin and points north, south, east and west of these.

In amassing these notes I have eavesdropped shamelessly, sitting in trains and airplanes, in hotel lobbies, on transatlantic steamers, at breakfast, lunch and dinner during road tours after George Lewis and his men had come to accept me as an equal and a friend, and—what was more important—frequently merely a forgotten part of the general surroundings.

There is no trustworthy documentation available, either for a biography of George Lewis or a true history of the music which he plays. I saw the members of the George Lewis band while away a five-hour train trip from Cincinnati to Chicago one day, figuratively tearing to bits a supposedly "factual" book on New Orleans music, written by a self-styled expert. (There are no true experts on this music except the musicians themselves.) When George and the men had finished with the book, I estimated roughly that at least sixty per cent of it had been erroneous, and that errors regarding George Lewis accounted for about twenty per cent of that sixty per cent. The men in many instances spotted unerringly the sources of the mistakes. A great deal of it had obviously been obtained from a single source, and no attempt made to re-check the stories.

For a goodly part of my adult life I was a newspaper reporter and writer, working for conservative and what might be called by the captious "pernickety" editors. I had grown to regard facts with deep respect, if not downright affection.

I cringed when I read, in 1956, the phrase of an American critic: "Lewis's decade as a leader." I had sat quietly by on many occasions when George Lewis and Henry Allen, Jr., had reminisced about the first time Henry had played a professional

date with a band led by George Lewis in 1923. Playing not ten feet away from the critic a few nights before the "decade as a leader" phrase was written were George and his trumpeter, Thomas Jefferson, who had played his first professional date with a band led by George twenty-four years before, when Jefferson was in his teens, and Lewis thirty-two.

A monograph purporting to deal with Lewis, published in England, sent my blood pressure soaring, yet it was unfair of me to criticise for I knew that it could only be a re-hash of other equally erroneous accounts, some of them definitely biased. Much of the misinformation is traceable to one bitter source, but a great deal unfortunately appears to be the result of sheer laziness, and lack of an all-essential instinct for accuracy on the part of the writers. Only very few writers—they can be counted on less than the fingers of one hand—have ever bothered to check with what should have been the primary source of their biographical sketches of George Lewis—the man himself.

Therefore those who dote on such things will look in vain for a bibliography. Except for general historical data regarding the city of New Orleans, the material in this book has come from the tenacious and almost photographic memory of its subject, a man who prefers silence to talk, and truth above all else. It has come also from the memories and knowledge of his family, and of his contemporaries and friends of both races, not only in New Orleans but scattered throughout the United States. When I had reason to doubt the accuracy of the information or to believe that it was given either from a desire to please, or from more ulterior motives, I have discarded it. Not all of the information, by any means, came from George Lewis. Certain incidents were checked and re-checked with other persons involved, many of them incidents about which George was reluctant to go into detail because he felt that by doing so he might hurt others—or the surviving members of a family that might be involved.

Writing a biography of a living person is a difficult task at best. Everywhere sensitive toes obtrude themselves, and seem to beg to be stepped on. Where I have felt the stepping-on to be deserved I have done so without hesitation. But I sincerely hope that those to whom the toes belong will realize that the offending feet that tread upon their sensitiveness are the feet of the writer of this book, and not its subject; that their inevitable anger because of their trod-upon toes will vent itself upon the treader and not

upon the person who made this book possible—a man who would not willingly tread upon the toes of his worst enemy.

To attempt to thank all of those who helped me along the way would be impossible. To acknowledge my debt to a few and not to all would be distasteful. But there are no words strong enough to describe the magnitude of my debt to one of the greatest human beings I have ever known—George Lewis's mother, Mrs Alice Zeno. There can be no forgetting the days I spent in George's home in Algiers, listening while her incredibly active mind ranged back to her childhood with her grandmother, Zaier, and her mother, Mrs Urania Pacquet, through her girlhood and womanhood, and on through the infancy and childhood of "her boy." Yet the information which she gave me is not the sole reason for my gratitude, for Alice Zeno showed me vistas of life I had never seen before, the horizonless vistas of the faith and courage and indomitable spirit of her people.

And my thankfulness is infinite when I consider the kind Providence that set my feet on the strange path that led to this inevitable destination—a book about George Lewis.

The first discussion of the book was held in London in the spring of 1959, a few weeks after the questing young Dane had kindled the fire beneath it. When Mr Nicholas Davies expressed sincere interest in its publication, I returned to the hotel where George, his band, and I were staying. George, by then (his second trip to England) a confirmed and habitual afternoon-tea drinker, was sitting in the lounge contentedly consuming large quantities of that beverage.

"There may be a book about you published before too long, George," I said to him.

George's reaction to good news of any kind is almost invariable. The news is first taken in, there is a brief pause while it is examined mentally for flaws, for possible falseness, for hidden pitfalls of disappointment, then—if it passes muster—there is a quick, wide smile, and happy acceptance. This time the smile came a little more slowly and was preceded by a small frown of puzzlement. When at last it did appear, warm and glowing, it was composed of equal parts of incredulity, delight, and bewilderment.

"A book about *me*?" said George Lewis. "Why?"

If I have answered that question I shall be content.

Book One

"Has thou known how I fashioned thee,
Child, underground;
Fire that impassioned thee,
Iron that bound,
Dim changes of water, what thing of all
these hast thou known of or found?"

CHARLES ALGERNON SWINBURNE
"Hertha"

one

ZAIER, the Senegalese woman, was in her hundredth year when she delivered her granddaughter, Alice Zeno, of her third child. The birth took place on July 13, 1900, just as the first grey streaks of a muggy dawn struggled through the shutters of an old house on St Claude Street, in the French Quarter of New Orleans.

Evidences of poverty were everywhere: in the tightly folded newspapers used to stuff the wide cracks in the walls; the primitive, charcoal burning, brazier-type stove on which a pan of water was heating, and the larger pan of water on the floor, filled from the cistern in the yard. The house was without plumbing or drains. An oil lamp furnished the only light. But it was spotlessly clean. The floor was freshly scrubbed, and because Alice and her husband, Henry Zeno, had been battling a persistent invasion of ants, the area around the makeshift, carefully prepared crib showed signs of extra hard scrubbing. So worried had Alice been that the devilish red insects would return and find the baby it had almost been necessary for the women present—her grandmother, her mother, and a midwife—to force her to bed when her time came.

Her frenzied concern for this child was understandable. Although she had borne two children previously, both had died within a short time after they first glimpsed the world that lay in wait for them. Because of this she had been praying incessantly to God and most of His saints, in particular St Joseph and St Francis, that this baby be permitted to live.

She had promised the saints that if she was granted this boon, and the child was a boy, she would name him Joseph Lewis Francis Zeno.

Although Zaier had delivered many scores of babies in her

lifetime, she urged that a younger woman be called in to handle this birth. Alice, who adored her grandmother, had protested, but finally consented reluctantly, demanding, however, that Zaier at least be present.

The bells of nearby St Augustine's Church were tolling the Angelus when the midwife found herself in difficulties, and called Zaier from her chair in the corner to assist her. The old woman's long-fingered black hands were extraordinarily deft and skilful, even after a hundred years, and now they ministered expertly to her granddaughter.

At her side was her daughter, Urania, Alice's mother, and when the baby was safely delivered Zaier handed him to his grandmother, murmuring in Creole, "He's a little one, this one." And, more loudly, to the mother: "But he's a fighter, Alice. Don't fret. The Angelus is ringing."

When Urania came to her mother's side a little later, carrying the newly-bathed baby, the child sneezed loudly and unmistakeably. Urania laughed with delight. The sneeze was a good omen. She could not explain then or in the years to come why she said what she did at that particular moment. Perhaps during her childhood, in the home in which she and her mother had grown up as slaves, she had heard tales of a famous dragon-killer told to the children; perhaps she had seen in their story-books pictures of a man slaying with his sword a fire-breathing monster that destroyed all who came near. Certainly the grandson she held in strong, graceful hands was to need the courage of a St George, for the dragons lying in wait on the road ahead were many. Whatever her motivation, as she laid the baby in his mother's arms Urania said:

"Call him George. This one will live!"

two

MORE than a century and a half ago an eight-year-old girl crouched in a cage on the deck of a slave ship bound for the Port of New Orleans from Senegal, West Africa. The sound of the drums of her tribe, spreading the news of the slave raid, had come

over the water throughout a long night, and she had huddled wide-awake, breath almost stopped in an anguish of listening. At daybreak a dark green shadow on the horizon was still recognizable as home, but the drum beats had faded entirely. She never heard them again.

Her name was Zaier, and little more than twelve hours before she and five of her playmates had climbed the bank of a reed-bordered stream, dripping from a swim. Their shouts and laughter as they played in the water had kept them from hearing the bearded man approach, and the children did not see him until they were on the bank. The bright beads he showed them dangled from pudgy, thick fingers, and the children sidled toward him in cautious wonderment. None of them was more than nine years old, some were less.

In later years Zaier described the man to her children and grandchildren. She told them how amazed she and her playmates had been at his light skin and eyes, and strangeness of his outer clothing. She described, too, the clumsy way he moved through the grass and foliage, so unlike the grace and swiftness of her people. And she told how the sure-footed children had followed him with the wary, tentative curiosity of kittens. Until that day they had never been afraid of any living thing except reptiles and predatory animals.

The bearded man led them to a small boat on the river and with smiles and gestures promised them he would give them the beads if they would come aboard. The other white-skinned men at the rail of the boat were smiling, too, and the children's wet brown feet padded up the gangplank to the deck.

There may be a credit somewhere on the bearded man's record, for he tossed each of them a string of the gaudy trinkets before the boat pulled away, and after their cages had been made secure. He and the others were panting before the job was done, Zaier said. It had not been easy to secure the cages, for the children of Zaier's tribe were strong, and they fought their captors like wild animals.

They were not released again, even when the small boat rendezvoused with the larger boat, its hold already crammed with captives, to which they were transferred.

The eight years of Zaier's life had been happy ones. Her slim, straight body had thrived under the warm tropic sun and the sudden, cooling rains. Even the steaming heat that flowed from

the earth had been a pleasant thing, bringing the growth of tall grasses and gay, splendid flowers. From these Zaier made garlands for her mother, her slender, long-boned hands plaiting them with lightning speed. Zaier's descendants were to inherit these hands, and a hundred and fifty years later her great-grandson, George Lewis, was to raise them imploringly before clamorous audiences in great cities, begging silence so that he could continue to play his music.

Shock, numbing terror, homesickness, and finally dumb resignation to a fate she could not understand or change, obliterated many of the details of those caged weeks from Zaier's mind. She recalled body-racking illness, and that her mother's name, Bi-a, was constantly on her lips. She remembered what must have been a fever, and that three of her playmates were carried away, no longer sobbing, grey now instead of black, looking more like their captors in those first moments of death than like those of their own race. But a toughness of spirit, a tenacity of will, carried Zaier through, while adults, healthy and strong a few weeks before, died by the score in the hold of the ship.

The New Orleans to which Zaier was brought had only recently come under American rule. It was a comparatively small community, still under the influences of previous French and Spanish administrations. In 1803, five years before Zaier's involuntary arrival, it had consisted of about 4,000 houses, and 10,000 inhabitants. Approximately 5,000 of these were whites and 2,000 free Negroes. The remainder were slaves. Law enforcement was lax, and a criminal element of multiple origins was in almost full control of the swampy settlement, an element destined to remain in virtual control for nearly a hundred years. Starting at Levee (Decatur Street), the town was 600 yards in depth, with only a few houses beyond Dauphine Street. The most heavily settled area sprawled for 1200 yards along the Mississippi River front, and a stockade enclosed the town. Forts stood at all four corners, and what is now Canal Street was a water-filled moat. A gallows was erected on the site where the statue of General Jackson now stands. Pillories, usually occupied, stood on Chartres Street, facing the Cabildo. These pillories, abolished as punishment for whites in 1827, continued to be used as a means of punishing and humiliating Negroes until 1847.

Zaier was never permitted to see those of her people who had survived the voyage in the hold of the ship, but was sold almost

immediately to a Creole family living in the city. They clothed her and brought her to another of their slaves, an old man from Senegal, who spoke to her in her own dialect. After the hell of the ship, happiness had become a relative thing. Zaier told her children that when she met the old man from her own country her joy was so great she thought her heart would burst. She never forgot him, and spoke his name even in the last years of her life when, after ten decades of absence, she slipped gradually and peacefully back to her childhood in Senegal; while the world around her became as strange as it had been when she was first freed from the cage that brought her to it.

The old man, and others of her country owned by the same family, told the child what she must and must not do to ensure a minimum of hardship. They tried to explain the ways of the white people, many of them ways that would never have been tolerated in the simple, fundamentally ethical life of the tribe from which she came. Once her fear had gone, she learned rapidly. Her new owners were kindly; good to her within the limitations of minds that could accept slavery, practise it, subsist upon its profits, and enjoy the comforts which its labour made possible. She never knew abuse, and was treated more as servant than slave. Scores of thousands of her countrymen were less fortunate.

But there remained within Zaier, as there remained within all her people, a fierce fire of independence, a feeling of individuality so strong that she was never able to acknowledge that she was any less a human being because she was a slave and black. And so she learned, as did all her race, a craft and method of meeting the world that showed only what she wished to show of her thoughts and feelings, and kept the others hidden or masked beyond recognition. Today in the deep South the people of her race are equally skilled. Although legally free for almost a hundred years, they have remained captives of a colour slavery as spiritually humiliating and almost as restrictive materially as the slavery of Zaier's time. They, too, know and use with consummate skill the art of masking fear with a show of respect, resentment with deference, and contempt with good-natured laughter. In this respect the Negro of the South has always resembled the iceberg of arctic waters, which shows a scant one-tenth of its substance above the surface, while the remaining nine-tenths, which give it direction and movement, lie submerged and hidden from sight. It has had to be so for survival.

There is, however an exception to this rule: The rising generation of young college students, just emerging from adolescence, which has discarded forever the masks and posturings earlier generations assumed for survival's sake. In earlier times their counterparts, refusing to adapt, would have been killed in the riots and uprisings they instigated; or, if they had escaped, lived out their lives perpetually hunted, in swamp and bayou, like animals. But today's young Negro of the South is pulling himself up by bootstraps his ancestors never had—education and learning—and, his back turned against violence, has begun a quiet, dignified, inexorable march toward freedom. There is abundant evidence that the greater part of the thinking world is with him.

In Zaier's youth New Orleans was a city in which three languages were spoken interchangeably: French, Spanish, and English. Zaier learned rapidly all that she needed to know of them. She grew up speaking what is known as "Creole," a patois of French and Spanish, to which she added many of the "gombo" phrases of her native country.

After she had learned the language, religious instruction followed. During the French régime the Bienville Black Code had required that all slave-owners give religious instruction to their slaves. Even those slave-owners who were not particularly religious themselves saw the merit in this, and throughout the South it became their custom to see that their chattels were thoroughly indoctrinated with the principles of Christianity. Although they were unschooled in the academic psychology of modern times, they were nevertheless well aware that religion could become a far more effective weapon than guns or whips against the rebellions of the human spirit.

Zaier's master, a Roman Catholic, taught her about a God, just and kind, though stern, who ruled the universe and was the Father of all men. She was instructed in the manner in which she must address Him if she wanted her prayers to be well received. She was told that her prayers would be answered only if it was for her own good, and, therefore, in accordance with His will. If at times these teachings were dimmed by resurgent memories of tribal rites, it might have been because the mind of a child could not understand why it was not for her own good that she be returned to a reed-bordered stream in Senegal, and the warm, protective love of her mother. There were still nights when she would sob herself to sleep with the word "Bi-a" on her lips.

But eventually she learned not to question the contradictions of the Christian doctrine inherent in the customs of those times. Whether Roman Catholic or Protestant, the religion of Christianity gave to an enslaved people an anchor to windward that kept them from destruction. The Christian teaching of a happy after-life for the good was necessary to maintain reason. Somewhere the burden would be lifted; some time they could lay it down. It would not be here and now, in the world in which they lived and toiled. That much was made clear to them. But God had promised it, and "let it be, dear Lord, let it be." When a group of Negroes sings "Walking With the King" it is without the reservations that exist in the minds of those who have permitted their intellects to carry them beyond the simplicity of blind faith. They sing it with a knowledge no man can take from them that on a long, lonely road there is a Royal Companion, who will not leave them. When they sing "Take my hand, Precious Lord" it is with supreme faith that He will do just that.

And the religion of their captors gave them another teaching, something they could understand and grasp even better than generalizations about God. It was that God so loved His people that He sent His only son into the world to suffer and die for them. This was a concrete thing, a teaching which personalized their faith, and brought it into their cabins, and into the fields and the kitchens where they worked. It gave them a friend who was human, as they were human, with the added grace of divinity; a friend who was not so preoccupied with affairs of the universe that He could not lay an arm across their shoulders and ease their burden. Nowhere in this teaching did it say that this man who had come to help the world and the poor people in it had ever said "Suffer little white children to come unto me . . ." but only that he had said "Suffer little children . . .", and what else could they possibly assume but that when He said "As ye have done it unto the least of these . . ." He meant them?

Anyone who has ever attended a Good Friday service in a Negro church must have sensed the identification of these people with their Saviour. The tears and groans are not maudlin emotionalism. They are, rather, the tears and groans of a people for a man whose sufferings they believe paralleled their own; and they bring to the long, agonizing walk to Calvary their own knowledge of the burden of a cross as heavy as was their Saviour's. Because of this he is peculiarly *their* Saviour, *their* Jesus, *their* friend.

That the Negro of the South remained tractable for many generations because of the spiritual and emotional fervour with which he embraced the "no cross, no crown" theory of salvation almost goes without saying.

Eventually Zaier accepted the religion of her masters with a burning faith that she passed undiminished to her descendants. Although in later years her great-grandson was to turn from the strict orthodoxy of this religion, its basic tenet of faith in God was to sustain him and keep him going when, in the opinions of medical experts and laymen alike, he had reached the end of the road.

three

ZAIER'S owners never had cause to regret their purchase of the Senegalese child. It had been a good bargain. Much of the soundness of the bargain was due to Zaier's own attitude. She was always aware that sale to other masters could become a possibility, and she feared this more than she feared anything in the world. Friends she had grown fond of were sent away, and her first love affair ended abruptly when the young man was sold to owners of a rural plantation who needed strong labourers. News of these friends trickled back to the slave quarters through the grapevine that always exists in any community, from city to prison, where groups of people live under repressive legal and social restrictions. Sometimes the news was good, sometimes it was bad. Then, too, as the years went on she developed a reserved affection for the white people who, if they did not give her the type of love a child craves and needs, did at least give her security and genuine kindness. Like many other slaves in the same circumstances her loyalty to the family she served was as strong as, and often stronger than, that of their own relatives.

A son, Arthur, was not destined for the good fortune she had enjoyed, for he was sold when only a boy to relatives of Zaier's owner. Although he had been born in slavery he had never accepted it or its implications, and his new owners were not appreciative of his independence. He was badly mistreated, and

frequently beaten—a situation that eventually came to Zaier's ears, and haunted her through long nights. Yet when the boy escaped from the slave quarters of his master's house and somehow found his way back to his mother, through the ill-lighted streets and by-ways, she held him close and comforted him, but then thrust him away and told him he must return to his owners. Frightened and sobbing, he refused, and then she ordered him sternly to obey her, and, as all of Zaier's children were wont to do, he followed her orders. He was too young to know the pain that twisted her heart when she saw him slip away into the darkness, the depth of anguish in her prayers to God that he return safely before his escape was discovered. And far too young to take comfort then from the words that followed him into the dark: "God will make it good."

Most of the provisions of Bienville's infamous Black Code were made the basis of laws passed by the Louisiana Legislature after the Americans assumed control. The first article of the original Code drawn up by Bienville when the colony was administered by the French provided for the expulsion of all Jews. The succeeding four articles dealt with compulsory religious instruction. Forty-nine additional articles dealt entirely with the conduct and government of the Negroes, and it was the spirit of these which remained in effect as state laws. Laws on the statute books today, while they cannot deal with Negroes as slaves, still embody much of the spirit of that code.

Among the repressive measures of this code were several which forbade, in various forms, any assemblage of Negroes belonging to different masters, under any pretext. The thirteenth article specifically provided for severe punishment for Negroes found gathering "in crowds, either by day or night, under the pretext of a wedding or any other cause, either at the dwelling or on the grounds of one of their masters, much less the highways or secluded places." Such transgressors were to be whipped, and for frequent offences were to be branded, and "should there be aggravating circumstances" killed.

Nor were white slave owners exempt from punishment if they permitted assemblages of Negroes on their property. Penalties for the whites were: for the first offence, a fine of one hundred crowns to the treasury of the church, and, for the next offence, a life sentence of work on the King's galleys. Whites continue to be held accountable for violations of today's "Jim Crow" laws in

the South, although the King's galleys have long since become history.

Bienville's *Code Noir* was to reach far into the future. More than two hundred years after the fear-provoking conditions which brought it into being, conditions which were, in the eyes of many a part of the glamour of old New Orleans, the Negroes of the South know that to openly defy the spirit of its laws is to invite disaster.

The New Orleans in which Zaier grew to womanhood was a city teeming with vice, rotten with corruption, its streets bloodied daily by violence. Although the strict curfew imposed on Negroes kept her from any first-hand knowledge of these conditions, she learned of them through the conversations of the whites, the warnings of her master, and through the grapevine of the slave quarters. Her revulsion against them was shown in the strictness with which she brought up her children, and the moral precepts she instilled so sternly in them and in her grandchildren.

She saw many things as she grew into womanhood in New Orleans: The marching soldiers on their way to repel the British in the battle of New Orleans; the slave dances in Congo Square; the beginnings of what was to become the internationally famous New Orleans Mardi Gras; the public punishment of slaves by whip and pillory; and later, the bewildering days of Union occupation, and the corruption of the Reconstruction period.

It is from the Negro of Zaier's day, and earlier days, that the injunction has been handed down from generation to generation: "Let the white man alone. Stay out of his business, and mind your own." Although up to a certain age Negro and white children play together in the South, Alice Zeno, Zaier's granddaughter, phrased the injunction to her son, making a little tune of it: "Play in your own back yard; never mind what the white child do."

There was one amelioration of the Black Code, however, after the Louisiana Purchase. Although the Americans who took over the reins of government then were by no means averse to slavery, recognizing it as the bulwark of the South's economy, they realized the serious danger inherent in the prevailing treatment of a constantly increasing number of blacks. They believed that a certain amount of social intercourse and mingling with his kind was essential if trouble from the Negroes was to be averted. Nothing seems to indicate that their actions were dictated by

anything other than a sort of enlightened self-interest, a self-interest which required that the Negro be kept reasonably content with his lot. And so, shortly after the Louisiana Purchase, slaves were permitted by the American authorities to gather in public on one day a week for dancing and singing.

The largest and most famous of the gathering places for the slaves was at Rampart and Orleans Street. First known as the *Place des Nègres*, it later became known as Congo Plains, and finally as Congo Square, a name given to it by the Negroes.

Here Zaier heard, at last, the counterpart of the drums she had listened to so helplessly in a cage on the deck of a slave ship. Here she saw again the native dances of the people of her country.

The dances were closely supervised by a considerable number of police. In fact, it was not until a police official gave the signal that the slaves were summoned to the centre of the square by one of their number, who did this by rattling two huge beef bones on the head of a cask which had been fashioned into a drum called a bamboula. Not only did the presence of the police serve to reassure the white people, fearful of consequences when so many Africans were allowed to congregate, but also served as a constant reminder to the slaves that this recreation was provided by the grace and favour of the white people, and that they played when permitted only, just as they worked when told.

Some of the dances lasted all day at first, but later settled into a routine of approximately three hours on Sunday afternoons, between four and seven o'clock.

As might have been expected, the reaction of most of the white citizens to this exhibition was definitely unfavourable. Yet crowds of them attended, watching in a sort of fascinated disapproval something they made no attempt to understand. On the outer edge of the square the little Negro children danced and leapt in unison with their elders, in a forerunner of the "second line" which still follows Negro parades in New Orleans today.

A few years ago Warren Dodds, known better as 'Baby' Dodds throughout his life, and one of the great drummers of modern times, said to the writer: "You white people who write and make talks about the music are mighty fine people. But you know, don't you, that none of you *really* knows anything about it?"

No one was better qualified to make that statement than Baby Dodds. His great-grandfather had been one of those drummers in

Congo Square, and passed down to Baby from him were the complicated rhythmic patterns of the drums so many white musicians have attempted to imitate, no one of them with any notable success.

Authorities on language have stated that in West Africa meaning is conveyed to a large extent by tone and accent, with the tone level of each single-voiced vowel carrying this meaning. A nineteenth-century Northern writer, attempting to describe the songs of Congo Square, referred to their "many-vowelled syllabification."

This tongue-twisting phrase, obscure though it sounds, does to a certain extent define the derivation of Negro music. To ears accustomed to speech dependent upon intonation and accent for meaning, the subtle changes to the quarter and even eighth tones were only natural in the music through which they expressed what they would not, or dared not, express in speech. It was possible in a phrase to convey so many things that could not be expressed with only whole and half tones to rely on. When later the Negroes found instruments through which to voice their emotions it is not surprising that from these instruments they brought tones impossible for other musicians to duplicate.

Once it is recognized that American Negro music is far more than the dictionary definition of the word "music" the truth of Baby Dodds's remark becomes clear. For the music of the Negro of the South has always been a language. Because it is a form of speech, of idea communication, its free improvisations are not surprising phenomena, but instead as natural as a conversation between two like-minded people. The world would be full of strange and stilted sounds if the everyday speech of humans was read from a book or score, instead of springing spontaneously from mind and heart.

There was no emotion or thought which was not expressed by the Negro through some form of music. Until he had access to instruments, these forms were confined for the most part to drums and voice. In the cotton fields, and on the docks and levees, the ache in a man's back became the song on his lips. That it was a song of sorrow and pain, and of stillborn rebellion, was his secret; all the whites knew was that the "darkies were always singing" and, therefore, must be a happy, extroverted lot. A woman sang a lullaby, half-prayer, to her baby, or she sang of her jealousy of her man; the singing in the fields and in the slave

quarters frequently masked a message or a warning, and frequently told a story. The Negro had ears to hear the message or the story; but to the white man—it was merely a strangely disturbing sound.

Just as the Negro made the religion of his master his own, giving to it a meaning incomprehensible to his instructor, so he made the music of that religion his own, enriching it and vitalizing it. Into the spirituals, so completely Negroid, were poured the whole history of his race, his faith, his longing for escape and freedom, and his belief in a God who would bring him that freedom, a Saviour who would comfort him, and a far-off land where he could at last lay down his burden of shame and servitude.

The words of many Negro spirituals not only envision the defeat of the enemy, shown symbolically in various forms, but also their complete faith that when they reach the other side of "the river" they will be welcomed by a Heavenly host all of whom will be colour blind. The spiritual "Pharaoh's Army Got Drownded" shows this as clearly as any.

"O Mary! don't you weep, don't you moan;
O Mary! don't you weep, don't you moan;
Pharaoh's army got drownded—
O Mary! don't you weep!

When we get to Heaven gonna sing and shout—
Ain't nobody in Heaven gonna throw us out—
Pharaoh's army got drownded—
O Mary! don't you weep!

Small wonder that the whites who watched the dancing and heard the singing in Congo Square came away amazed and bewildered, and that Baby Dodds said to me:

"You know, don't you, that none of you *really* knows anything about it?"

four

DANCING in Congo Square was abandoned during the troubled days following the capture and occupation of New Orleans by Union forces during the Civil War. But as late as 1880, the backyard of a property on Dumaine Street was still the scene of similar, though smaller, Negro gatherings.

Shortly before the Emancipation Proclamation was signed Zaier's master called her to him and told her that within a short time she and her family would be freed. She accepted the news calmly; the Negroes had long known the great day was coming, and she did not want to hurt her master's feelings by too great a show of joy. But her daughter Urania said that her mother's happiness was unbounded. Yet, there were reservations in that happiness. Zaier was too intelligent and too observant not to realize that the freedom they were being offered would be a limited one, and that for generations to come they would carry their fate in their colour. It had come too late to mean much to her or to her children. It was for her grandchildren her happiness was greatest. Zaier would have understood the incident that happened in Montgomery, Alabama, more than ninety years later, during the Negro boycott of segregated city buses.

A reporter from the North, sent to cover the boycott, stood one morning on a corner at which a group of Negroes gathered daily to meet the pool car that would take them to work. The meeting place was at a bus stop, and an empty city bus rolled slowly up. By this time the bus company was in such economic pain from the success of the boycott, drivers were not above such broad hints. As it drew up to the corner an aged Negro woman, bent, and walking with a cane, hobbled past, ignoring the bus. One of the young Negroes called to her:

"Hey, granmaw! Go on—git on the bus. This ain't for old

folks like you. Go on, you too old to be walkin' all that way to work. We're young—we can take it."

The old lady turned to the group of young men, and, shaking her cane, replied sharply, "Son, you mind your own business, hear? I ain't walkin' for myself. I'm walkin' for my grandbaby."

By 1862 Zaier's grandbabies were being born with great regularity. She knew her next grandchild, which her daughter Urania was expecting, would be born free, but she also knew that freedom would exact its price from her people. Refused the education they had begged for, forbidden to learn to read and write lest reading give them ideas and writing a means of communication difficult to control; denied any part in community life or responsibility for community government, they would be ill-prepared to take their place in a world in which they were believed to be inferior.

She knew that it rested upon her shoulders, and her children's shoulders to rear the coming generation to live safely in that limited freedom without rousing the always latent fears and antagonisms of the white people. It has rested on the shoulders of every Negro parent since that time to give their children that same rearing.

When the day of freedom came Zaier's master told her: "If you want to leave us we can't hold you. But freedom is not a good thing for the black. It is a bad thing, and if you leave you will live to see the day when you'll wish for the old days back."

He could have saved his breath. It had never occurred to Zaier to leave, to break the ties between herself and her master's family, now grown almost as strong as the ties of blood. Her daughter Urania chose to remain with her, and the two women continued to occupy the quarters they had always lived in, and to carry on the work they had always done.

Alice, Urania's first child, was born on June 6, 1863. Urania, who had married a man named Alfonse Pacquet, was to have five more children, one of whom died, but all of whom remained devoted to her throughout her life.

Zaier was remembered by Alice as a tall, handsome woman, even in her seventies, and Urania is quoted as saying that when her mother was young she "was as fine a looking dark-skinned woman as there was in all New Orleans." She was never seen, even by her children and grandchildren, without that indication of servitude so sentimentally loved by the whites—the bandana,

called by the Creoles a "tignon." The head that wore it was always carried high above a tall, lithe, proud body.

Alice always talked as much about her grandmother as she did about her mother. She adored the tall black woman and stole every moment she could to be with her.

"I used to beg her to tell me stories about the old days, when they were slaves," said Alice. "My mother would try and stop me, and she'd say to my grandmother, 'Don't fill the child with stories of a past that's best forgotten—.' But my grandmother would say, 'It won't hurt the child, Urania.' She was a wonderful woman, and if I'd been her own she couldn't have loved me more."

Zaier had become skilled in nursing and midwifery, and her services were in demand for both. During the numerous plagues and epidemics that swept New Orleans during the nineteenth century, Zaier and Urania voluntarily went into the streets and the homes where disease was striking with a speed that defied all efforts at treatment, nursing the sick, preparing the dead for burial.

An almost complete lack of a system of sewers, with open gutters taking its place, and a refusal on the part of the city fathers to undertake a daily flushing of the gutters—urgently petitioned by the populace—was, of course, the primary cause for these recurring epidemics.

The first sewer to be laid was a private main serving the swank St Charles Hotel, which, incidentally, at one time varied its social functions by public auctions of slaves. This main was followed in a few years by another private main laid by a department store. In 1892, forty years after the Great Epidemic, five miles of drains were installed,intended to serve the needs of a city which by that time had almost two hundred and fifty thousand inhabitants.

As a consequence, in the early 1900's the young George Lewis was able to wade ankle deep in water in the gutters of the old French Quarter, splashing gleefully with his playmates as they tried to catch tadpoles and minnows, finding all manner of interesting creatures in the stagnant pools that abounded. Drinking water continued to be taken from cisterns in the yards, cisterns which had been filled by the drip and flow of rainwater from the roof gutters. Wash water came from the river, and had to be allowed to "settle" before it could be used. Such settling always developed an inch or so of sand and filth at the bottom of the tub.

And there were the rats. The brave, insolent, defiant rats. An unconditional guarantee of nightmare can be given anyone who has ever eavesdropped on a group of old-time residents of the French Quarter as they reminisce about rats, reminiscences which extend down to the nineteen thirties and early forties. They met them on the stairs when they came home from work, and frequently the human gave way before the rat. They fought them in the kitchens, the bedrooms, and the outdoor privies, for indoor plumbing is a comparatively recent innovation for the poorer residents of that area. They battled them in the yards, the alleys and the areaways, and never slept at night without the fear, too often realized, that the obscene rodents would find their sleeping children. The "glamour" of the French Quarter has been mostly in the eyes of the tourists and of New Orleans' more fortunate residents, and, of course, in the eyes of those who love the "Bohemian life" for its own sake and find in the Quarter's continental atmosphere a general attitude of *laissez faire* in tune with their temperaments. It had never been glamorous in the eyes of its coloured residents, though they have been grateful for its low rents, yet the French Quarter Negroes who have remained in New Orleans have clung to it. It holds many memories, and here are their families and their friends, to whom they are bound by the powerful ties of shared experiences and a common destiny.

As Alice grew into childhood the need for additional money in the family became imperative. As slaves neither Urania nor her mother had known what it was to have money of their own, earned or unearned, except when it was given in small amounts by their masters to purchase necessities. But there were few challenges that Urania and her people were unequipped to meet, particularly if they involved survival or the care of their children, and Urania tackled this one head on.

To relate that Urania had learned to cook would appear to be a simple statement, applicable to almost any young daughter of any family. But in New Orleans learning to cook meant far more than mastering the principle that the application of heat to certain foods will make them edible. It meant, and still means, learning a craft, an art, and it embodies the lore of many cultures, French, Spanish, West Indian, Italian, and the African. Zaier's people brought to the French and Spanish cooking of the day a knowledge of herbs and condiments, as well as fertile imaginations and discerning palates, and made New Orleans cookery a

synonym for wizardry. There were some dishes they prepared just for themselves, and only those who have tasted the cooking of the New Orleans Negro, whose antecedents can be traced to slave times, knows what the snobbish whites are missing when they dismiss these subtle preparations as "Nigra cooking."

Their skill was not confined to gourmet dishes, and they learned to make mouth-watering candies with the same delicate touch. Urania had been an unusually apt pupil in candy-making. Because she did not want to leave her children and her mother, now nearing eighty, for a live-in job as a cook, or be absent from them for the long twelve and fourteen hour days, seven day weeks, required of domestic day workers, she decided to find a market for her candies. She specialized in two, the well-known praline and another confection of her own creation, lighter than any breeze and snowy white, which her grandson still mentions with awe.

She sold her candy on the streets each day, gradually adding to the pennies from these sales the money she received from families who ordered from her regularly. Yet the income remained inadequate. Her family had grown in size, her husband was unable to find work except spasmodically, and more money was needed.

And so Alice, her oldest daughter, started working at an age when most children are too young to enter school. Every day she started out, accompanied by a still younger brother, carrying her mother's candies spread out on a spotless tray, with a supply of equally spotless containers which her mother made at night. The children would take turns carrying the tray. They did very well; almost, in fact, as well as their mother. It is hard to resist two small brown children offering pralines for sale, especially when the price they ask can be counted in pennies. Each evening when they returned Urania would require a full accounting of every sale, and every penny made, especially if the amount of money brought back was more than it should be. Zaier's daughter would not have her children begging, and if word came to her that they had done this, punishment was quick and severe. And she told them constantly, as Alice told her son years later: "If I catch you stealing, God help you. I'd rather see you dead than a thief."

After a year or so Urania found more work, fine ironing and some washing. As soon as this additional income was assured she was able to send Alice to convent school, even paying a little for

her tuition. The child soaked up her studies like a thirsty sponge. She had a drive and nervous energy, even then, that sent her into every task, whether it was selling candy on the streets or studying, with an intentness and single-mindedness that frightened even her mother at times. Possessed of an intelligence that quickly grasped every phase of a subject, she learned far more quickly than most the simple lessons of the convent school curriculum. And learned them in French, translating them into English when she went home.

But the schooling could not last long. Again a drop in the family fortunes made it necessary for Alice to go to work. Although the Negro parents wanted above all else to give their children the education that had been denied them, they knew that the mere rudiments of education were all they could expect. This, in the opinion of the whites, was seemly and eminently practical. Why should a coloured child waste precious time acquiring an education? It would be of no use to him. It was far better that at an early age he learn to work and become useful in the only fields open to him—labour and domestic service.

Enough reading and writing so they could understand notes from their masters and mistresses, and comprehend simple signs; enough figuring so they could make change and perform simple tasks requiring the elementals of arithmetic—what more could a "darkie" want?

But despite the handicap of her colour and of poverty, and the need to work on the streets selling candy at an age when most white children string beads in kindergarten, Alice fooled them. Before she was twenty-one she had acquired learning and knowledge far beyond the wildest dreams of her contemporaries.

Although her grandmother Zaier protested vigorously, Urania had no choice but to take Alice out of convent school and send her to work for a white woman who, Urania had cause to know, was kind and considerate. The woman was Miss Grace King, one of the early New Orleans historians, whose home was filled the major part of the time with other writers and intellectuals.

Grace King abhorred ignorance or illiteracy in any form. To her a mind empty of learning was one that must be filled, and quickly. That the body which that mind occupied was black was of no consequence whatsoever. When she saw the child Alice looking at picture books with a minimum of text, she took them away from her. In their place she gave her the classics. When Alice protested

that she could not understand them, Miss King would reply with unsympathetic firmness: "Never mind. Read them whether you understand or not. What you don't understand I'll help you with. But read!"

If reading meant that Alice neglected the work she had been hired to do, Miss King did not complain. An undusted table was a small price to pay for the acquisition of knowledge by a growing human being. And she was seldom too busy to help the child when questions came up.

One of the most frequent visitors to the King home was Joaquin Miller, who found the eager, grasping mind of the Negro child fascinating to explore, and even more fascinating to enrich. He would sit with her for hours in the garden of the Kings' home, reading aloud from a book open on his knee, instilling in the thirsty young mind a love of words and their meanings, unlocking doors to treasure houses of literature that otherwise would have remained closed to her for ever.

Once Alice's son, George Lewis, quoted to me, almost in its entirety, the speech of Iago: "Who steals my purse steals trash . . .". When I asked him where he had learned it, he replied that he had heard his mother recite it so many times, he had memorized it without trying.

Eventually Alice left Miss King, to return home to help her mother, whose work load had grown greatly. The few years she had spent with the author had been fruitful ones. She had become an omnivorous reader. It made no difference what it was—if it was in print, Alice read it. She read with equal ease in French and English. Her catechism, prayer book, and Bible were in French. Many French publications were available in New Orleans, and French magazines and books were as much part of her self-imposed curriculum as were English publications.

Alice grew to be above medium height, though not as tall as her grandmother, Zaier. Her skin was very dark, her nose thin and straight, her lower lip full. She had added sewing to her list of accomplishments, and made all of her own clothes, which were invariably in good taste. Her son remembers one dress she had worn as a young woman, and kept for many years carefully wrapped in tissue paper—light tan, with a myriad tiny tucks across the bodice, and a row of finely pleated ruffles low on the skirt, the ruching at the high neck and wrists set off with a narrow turquoise ribbon.

She was quick-spoken, with the high, clear voice she retained throughout her life, and when she spoke in English it was with the accent of a person who has learned it as a second language, precisely and correctly.

Her movements were quick, like her speech, and as a child she never walked when she could run. Her son says she "never did stop running" and when she was older her long, quick strides frequently left companions panting behind her. He remembers that not many years ago, when she was in her ninetieth year, he had to "go like five hundred" to catch up with her when he saw her crossing Canal Street, alone and unaided, splendidly defying the frantic horns of passing cars. She was on her way to a store to buy a present for him; something she had seen advertised in the paper. When he finally managed to overtake her she shook his protecting hand off with considerable ferocity, and throughout the shopping trip and all the way home to her apartment on St Phillip Street, scolded him roundly for his interference.

It took a brave young man to court the high-spirited independent young woman that Alice was in her youth, but apparently New Orleans was full of brave young men, for she never lacked suitors. But she cared very little for any of them. She enjoyed their company as escorts to the balls and picnics, and certainly it was more pleasant to have a young man to walk out with on warm Sundays than to walk alone. Beyond these relationships she had no particular interest in them.

The religion that Zaier and Urania had given her grew to mean more than any outside interest, and she was convinced that, if He thought it right, God would send her a man she could love, and the children she wanted so intensely.

Meanwhile there was work, and when the work was done there were books to be read, and there were the balls and picnics and parades, and the excitements of the long Mardi Gras season. And there was always God and His family, and a whole host of interesting saints, with whose lives she was as familiar as she was with the lives of her own relatives, and with whom she talked daily, on intimate, friendly terms.

five

THE small summer resort of Mandeville lies directly across Lake Pontchartain from New Orleans. In the summer all its cottages and houses are filled, for the year-round population is augmented then by vacationing Orleanians and other Louisianans escaping the heat of the cities. It is generally regarded as being more healthful than New Orleans, possibly because it is a little farther from the river. Surrounding it is some of the best hunting and fishing country in the area.

Near here, just before the Emancipation Proclamation, Henry Lewis Zeno was born, the first child of a Negro slave and his full-blooded Choctaw Indian wife, also a slave.

Henry Zeno did not remember the details of his life before his mother and father were freed. His first memory was of the cabin in which they lived in Mandeville, and of the woods and bayous which surrounded the town. It was to this cabin Henry's father brought his wife and three children. Unlike Zaier who, at the same time, just across the lake, was content to remain in the security of her master's home, it is doubtful if the elder Zeno wasted twenty-four hours before putting as many miles as possible between his family and their former owners.

He was a small, gentle man, whose bent and twisted spine was eloquent evidence of the reasons he had fled his owners with such rapidity when freedom came. He never talked about the injury that had crippled him, but, from his mother, Henry Zeno learned that it had occurred when his father was young and hot-blooded and before his pride and fiery independence had cooled sufficiently to make him the model slave his master required. When his grandson, George Lewis, would ask his parents, as he did persistently, how his grandfather had become crippled, both his father and mother would brush him aside.

"He was a good man, son, but he had a hard time. Now run away and find something to do." And that was all they would say.

But they did tell the child what they believed to be the reason his own father bore throughout his life the disfigurement of a

badly deformed jaw. Henry Zeno's Indian mother was no less difficult than other Indians whom the early settlers had attempted to enslave. Most slave owners gave it up as hopeless, but some persisted. A few days before the young Choctaw's first child was born, sired by the gentle, crippled man who loved her so undemandingly, she had displeased her master. She took the heavy blow across the abdomen, dealt with the handle of a broom, without a whimper or a sound. Then she barricaded herself in the cabin she shared with her husband, and not even the white people dared come near. A few days later she gave birth to her first child, perfect in every respect except for a badly deformed jaw.

The cabin to which the elder Zeno brought his family was small. He enlarged it as best he could, but his capacity for physical work was limited, and the rapidly growing family of the Zenos soon overcrowded it. There was only one regulation bed, in which all the children slept. It was not a large bed, and there were always casualties at night as some insecurely based youngster would be crowded to the edge by another's squirming, and would tumble off. Sometimes the fall didn't even wake the tumbler, but no matter how quiet the landing, how soundly all the children slept through it, their father never slept so soundly he did not hear the soft thud as the child's body hit the floor. Each time, and it often ran to many times a night, his small, bent figure would come softly into the room and he would lift the child from the floor and tenderly place it back in bed. Then he would re-arrange all the youngsters and, as best he could, secure them with the patchwork quilts he tucked around them.

Neither his wife nor his children ever heard him raise his voice, or felt his hand. Yet his anger was quickly aroused by outsiders, and once roused was all-consuming. He had a fierce and uncompromising pride that would not let him ask favours of any man, nor did he accept voluntary offers of help with too good a grace. He was never known to truckle or beg. The mental and spiritual suffering he endured under slavery must have been far harder for this man to bear than any physical sufferings.

The children worshipped him and their need of him grew greater as the years went on and their mother grew farther and farther from them. At first she would disappear for a day, and then for a day and a night, leaving no word to indicate where she had gone or when she would return. Eventually the absences

stretched to a week or more. There was never any thought that she was slipping off for any pleasures the region might offer, or for a rendezvous with a man. Her husband knew, and her children sensed, that her absences were as inevitable as the returning to the wild of an animal only partly domesticated, who slips off to his own kind when the urge becomes too strong to resist. The elder Zeno understood that in this Indian woman, enslaved since childhood, there was a need for solitude, an irresistible compulsion to return to the bayous and the swamps, and, perhaps, to her own people. He never reprimanded or questioned her, and accepted her return with the same gentle tolerance with which he had accepted her absence. She died before any of the children reached maturity.

Henry Zeno talked of his father constantly, even after he was a grown man. He used one anecdote in particular to illustrate the older man's character. One late afternoon, when the sun had set and a cool damp evening was creeping in, the Zeno children returned in a body from an afternoon of fishing. As they approached the cabin they heard a thrashing in the underbrush behind it. Then their father emerged, twisted figure bent double, panting, trying to "tote a log twice as big as he was."

"He couldn't carry that log," said Henry. "Take a strong man twice his size to tote that one, but he was doin' it. Said he had to bring it home for firewood to keep us young 'uns warm. That's like he was—a mighty good man."

After his wife's death the elder Zeno faced the full-time job of feeding and caring for a brood of growing children. He was seriously handicapped physically, and without education or training. Yet, his son said, this gentle man never complained.

"He always could smile, no matter how bad things was," Henry said. "But you'd only hear him laugh once in a while. Mostly it was when he managed to get a little piece of change in the house and he knew us kids would eat good. We was the hungriest, eatin'est kids in the parish."

Unable to handle hard physical work, the father of the Zeno children made use of the skills and knowledge he possessed that did not require muscle or a strong back. At some time, perhaps when he was unable to do hard labour because of his back injury, he had learned to sew. For several years he had been making all the children's clothes. Now, working late at night with only a home-made oil lamp for light, he made with painstaking care

some of the finest patchwork quilts anyone around those parts had seen. His son said his father's stitches were so fine and straight you'd have thought them a woman's work. Then early in the morning he would start into the woods to gather herbs, and sassafras for filet powder.

Customers who came to the little cabin to buy his quilts or filet powder soon found that the quiet, gentle man who greeted them became a totally different person when negotiations were opened. He had one price for his wares, and only one. It was in those early days of freedom that the Negro developed his methods of doing business with the white people. There has always been an immovable mental block in the white Southern mentality that refuses to accept the idea of a Negro receiving as much for his labour or merchandise as a white man would receive for the same commodity. One reason for that attitude has been the viewpoint: "The Nigra doesn't need that much money—it doesn't cost him half as much to live." It is the basis of much of the racial tension in the South and in the industrial border cities to which the Negro has migrated in large numbers. If the day ever comes when the Negro is as highly paid as the white, the South feels that complete economic deterioration will be just around the corner.

The elder Zeno learned this, his son learned it through observation, and, in New Orleans, Urania and her daughter Alice were learning it.

When white customers, certain that the crippled little coloured man would not argue price with them, tried to get his filet powder for less than the few pennies he asked for it, he would jump to his feet, face taut with anger, eyes blazing, and holding the little container of powder over his head he would shout:

"Before I'll sell what I wukked for for less I'll throw it on the ground!" And hobbling to the door, would prove his words.

But they usually came back. It was the finest filet powder to be bought anywhere in the region.

He would hold a quilt in one shaking hand, and a pair of scissors in the other, and tell his astounded customer:

"Before I'll take that little bit of change for this quilt, I'll cut it in pieces—an' give you the smallest piece."

The Zeno children did not hunt and fish as most children do—for fun. There was no question of "sneaking off" for a day in the woods or along the lakefront or bayous. They were more apt to

be told gently by their father that there'd be no meat for dinner if they didn't stir themselves and go fetch some. If there was a school for them to attend, they never saw the inside of it, for they were needed too badly around the little house, and in the truck garden, or out tracking down or catching the main course for dinner.

At twenty-one Henry Zeno stood six feet tall. His hair was coal-black and straight, like his mother's; his skin light, more red than tan. When he was old enough to grow a moustache its sweeping width terminated in points waxed to the sharpness of a needle. His son says he never saw his father's moustache with a hair out of place, even early in the morning. It hid to some extent, but not entirely, the deformity of his jaw. Those living today who knew Henry Zeno say that without that deformity a handsomer man would have been hard to find. He walked slowly, with a soft, graceful tread, and early in life acquired the habit of clasping his hands behind him as he strolled along the streets of Mandeville, or the banquettes of New Orleans.

He did whatever he could to make money. Every foot of the woods and the bayous, every stream and lagoon, were as familiar to him as her kitchen is to a careful housewife. When hunting and fishing were not enough, he did labouring jobs and finally, taught by his father, he developed a flair for cooking. Work was not too hard to find after that, for if there was not a house to be painted, a privy to be built, or a well to be dug, there was usually a restaurant or lake boat in need of a good cook.

In spite of more than the average number of opportunities, Henry Zeno let women strictly alone. He never went into detail on the reasons for his celibacy. It may have been that the fierce pride he inherited from his father, and which was to become one of the salient characteristics of his son, would not permit him to risk a rebuff because of his facial deformity. Certainly it was not a common trait among a people who recognized procreation, birth, and death as the three basic realities, and it was the cause of considerable frustration among the young women of the community.

Like his father he spoke softly and gently, though the softness and gentleness hid the same volcanic fires of burning pride and independence, dangerously near the surface, but never displayed toward a weaker person or a child.

As Henry grew older he became canny, and wise in the ways

of the world as far as business matters were concerned. He was thrifty, and as uncompromising in a deal for his labour as his father was in a deal for his handiwork. He attended the Baptist Church. His clothes were always immaculate, and as close to the last word in style as his pocketbook would permit, though he never dressed loudly or garishly. But he remained naïve in social relationships, and he continued to keep a safe distance between himself and the opposite sex.

It was much against his will, after strong urging by a friend, that he attended, in 1896, a ball in the French Quarter of New Orleans. Zaier's granddaughter, Alice, was at the ball, and angry at her escort.

"I let Henry walk me home for spite," she said.

A short time later they were married.

six

ONLY an incurable optimist would have predicted a completely smooth course for the marriage of Henry and Alice Zeno, yet for several years they were as happy as their poverty and the tragedies that dogged them would allow. Each was the reverse of the other. Henry was gentle, slow-moving, soft-spoken, patient. His anger was roused only when he considered an attempt was being made to take advantage of him. He could drive a sharp bargain, and could understand the same attribute in another, but if he believed the sharpness of the bargain was related to his race, he became fiercely adamant and unceremoniously ended negotiations. Never surly, or bad-tempered, his anger remained with him in the form of a deep distrust, and he viewed with the wary eye of his father all dealings with those who held the economic whip-hand.

Alice, by contrast, was quick-moving, quick-spoken, and her own immediacy of perception and comprehension tended to make her impatient. With those close to her she did not hesitate to express anger or displeasure, forgetting it, however, as soon as it was displayed. But where Henry Zeno had been reared by a father and mother who had never been able to learn the lessons of adaptability so essential to the society in which they lived,

Alice had been trained—and well trained—by Zaier and her mother in what was as much a "survival course" as is any atom-age military survival course.

As a consequence, where Henry rejected, with no attempt to conceal his reasons, any attempt to humiliate or take advantage of him, Alice, with the same inner reactions, continued to express herself to her adversary with an unfailing charm of manner which was never humble, but always polite. Yet the end result of Alice's approach to these problems was the same as the end result of Henry's approach, the difference being that no one could tell what Alice was thinking, but Henry left no doubt.

They lived close to Zaier and Urania, who still remained in the house on the property of the family who had bought Zaier almost ninety years before. Two maiden sisters, the last descendants of the family, were still alive and occupied the main homestead, and to Urania's already over-crowded schedule of washing, ironing, and cooking, was added the work of caring for the two old ladies.

The poverty that was such an integral part of the Zenos' life was accepted as foreordained. During the early years of her marriage Alice went out to work only occasionally, but took in washing and ironing and grew more adept every year. Like Urania, she was a perfectionist, and no matter how fine or minute the tucks and ruffles, there were no flaws in her work.

On hot summer evenings, before the dark set in, Henry and Alice would sit on the low gallery of their St Claude street home while the teeming, multi-coloured life of the French Quarter swirled around them. The sound of the street vendor's cries, the raucous "ST-O-O-O-N-E C-O-A-L!" of the coal-cart driver, the cries and shouts of the children as they played in the filthy, stagnant water of the gutters, the occasional sharp, tearing sound of a woman screaming in anger, the wails of babies miserable in the sticky heat, and the assorted smells from steaming pots of filet gumbo and of red beans, and from the carts of peddlers of fish and sweets, were to Alice the very warp and woof of her existence. To Henry they were sometimes an irritant, and when they finally rose and turned their backs on the steaming, noisy life of the never-sleeping French Quarter and went inside, Henry would hear in his mind and heart the sounds of the forests and the smells of the bayous and lagoons where he had grown to manhood.

Out of the few dollars he and Alice were able to make Henry managed somehow to help the gentle little cripple on the other side of the lake who had cared for him so tenderly when he was a child. Hortense, Henry's sister, had stayed with her father in the little cabin in Mandeville, married, and become the mother of several children. Later her husband developed a chronic illness and his work capacity became limited. Henry had known what it was to sit on the floor with his brothers and sisters and eat an inadequate meal when slashing rain and wind had made hunting or fishing impossible, a meal that never seemed to last until bed-time inside a young stomach. As long as he was able to help, his sister's children would be spared that all-gone feeling as much as possible. Alice, to whom a hungry child was a sin against God and all old people the special trust of the young, deprived her-self without complaint to make the old man's last years as comfortable as she could, and to save her sister-in-law's children from hunger.

Alice and Henry's first child was born a little more than a year after they were married. Like many men who for years avoid the responsibilities of marriage as they avoid prison, Henry did an abrupt about-face and was bewildered with happiness over what seemed to him a miracle. He had viewed his approaching father-hood with some misgivings, but these were lost in amazement that he, with the help of Alice, had produced anything as perfect as a baby.

It was agony for them both to watch the child fade before their eyes. She did not gain after the first few months, and then began to lose. Each day they watched the baby's vitality grow less, and each night they prayed, according to their own creeds.

The baby died before a year had passed. Within a few days of her death Henry's father loosened his grip at last on a life that had brought him much pain and unrelenting need, yet which had been enriched so greatly by his love for his children and theirs for him.

On Henry's shoulders fell the burden of the expenses for both funerals. Alice, sick with grief, worn out with days and nights of nursing the baby, almost—but not quite—weary of prayer, had little time to indulge in self-pity or mourning. With this double expense there was double work to be done to get the necessary money. And even with double work, it could only be done by going into debt, and for months she and Henry ate sparingly and

worked night and day to repay the loan company they had been forced to call on.

She felt that her second pregnancy was a sign from God that He would bring her comfort. The child would make up to them for their grief over the loss of their firstborn. Urania and Zaier helped her as much as they could, taking from her shoulders some of the heavy work of washing and ironing. Henry drew the water for the washing from the "plug" in the street, drawing the clear water into pans after it had settled, lifting the heavy pans to the primitive stove for heating, and hanging up the larger pieces.

He worked at whatever jobs he could find, labouring or cooking, never for more than a few dollars a day. Alice spent much of her time with her mother and grandmother, frequently bringing her ironing to their home. As they worked the women often heard the high, clear, brassy sound of a marching band in the street. If it happened to be a funeral cortège on the way to the cemetery the sounds would be slow and dirge-like, the drums muffled, and the tones of ineffable sorrow from the lead horns would stop the women in their work, and they would wonder aloud who among their people had lost a husband, a father or—Mary, comfort them!—a son.* High like the wail of a woman, the tones of an E-flat clarinet would cut through the lamentations of the brass, and Zaier would stop what she was doing to listen, and to moan softly, and sometimes to say in Creole: "We hear you. Jesus give him peace!"

When the sounds died away they knew that in an hour or so they would hear the same band again, differently this time, on the way back from the cemetery, and they would stop work again to go into the yard to watch. Zaier, almost a hundred years old, would stand at the gate, foot tapping, body swaying. They would clap their hands to the beat of the drums, and all three women would laugh with delight at the capering, dancing children the band was drawing in its wake, as the Pied Piper of old had drawn the children of Hamelin.

There was no grief or sorrow in the sound of the band now; the clarinet had stopped keening and was leaping, dancing, flirting in and out among the loud, exultant brasses like a coquet-

---

* Funeral parades with bands are held only for men. The parade is always arranged and carried out by some lodge or society, usually restricted to masculine membership. Women's auxiliary groups sometimes march in these parades.

tish woman. In the sound of the drums, unmuffled now and snares released, Zaier heard the same rhythmic patterns she had heard long ago in Senegal, before a bearded white man had approached the reed-bordered stream and offered her a string of beads to come aboard a strange craft. Not a foot or a hand within hearing distance of those drums but what was keeping time in some way.

They had brought this music with them when they were born, these bandsmen, in their hearts, and their muscles, their blood and their bones and their very guts; it had come to them from their fathers and their fathers' fathers down untold thousands of years, and these ancestors had made it a part of their worship of strange gods. They vitalized the tunes and airs they learned in this country with the gifts that were within them, and in doing so made them completely their own. In later years, young white musicians were to sit at their feet and the feet of their sons, in the North and South alike, to learn these rhythmic patterns, to try and understand these disciplined yet free-flowing improvisations. They gave what they could as teachers generously, but never succeeded in giving the thing they themselves would not define—the message from within that gave the music validity. The white musicians were to return to their own bands to play the same tunes and the same airs, with the same basic beats, in the same manner, yet never with the same sounds. They captured the glow from the fire, but never the fire itself; the drive of the beat, but never its subtle, interwoven counter-beats; the warmth and the heat, but never the coolness and the shade; the flamboyant joy and skittish happiness, but never the sorrow and the pain. They were like men speaking a foreign language, who have mastered only the basic nouns and verbs, but not the niceties of the rules of grammar.

White people who heard the band came hurrying to watch, too, lining the sidewalks or leaning over fences. Their feet tapped and their heads bobbed as the Negroes' did, but they would say to each other:

"They sure forget their grief quick. That man's body isn't cold yet."

The writer, who heard the gay, driving, pulsingly vital music of the return march from the cemetery called sacrilegious, asked an old-time Negro brass band musician of New Orleans what he had to say to the charge.

"Shucks," he replied. "Cain't do nothin' foh the brothuh that's gone. He's out of it. Might as well make the young 'uns happy on the way back."

The music of the marches to and from the cemetery expresses completely the basically realistic attitude of the Negro. It is a realism that has its roots in the past, in the fields and the levees, and the chains of the slave labour gangs; a realism that sees death without its trappings and its mask, as a release. It is the realism of the slave in the fields who, when his father or his brother or his friend dropped beside him, felt a double burden: the burden of grief at the loss and the burden of double work until the one who had gone could be replaced. There were tears to be shed, and wailing to be done, but the row stretched ahead and the bag on the back had to be filled. So a song must be sung, a story told, to ease the weight. All songs are not happy songs, and all stories are not happy stories.

And so at Negro funerals the preacher goes on and on, and the grief and hysteria mount to an almost unbearable pitch; women faint and men shout, and the preacher himself becomes a being possessed. It is grief, but it is far more than grief: it is the release the slaves found, in a prior generation, in the dances and rituals of the Congo Square.

Then, the service over, pent-up emotions liberated, the spent and exhausted mourners follow the band to the graveside. When the body is committed and the musicians and the mourners make their way out of the cemetery, they know they have left the brother who has gone in good hands; whatever his sins may have been of thievery, or drinking, or lechery, Jesus has taken over now, and no one will "run him out." There may be payment exacted for the sins committed while on earth, but he would pay no higher price in the hereafter because in this life his skin had been dark. He was at last equal for God does not judge as man judges. If one listens carefully one hears in the brasses and the reeds of the home-coming funeral band a tone that sounds strangely like triumph.

Their brother has gone, his Lord has him now, his troubles are past; grief has shaken them as a dog shakes a rag doll, but the days and the months and the years of the future lie ahead for them, each with its obstacles, its joys, its sorrow, and its cross.

"Might as well make the young 'uns happy on the way back!"

seven

DURING the months of her second pregnancy Alice continued a routine she had started early in her marriage—the daily job of patiently correcting, with the limited time at her disposal, the shortcomings of her husband's education. At night, with only an oil lamp for light, she ironed the fine dresses and lingerie of her customers while Henry laboriously worked his way through simple reading exercises. When the lamp was not needed for Alice's work he would sit at the table and, tongue between teeth, stalk down arithmetic problems with the same determination he used in stalking game.

Her grandmother delivered their second baby, a small but apparently healthy child. After a few weeks they felt that God had answered their prayers. Alice scarcely let the infant out of her sight and, when it did become necessary for her to go out to work occasionally, brought it to Zaier and Urania with the minute and detailed instructions regarding its care. It was Zaier who saw the first signs of faltering vitality in the baby, and it was Zaier's comforting arms that held the heartbroken mother close when that vitality ebbed away. When the first baby had died Alice had not questioned God's will. This time she did, and for weeks neither her family nor her priest were able to comfort her. Henry became more quiet than ever during those days, and as he walked along the banquettes of the French Quarter, hands characteristically clasped behind him, friends noticed that for the first time his head was bent, his shoulders not quite as straight as they had been.

But when she was pregnant for the third time, Alice looked upon it as another promise from God. She began to wonder if perhaps she had somehow failed Him, and the loss of the other two babies had been a punishment. Alice believed firmly in the strong, disciplinary hand of God, and looked first to herself for the reasons for the troubles she had. If they were not punishment,

then they must be trials sent to test her, or lessons to be learned. She felt ashamed that she had grieved so wildly for the baby she had lost, and that she had ever questioned His wisdom.

During the entire nine months of her third pregnancy she went to Mass daily, and made frequent Novenas to the saints she felt could be the most helpful. She prayed for a son because she thought a male child might be stronger and better able to cope with the perils of the first year of life. And because she wanted a unified home, she prayed especially to St Joseph, patron saint of families. He who had been a good and happy father, albeit in locum tenens, would surely hear her prayers and intercede for her.

And because St Francis was the patron saint of the poor she knew that the ears of this kind and compassionate man would be attuned to the entreaties. And as she had prayed to the mother of the infant Jesus for strength to bear her losses before, Alice prayed to her now for strength to bear a healthy child, as she herself had borne one. At her urging Henry, too, prayed to the mother and father of the Saviour he also believed in. It did not seem too illogical to Henry that they would hear, and while he could not go along with Novenas and prayers to various saints, he could give in to his wife's urging with a certain amount of faith that prayers to Joseph and his wife Mary would be heard. Alice felt that she had covered just about all the ground she was able to in these preliminaries, plus a promise that her child would be named Joseph, as his patron saint, and that Francis would also be included.

Thus it was that when the boy delivered by Zaier on July 13, 1900, was christened in St Augustine's Church the baptismal certificate bore the name Joseph Lewis Francis Zeno.

It was probably the only time the child was formally addressed by that name. Alice had heard her mother predict before, and she was not disposed to ignore Urania's words when she had first placed the baby in her arms:

"Call him George. This one will live!"

The use of double names is common in the South, and from the first the child was called George Lewis. When he was asked his name, after he learned to talk, he invariably responded "George Lewis." And never by so much as a nod in its direction acknowledged the existence of the letter "R" in its make-up.

There was a different look about this child; when he cried it

was determinedly and with gusto, and he never whimpered. True, he was smaller than most babies, but he had the look and feel of the fighter Zaier had said he was when he was born. Both Henry and Alice felt strangely confident that God was going to permit this son that they had prayed for to remain with them.

The baby lived, but with each infant illness he was nursed unduly, and candles burned in considerable profusion in St Augustine's Church during the early years of the 1900's. Whether it was the candles, the prayers, or the gentle stubbornness within the youngster that pulled him through there is no way of knowing.

The saints, though, were not to be let alone as far as George Lewis was concerned. Even as the Zenos began to realize that their son stood a good chance of living to become a man, it became evident that, while man he might become, it was going to take a little more effort on the part of the saints to make of him anything but a man with a boy's stature. Once again Alice made Novenas and lit candles and prayed unceasingly that this son would some day be large enough so that at least the clothes of a boy three years younger would fit him; never, however, forgetting to thank the saints that he had been spared, and asking a trifle diffidently for this added favour lest they think her ungrateful.

It was during his infancy that an event occurred that seriously affected every member of his race in the Crescent City. It was as though the ordinary struggles of existence, which were many and bitter, were not deemed enough by an unkind fate, and this added trial was sent as a major test of their further ability to absorb hardship. Known as the "Robert Charles Case," for weeks it sent every Negro in New Orleans into virtual hiding.

Robert Charles, a Negro of late middle age, born in slavery, had gone berserk one afternoon, and by the time the police arrived at his home he had terrorized everyone within a radius of blocks. In the struggle to subdue him he was shot. If his death had ended the incident, weeks of terror for the New Orleans Negroes would have been avoided. Instead, the incident sparked an all-out campaign of persecution and brutality by certain segments of the white population, directed at the Negroes. Every Negro in the city seemed to be held personally accountable for the acts of one psychopathically deranged member of his race, and no Negro, man or woman, was safe on the streets. Negroes who did dare venture abroad were quickly ordered off the streets

by the police, and many alive today recall that even those who sat on their own doorsteps, or courtyards, were abruptly and peremptorily ordered inside. There was no defying these orders. To do so could mean arrest.

Many white citizens of the glamour city of the South deplored the conditions. Yet they differed in no way from a number of the white citizens of the South today, who give lip service to integration, talk devoutly about the Christian ethic, yet remain for the most part passive because of their unwillingness to incur the censure of their fellows, the loss of their social standing, and the pointing of a scornful finger at them by those of their own caste who would consider them traitors. Like Mark Twain's weather, it is talked about, but except among some members of the younger generations, not much is done about it. The white rain-makers of the South who actively seek to bring the healing rains of tolerance to the parched desert of Negro segregated life are among the most morally courageous of any of our citizens.

Yet it was a white resident of New Orleans, sickened beyond bearing by what was going on, who brought about the break in the tension and ended, once and for all, any concerted harassment of Negroes as a race by the people and police of that city.

During those dark days Alice bore the major part of the burden of making money for the little family. Her customers would bring her the work to be done and Zaier and Urania would help her. She was once again pregnant, but there could be no slowing down. Henry was close to mania himself, and only Alice's tearful pleadings kept him at home and off the streets in search of work. Of all the Negroes in New Orleans, Henry, with his quick temper, his refusal to knuckle under, his instantaneous defiance of any tyrannous act, however slight, would have been one of the first to suffer reprisals. No one appreciated better than Alice the fact that he probably would not have been a live man for more than a few blocks. They made out somehow, but it was a period in their lives they seldom talked about, so dreadful had it been.

It was after the situation had lasted for some time that the entire city rocked with amazement one morning when there appeared in the daily paper an advertisement, placed by the white owner of a hardware store, offering free to any Negro who felt the need of one to protect himself and his family— a Winchester rifle. Plus sufficient ammunition to do the job. Centred in the advertisement was a sketch of a lethal-looking rifle.

Overnight mass persecutions stopped. Since the appearance of that advertisement in the early 1900's, that public avowal of a white man to give to the Negro lethal weapons with which to fight for his home and his self-respect, there has never been another "drive" of such magnitude against the Negro population as a whole.

It would be wishful thinking to say that all persecution stopped. There is not an adult Negro in Louisiana who has not at some time felt the Bienville Black Code stirring in its slumbers, who does not realize its spirit still lives, particularly those provisions which provide quick retaliation against a Negro guilty of any action that might tend to "endanger the absolute supremacy of the white race."

George Lewis, even in the first five years of his life, showed signs of being a headstrong youngster, with the quick reactions of his mother, leavened by the gentleness of his father and grandfather. His two most outstanding characteristics were an almost abnormal sensitivity, his emotions so close to the surface he could be unbearably hurt almost by the flick of an eyelash; and a fiery, lightning-quick temper. And his mother has said that even then he had the devastating, gentle smile that was in later years to open the doors of hearts all over the world.

In Alice Zeno's mind her son was no different than the son of any other mother, and as long as God would give her the strength and wisdom for which she prayed daily, he would grow to be as well-mannered and as much a gentleman as any child in New Orleans. She had learned from Zaier and her mother, from Grace King and other white people for whom she had worked, the niceties of a way of life from which she must always be shut out. With an inherent selectivity she discarded those things that did not measure up to her exacting standards. She had learned the fine points of manners, the graciousness of the courteous phrase, the way to set a table, and how to conduct oneself at it, and the way in which the gentlemen of the era deported themselves—and she knew the difference between a gentleman and a man who was not. These things she made her own and started to impart to her son before he could even say the words "Merci," or "thank you," or "s'il vous plaît" or "please." She wanted fiercely, with every fibre of her being, to give him the best, and she knew that she could not. But what Alice did know was that with God's help

and her own unrelenting discipline she would mould his character so that in God's eyes he would be wealthy.

To this end discipline started early, but the fierceness of her love for this tiny child, so miraculously permitted to live, tempered the severe punishments, and he never closed his eyes at night doubting the bottomless, protective depths of that love. It remained for sixty years the one security to which he could always return.

Left to himself, Henry would have spoiled his son. He gave the boy gentleness, a quiet, whimsical mirth, and a brooding compassionate love. The boy worshipped him, and his father's calm voice and gentle touch could stop a tantrum before it ever got a running start.

The inevitable clashes of temperament between Henry and Alice were becoming more frequent now. It was not that they quarrelled, for Henry was not a man to quarrel, but rather that instead of bridging the gulf of temperament that had always lain between them, they had somehow widened it. It would have been difficult for them to have found peace under the most favourable circumstances. Under the grinding strain of years of unrelieved poverty and frequent illness it was practically impossible.

When George was five Henry left the house on St Claude Street. Alice never hesitated to tell the reason: There was another woman. Perhaps a woman who seemed to have less driving, relentless force; a softer, more biddable spirit; a woman who could never have reared a George Lewis but who might have seemed easier to come home to. Alice never forgave her husband. If the woman involved had been a stranger she might have, but she was a close friend and distant relative of Alice's, a frequent visitor in their home. And Henry, when he had met and married Alice, had been as naïve and unsophisticated as a child, with no prior experiences with women to give him tolerance, or by which he could be guided.

George remembers little of the circumstances, except bewilderment and loneliness. But these emotions must have been very strong in the child's mind and heart, for within a short time he found his way to his father's new lodgings. There he sat on the lap of the tall man he called "Pappa," and ate the feather-light, buttery, honey-laden biscuits Henry made especially for him in honour of the occasion. After that first visit he trudged to his father's house as often as he could, and eventually Henry came

to visit Alice and their son whenever the urge to see the boy became more than he could withstand. But evident though it was, within a short time after Henry had left their home, that his heart was still within it, Alice always met her son's anxious pleading questions about when Pappa was coming back with a quiet "Never."

eight

A five-year-old boy stood at the edge of a long, high table, his head barely reaching the top, in the kitchen of a house on Treme, now Liberty, Street, in New Orleans. The boy's skin was the colour of milk chocolate; the cheek-bones high under the overlay of childhood's chubbiness; the nose long, thin, with flaring nostrils; the mouth generous with finely formed upper lip, the lower lip slightly over-full. The head was small, round, and the kinky black hair was cut close, like a cap. The diminutive, small-boned frame was well proportioned and he carried it, even at that age, erect, with shoulders squared, in unconscious imitation of his father.

Small, thin fingers, preternaturally long for a child his age, gripped the table edge and served to pull the tiny body higher so the black eyes could watch every movement in a process which would have fascinated any small boy. His grandmother, Mrs Urania Pacquet, stood opposite him; her long, deft fingers—younger editions of her mother's and older editions of the boy's—delicately patting and turning row after row of pralines and candies laid out on the table top. She had finished preparing the supplies of head cheese and sausage her customers had ordered and now she had time for her favourite work—making candy. One of her candies she called *Tante Betsies,* luscious, mouth-watering confections calculated to keep any five-year-old quiet in anticipation of being given one. The white people to whom she sold them called them "Aunt Betsys." Every move she made showed pride of craftsmanship, particularly when she handled the *Tante Betsies,* for she had been the first in New Orleans to make them, and had acquired a certain fame on that account.

The cypress table on which she worked was spotlessly clean. It had been made for her by her husband, dead now, who had been a baker by trade and a carpenter by hobby. Days of painstaking labour had gone into finishing the top, which was mirror-smooth, without flaw, crack, or suspicion of splinter.

As her swift, graceful fingers worked she whistled tonelessly, never stopping. Her family always knew when Urania was finishing her candies by the sound of that constant, low, unvarying whistle, and only her grandson, George Lewis, ever interrupted her.

This day as his round, yearning, black eyes watched intently over the table's edge, his own lips were pursed. Urania did not hear at first, and then she stopped her own whistling to listen, quick fingers still turning the candies on the table. Across from her her grandson was whistling, not in toneless monotony, as she did, but a clearly recognizable tune. He did not miss a note. Urania spoke to him quietly, as she always had. She made a special effort to speak quietly now, though, in order not to make the boy self-conscious, and she did not look up or stop work.

"Where did you learn that, baby?"

The child shrugged.

"Can I have one, Da. Can I? A *Tante Betsie*. Can I, Da?"

Urania picked up one of the light, mouth-watering candies, and held it just out of reach in long black fingers.

"Whistle another tune for Da, baby, and you can have it."

The child laughed happily.

"That's easy, Da! That's easy! Listen!"

And, faltering once or twice because he was trying now, he whistled from first to last the simply stated melody "If I Ever Cease to Love."

As she handed the candy to him she called to her daughter, ironing in the next room.

"Alice! We have a musician here. Come and listen to him!" And to the boy: "Whistle it again for your mother, George Lewis."

The child's eyes rolled in the direction of Mrs Zeno, standing in the doorway now. He savoured the last morsel of his *Tante Betsie,* puckered his lips to whistle and then stopped. He knew the stern reprimands that followed any effort that even hinted of "showing off" or "acting smart." These were not tolerated. Even sharper reprimands were brought forth by bragging or any

semblance of what his mother considered the deadliest of all the seven deadly sins—self pride. But this wasn't showing off. Not really. And she was watching him expectantly. He whistled the tune again, half-fearfully. His mother caught him up and held him close, almost hurting him in the tightness of her embrace.

"That's fine, son. And you whistled it true. When you do anything, son, even if it's play, do it true and right. Who taught you to whistle that song?"

The boy wriggled delightedly, for praise from his mother was then, and always remained, the greatest joy of his life.

"No one, ma, no one. I heared it." He twisted around and pointed to the front door. "Over there. The men playing."

Alice let him wriggle down to the floor from her arms, to resume his hopeful vigil at the table. She knew how he would stand, entranced, for far longer periods than the average small boy can remain quiet, as the sound of the bands came loud and clear from Hopes (sic) Hall across the street. When the bands were playing for daytime functions in Hopes Hall she had no worries about her small, nervous, over-active son. A team of horses couldn't drag him from the yard or gallery then. His head would bob; tiny feet, long for his size like his hands, jigging or tapping; eyes shining like black gems in his ecstatic face. Yes, her son loved music. Perhaps some day God would make it possible for her to give him lessons on the violin and he could find honourable, clean work, more suited to the frailness of his small frame and small bones than the hard labour and back-breaking jobs that lay ahead for most black children. There would be no strain on a thin chest, and violins were always in demand for the musical groups that played at the continuing round of soirées and balls of her people. And she would teach him that he must play, whatever it was or wherever it was, for the glory of God, and not just for the pleasure of the crowd. Certainly a child who could whistle like that at his age must have a gift, and the fruits of any gift must be offered to the Giver.

She was pleased about anything that made this small son of hers happy, always provided that it was not something that would mar his character. She was glad that they lived now where the music from Hopes Hall could bring this shining joy to his eyes, and make him dance and whistle.

After Henry had left their home on St Claude Street the expense of keeping up the house had been too much for Alice, and

she had moved with her son to a room in a small brick house in the same courtyard on Treme Street in which her mother and grandmother lived. The room was very small and dark; so dark that it was necessary to keep a coal-oil lamp burning throughout the day. In the raw, damp weather of a New Orleans winter the lamp did double duty, for it was their only source of heat.

But there was one advantage. Her loneliness was not as poignant here with her family as it had been in the St Claude Street house, for like most Negro families of that day, their ties were extraordinarily close. Communal living was not theory, but fact. Poverty has a way of either separating people through bitterness or greed, or of bringing them together within the protective bulwarks of group-living. Zaier and her descendants were a closely-knit unit, bound by indissoluble ties of deep affection, shared hardship, and that feeling of security found only in the safety of the clan. Urania's husband was dead now, and her other daughters married, but her two sons and a nephew lived with her.

"We was all there. All my family," says George Lewis. "My great-grandmother, my grandmother, my mother, my two uncles, Alfonse and Willie, and my cousin Sydney."

No proper Bostonian ever spoke the word "family" with deeper pride.

Zaier was becoming feeble now, with nearly 106 years of living behind her. She spent most of her time in a great chair in the kitchen of their home, never without the spotless *tignon* on her head, wearing equally spotless, crisply starched dresses and aprons. She remembered many things she had forgotten during the busy active days of her life. Each year that had passed recently had taken her back farther and farther in time until she lived again her early days in the country to which she had been brought so unwillingly. She spoke often of the old man who had first talked to her in Senegalese, and given reassurance and comfort to a frightened, heart-broken child. Much of the time she herself spoke in the language of Senegal, as her childhood in her native country grew closer. She was, after nearly a century, eluding her captors at last.

Alice and Urania were never too busy to care for her, cooking special dishes, keeping her clothes fresh and crisp, seeing that she was never alone, and that her lively great-grandson, who held her in considerable awe, did not tire or bother her. They did not need

to worry, for Zaier had an inordinate fondness for this highly-strung, emotional, unpredictable child, and he would have had to make a special effort to do anything that would displease her.

George Lewis learned early in life the tricks and skills involved in making three cents do the work of five. Ingenious methods of providing plenty of nourishing food for the table when there was little or no money in the house were second nature to all three women. If you "had it to do" you had it to do—and you did it. Fish backs, with meat still clinging to them after filleting, could be picked up for a penny or so a big bagful, and formed a good base for a stew. In the yard there grew a weed, with a tangy, spicy flavour all its own, and Urania used it when she cooked turkey giblets discarded at the market. "When I was eatin' that," says George Lewis, "I wouldn't have traded places with no one!" Pepper grass grew wild and was good seasoned delicately and cooked plain, and even better pickled. At the French market the outer leaves of cabbage, lettuce, spinach, and mustard greens were easy to come by. Shrimps, oysters, fish of all kinds, and chicken and pork were cheap and plentiful. Beet tops and carrot tops, in the hands of Urania and Alice, became dishes no average cook—who would scorn them— could hope to prepare.

For two and one-half cents one could buy half a loaf of long French bread. If one gave the storekeeper a nickel one received in change a coupon good for another two and one-half cents worth of merchandise. With this coupon it was possible to buy a good-sized piece of salt meat, or a bag of red beans, or second grade barrelled rice. Twenty-five cents, with careful managing, could provide several meals for a family.

Alice never fully approved of her son's extravagant fondness for that New Orleans staple—red beans and rice. She did not believe they had enough nourishment in them for a growing boy, but there must have been a flaw in her reasoning somewhere, for many a Negro child in New Orleans knew little else in his childhood. Her son would have eaten them at every meal, and never tired of their creamy richness, tangy with seasonings of bay and garlic and the soaked-up flavours of sausage and ham, or good salt pork. They were always served with snowy rice, each grain standing apart from its fellows in properly steamed goodness.

And if George Lewis asked for them at every meal, so did another child, born nine days before George, who was growing up then on the other side of town, and who was to reach the

loftiest eminences any American musician has ever reached, both in his own country and abroad—Louis Armstrong. When Louis and George met backstage in a London theatre in 1959, each in his own way the idol of hundreds of thousands, it was of red beans and rice they spoke. In New York, in 1955, Louis came to the side of a prostrate and critically ill George Lewis a few moments after George had collapsed on the bandstand of a Broadway night club. By gentle, compassionate bullying Louis wore down the sick man's resistance to hospitalization with the argument: "If you ever want to get up from there and eat them good red beans and rice again, man, you'd better listen to reason!"

At last the smallness of the one room in which they lived, the cold and the perpetual darkness, proved too much for Alice, and as soon as she could find a vacancy near her mother and grandmother, she moved. The new room at 1226 St Phillip Street was not exactly an outstanding improvement over the old. But at least there was light, although there was no plumbing and, as in the house on St Claude Street, the wide cracks in the walls had to be stuffed with newspapers to keep out the cold and wet. Cooking facilities were primitive, and she had to build almost from scratch a coal-burning monstrosity, which George called a "furnish," on which to cook and heat water. A multitude of rats was included in the rent and the warfare against them was constant and frightening. It differed only in kind from hundreds of other dwelling places in the French Quarter occupied by their people. Somehow, the lovely iron lacework of the New Orleans balconies, the old world picturesqueness of its courtyards, held no "charm" for a man or woman chasing an obscene and vicious rat away from their home and children. And cobble-stoned streets were far from "quaint" to a woman washing the filth and slime of stagnant gutter water from her son's feet and legs before he could go to bed.

The neighbourhood teemed with children, and George Lewis was one of the fastest and quickest of them all. Like his mother, he never moved except at a dead run, and what his legs lacked in length they made up for in speed. Even before he was six years old he began worrying Alice to near-frenzy by the astounding frequency with which he acquired black eyes and a bloody nose. Reasoning with him, scolding, spanking—none of these methods did any good. George Lewis's first reaction to a taunt about his smallness continued to be an all-out effort to prove

that he could lick the one that made it. It was immaterial and irrelevant that the taunter might be twice his size.

And there was still the music from Hopes Hall. Fortunately it did not always come at night, when a small boy must be hustled protesting, into bed. Two or three times a week some one of the various ladies' or children's societies would give all-day parties, winding up with a "banquet" early in the evening. The members would meet first at one of the many Negro churches, and then go in a body to the hall for lunch and dancing in the afternoon, winding up with the banquet early in the evening. The bandstand in Hopes Hall was on a balcony above the dance floor, and at the rear of the stand a door led to another balcony outside. The house on St Phillip Street was directly in behind the hall and the music was as close as it had been when they lived on Treme Street. Whether it was a daytime or a night-time affair, the musicians would first play four or five numbers on the outside balcony, warming up their horns, warming up the neighbourhood, "callin' the chil'ren in."

Some mighty horns were blown on that balcony. In later years the too-few records on which they were heard were to be fought for by collectors all over the world. Men like King Oliver, Alphonse Picou, Willie Cornish, Lorenzo Tio, Jr., George Baquet —"he could make you cry on a E-flat clarinet, that man could" —, Big Eye Louis Nelson and Charlie McCurtis blew there, cheeks puffed, eyes bulging with exertion or closed tightly, the better to hear their own notes. The music reached far and wide, down the alleys and into the courtyards, bringing the women out of the kitchens and the dark rooms of their homes, and the men out of the saloons and off the delivery vans and the coal wagons and push carts; bringing the children from everywhere a child might be.

They played in bands like the Superior, Olympia, Imperial— magic, golden bands with sounds and rhythms that crept into a small Negro boy's blood and bones and marrow like licking flames, and fired the sleeping rhythms of his ancestors; that talked a language as real as speech, and rejoiced and wailed, and told stories to his heart. There was the joy of uninhibited release in their tones, and the sorrow of a hundred years of heartbreak. The surging gold of the brasses, the hot, liquid silver of the clarinets, the crying of the violins, and the drum's throbbing beat that held them all together, lived with the child long after the

music had stopped. At night, when he was supposed to be sleeping, he heard the music in his head and felt it coursing through his body and pulsing in his blood. High above all the other sounds, the last to die in his memory, were the clarion-clear tones of the clarinet, flowing like a river of flashing jewels through and around the other instruments, sobbing in its low register, sometimes wailing and sometimes singing in its high register, laughing in incredibly swift and intricate stop-time solos; mocking, weeping, rejoicing, mourning, but speaking always to something within him that answered.

"There wasn't any other instrument in the band, really, for me," says George Lewis. "Seems like the first time I ever heard the music, the clarinet got to me. I never wanted anything else."

And as the bands played the children gathered below in the streets to listen in ecstasy. When the musicians went inside and the music poured through the open windows the children would dance until stopped by sheer exhaustion. George would stand as close to the balcony as he could get, one knee flexing with the rhythm in a mannerism he never lost. When the band was outside his eyes would be riveted on the flashing fingers of the clarinetist, trying to search out his secret. He was always more quiet than the other children when the music was playing, and he would clap his hands softly, as he does today in front of his own band, in double time to the beat, pat-pat pat-pat pat-pat, eyes glowing. To play on the balconies of Hopes Hall must be the greatest height a musician could attain. Of this, young George Lewis was certain.

nine

ON most fine Sunday mornings in the years between 1905 and 1910 residents of St Phillip Street could look from their windows and see two familiar figures strolling purposefully along the banquette. One was tall and straight, with an impeccably waxed black moustache. He walked with a peculiar striding step, hands clasped behind him, head bent to catch the words of his companion, a small boy who, with unusual dignity, strove to

match the other's steps, making himself tall, feeling tall.

The Sunday suit of knee pants and jacket the boy wore was pressed to perfection, the blouse was starched and spotless, ironed by his mother at dawn that morning before she went to work. If it was winter he wore a cap, but in summer a sailor hat sat squarely on his head, not betraying by so much as a rumpled streamer the battle that had been waged between mother and son to assure its presence there.

Those were proud moments for George Lewis, and he felt every inch a man as he walked down St Phillip Street with his father on Sunday mornings on their way to Bee the Riders' shoe-shine parlour. For one thing, pappa never tried to hold his hand or anything silly like that, but talked with him as he would with another friend, and they held long, important, man-to-man conversations.

At Bee's they sat companionably side by side while their shoes were being shined. Henry Zeno always watched the process closely, catching the shoe-shine boy up sharply if he skimped the job. The brushes and rags snapped back and forth rhythmically, and Henry would talk and the boy would watch, as he did everything, with absorbed attention.

"Pappa, I could do that," he said one morning after they had left Bee's and were on their way to the child's eventual destination, church.

"Do what, son?"

"Shine shoes, pappa. I could make money and help maw and get a horn, too."

"Horn! Horn! Don't you ever think of nothin' but gettin' a horn, boy? What would a little tike like you do with a horn after you got it? Tell me that now."

But Henry only asked the question because he wanted to see the glow in the boy's eyes. He'd asked it many times before.

"Make music, pappa!" The child forgot his dignity and broke into a running step, half skip, half tap. "Make music, pappa. Like this. Listen!" His whistle, surer now than when Urania had first heard it in her kitchen, was loud and clear, and around the melody were flying, skylarking phrases the composer never would have recognized.

"That's the way they blow at Hopes Hall, pappa."

"Damn, boy, I believe you could make music at that. One of these days, son, we'll get you a horn."

But if the boy's notes were loud and clear in the sunlight, Henry Zeno knew that his own words were a form of whistling in the dark. He knew now that in leaving Alice he had exchanged freedom for bondage, left a woman who might be quick-spoken and sometimes imperious, but who let a man be a man. The woman he had gone to was not only without conscience, but harsh and demanding in money matters, and instead of having his own money as a man should have—even if it was only a couple of dimes to rub together in his pocket—he had to save carefully each week and hide safely the little bit of change he'd need to take this Sunday walk with his son and pay for their shoe shines, with perhaps a penny or two left over for candy or a soft drink.

Henry was beginning to be plagued by bad health, and sometimes as he and his son walked together down St Phillip Street a fine dew of sweat would break out on his forehead and lip, under the waxed black moustache, and he would turn his head so the boy could not see him wince from the lancing pains that stabbed through back and loins.

There were days at a time when he could not work because of pain and sickness. On those days he would sit outside on the gallery rocking miserably rather than lie in bed, a vulnerable target for the scorn of the woman he was living with.

If Alice knew of the conditions in which he lived, and she must have, she never indicated her knowledge. One Sunday night, after she had returned from work, her son said to her: "Pappa's sick, maw. He didn't come for me to get our shoes shined an' I went down there. Her was hurtin' real bad, maw."

"I'm sorry, son. And I'm glad you went to see him. That was right. Now wash up quickly and eat your supper. I swear, George Lewis, I don't see, I don't see indeed, how a young one so small can get so much dirt on him in one day. You been fighting again?"

"N-no m'am."

"Yes, you have. That eye's swelling. Don't lie to me. Not ever, or I'll whip you good, black eye or not. Now answer me. Have you been fighting?"

"Well—ma—jes' a little fight. Honest, ma, it wasn't nothin'. Willie Anderson called me a squirt. He hit me first."

"I suppose he did. After you dared him to." She was peeling a potato as she talked.

"Lord, Lord! What did I ever do to have a son so sweet and good around the house and so contrary when my back's turned. Hold still now—" and she deftly dabbed a raw potato poultice on his eye.

Alice's heart was as great and warm as her tongue was quick, and it embraced everyone she knew, but she would not have been human if she had not known moments of bitter resentment against the father of her son. There was not enough money to be made by taking in washing and ironing to pay the rent, buy coal, feed her boy and keep shoes on his feet, let alone provide for her own necessities—not when the pay was only 25 cents for a huge mosquito bar that took the better part of a day to wash, dry, iron and fold, using the combined efforts of herself and small son. And payments were correspondingly low for other work, for was not Alice, in the eyes of the employer class, a member of that group which "didn't need so much to live on"?

As a consequence at various times she worked out as cook for several different families, but her worry about the boy, left from daybreak until after dark, was so great she could not bear to continue with the jobs. It was better to stay at home and take in washing and ironing as long as she could, though when she did this she was troubled because she had to ask her son to work with her. It seemed a pity that a boy so young, so full of play, should be deprived of his freedom, but she remembered her own childhood, and her family's teachings, and the teachings of the church that, whatever the task, if it was done for the glory of God it brought you closer to Him. And she remembered Zaier's stern admonitions—that one did not gainsay God.

Being required to help his mother with her work made George Lewis no different than the vast majority of other children in the neighbourhood. Each day a constant procession of youngsters could be seen going to the "plug" in the street for water, for running water was a luxury very few of the households in that vicinity boasted, Alice taught him how to fold the mosquito bars —and it took them both—and how to stretch and shape the heavy lace curtains of that era. He learned to clear the water, and mix starch, and how to cope with the primitive stove on which the water must be heated. He hated the chores, but he did them because even at that age he sensed, as do most children reared in poverty, that work was somehow tied in with survival.

He was sick much of the time. Colds, fevers, and undiagnosed

ailments plagued him throughout infancy and childhood. There was no money for doctors and in common with most of her people Alice Zeno believed in calling doctors only *in extremis,* as one calls the priest. At an early age he learned the usefulness of mutton tallow and camphor, wild honeysuckle, Irish moss, "composte tea," senna leaves, tamarind bark, quinine weed, flaxseed tea and flaxseed poultices and—of course—sulphur and syrup. On the days when he was ill and she was forced to go out to work she left him in the house with an array of home remedies on the table beside the bed he shared with her, and stern instructions to remain where he was. She never knew how often those instructions were ignored, when the youngster would slip from the house, somehow evade the watchful eyes of the neighbours, and seek the source of the music that had come through the thin walls of their home. It might be blocks away. No matter. He always found it.

He was sent to deliver the laundry after she had finished it when he was still so young it took both hands and arms to carry the bundle. One of the houses to which he delivered laundry was on St Louis Street, between Dauphine and Bourbon Streets, then —as now— one of the historic homes of old New Orleans. Deeply imbedded in the beautifully waxed, gleaming hardwood floors of the lower story of the house are the hoofprints of a horse, and elsewhere the ugly scars of wanton damage.

The story is that from this house a slave who had been mistreated ran away and finally, escaping capture, joined the coloured forces fighting for the Union Army. After the Emancipation Proclamation, during the stormy days of the Reconstruction period, he returned in a uniform much embellished and bedecked with medals and rode a spirited horse up the steps of the house and throughout the lower floor, taking with him what he wanted of silver and valuables, destroying what he did not want. How long the plan had been growing in a mind made sick by circumstance there is no way of knowing, but the house remains in that city the symbol of a bitter harvest.

Sometimes a young girl cousin his own age, daughter of Alice's sister, helped him on these errands. When the washing was too large to be made into a bundle, Alice would pack it in a basket, and George's thin arms were stretched to their fullest extent to enable him to grasp both handles. When his cousin went with

him each child took a handle, and they trudged together down the street swinging the basket between them.

The route to one of Alice's customers led past a veterinarian's office and hospital. The veterinarian was a man of dark and dreadful hate, all of it concentrated on Negroes. He had several sons, and he taught them, as one teaches dogs, to rush the Negro children passing on the sidewalk, and if they could not run them off the sidewalk and into the street, to beat them up. But peril has always had a certain fascination for children, and while George and his cousin had always obeyed Alice's orders to go out of their way a block to avoid passing the establishment, eventually their curiosity led them past the building. They were both dressed in freshly laundered, starched clothes, for after the washing was delivered they were to attend a party given by his cousin's Sunday School class. It was a warm day, and the windows of the veterinarian's surgery were open. They could see him inside, and see an anaesthetized dog lying on the table undergoing surgery. The man was noted for his kindness to animals. On a small table beside the larger operating table was the usual basin for waste material, filled now with bloody sponges and organic matter. The veterinarian glanced up at the sound of footsteps on the banquette outside and his face reddened with venom at the sight of the two small, brown-skinned children. Quick as lightning, and with deadly aim, he picked up the basin of waste material and threw it from the window. Its contents scattered. Both children were covered with the material it contained. They were too terrified to scream, and fled the remaining four blocks to the haven of Alice Zeno's arms as though all the demons in hell were after them.

It was the first, but not the last, time George Lewis was to ask the question his people have been asking for more than two centuries, the question to which there can never be an answer they will understand—"Why?"

Lewis described the incident to this writer when he was fifty-six years old, and ended the recountal in gentle, unemotional, reasonable accents by saying: "But you know, a funny thing happened. Right after that, that man burned to death—I mean he really burned *up*—on account of a stove exploding in his house. Afterwards the coloured kids could walk down the block without bein' scared half to death. It's a mighty bad thing—to frighten a young 'un like that."

Alice Zeno was a wise woman, with the unspoiled wisdom lost

to many because of lack of its necessity. For every delivery of laundry that her son made, she paid him. True, it was in infinitesimal amounts, but it was pay, and he had worked for it, and it was his own. When he was so young the lisp of infancy was still in his speech he knew what it was to be able to say: "This is my money. I worked for it."

Eventually Alice had to face the inevitable necessity of going to work regularly on a daily job. She knew this must be done, not only because of the dollar or two more a month it would bring in, but because it would mean a definite sum periodically which could be divided up—a few cents here, a few cents there—for their needs. She faced the prospect with heartache and dread. It would mean leaving this small, emotional, hyperactive youngster all day, every day, seven days a week. He might be headstrong and disobedient and need frequent chastisement, but his dependence on her was absolute, and all the fire and passion and emotion of her being were centred on him. Who would comfort and care for him in his frequent illnesses? Who keep him off the streets? Who make sure that he did not stuff himself with red beans and candy in lieu of decent food?

She watched him one morning as he sat at the table in the one room that served all their needs. He was eating rice, tiny feet drumming on the chair rung, oblivious to everything except the need to hurry so he could run outside and play. He seemed so small, so frail, so helpless. Before she could control it a sob tore out of her throat and tears coursed down her cheeks. The boy's black eyes watched in amazement that turned quickly to panic. He had seen his mother cry before, but this time it was different. He jumped from his chair and ran to her, clasping her knees.

"Ma! What's wrong? Please, ma—" and he was sobbing himself—"Please, ma, don't cry! Please!"

Holding him close she had wept uncontrollably. "Who'll take care of you, baby, when mother's gone? Who'll care—"

"Please, ma, don't. I'll do it. I'll take care of me, ma. Just don't cry."

He never forgot it and while, as any other child might, he forgot a promise he would not have been able to keep in any event, he never throughout his life forgot his mother's tears, and even after he had grown to middle-age his own eyes would fill remembering them.

The first job which she secured seemed like a miracle, an

answer to her constant prayers that she might find work and still be able to be near her son.

A white family needed her services, a family with small children who were to be taken to the park each clear day for fresh air and play. Alice loved all children, knew how to play with them and become one with them, and yet maintain authority. Each day she would stop and pick up George and take him with her, and for those few hours she knew where he was, and that he was safe.

Her happiness did not last long. After three or four excursions to the park her employer called her aside as she was leaving the house with the children one afternoon.

"Alice, my boy tells me you pick your little boy up and take him to the park too, with our children?"

"Yes, madam." Alice had always used, and continued throughout her life to use, the French "madam" when she spoke to employers.

"But, Alice—"—and Mrs Zeno said the woman stumbled over her words as though they were 'hard to bring out' and that her face was flushed with embarrassment—"don't you think it would be—well—better—if you left him at home? Isn't it a little too much for you, with all those children?"

Alice's only reply was to say quietly: "Yes, madam." She herself had said too often to her son, in a sing-song chant: "Play in your own backyard, never mind what the white child do" not to realize that she should have known better. The woman's meaning was as clear as the signs "white" and "coloured" that were springing up like festering sores all over the city.

The next morning Alice sent a neighbour's child to the woman's house to say that she would not be able to work that day. The following day she sent word that she would not be returning at all. She utilized the day off to search for another job. But true to her "survival course" training by Zaier and Urania, she never disclosed her real reason for quitting the job she needed so badly; and the woman whose children Alice's son was not good enough to play in the park with because of the colour of his skin could chalk up another black mark against "Nigra servants" for their "unreliability."

When Henry Zeno learned of it his face tautened as his father's used to.

"A chile's a chile," said Henry. "An' a black chile needs the grass under his feet now and then as much as a white chile.

Mebbe more. I'd of told that woman. Before Gawd, I'd of told her."

And he would have.

More than forty years later George Lewis was to play in a fashionable hotel in New Orleans and be required, because of the colour of his skin, to ride in the freight elevator while white musicians took the passenger elevator to the floor on which the function was held. Henry Zeno's son never played there again, except once when he did so to accommodate a fellow Negro musician who was in trouble. Alice Zeno's son gave as an excuse, on each occasion he was asked to play, that he was sorry but he'd be out of town, or that he had promised to play elsewhere.

Alice found other work almost immediately. For several years she did not settle down to constant work with one family, but later she was to go to work for the family of Judge Harry Renshaw, and remain with them, off and on, during most of her working life, establishing an affectionate relationship with the family that remained unbroken for almost fifty years.

On the jobs which she took during George's childhood she left the house at seven in the morning, sometimes earlier if there was ironing or other extra work besides cooking to do for her employers. She was not free until after dinner, and if there were dinner guests and subsequent social activities she did not finish until late at night. The work week was seven days. For this she received twelve dollars a month and the privilege of "toting" home at the end of the day the left-overs from the meals, and two or three pieces of stone coal. She paid her own carfare.

There was no compensatory time off on the morning following a night when she had worked late, and she would often arrive at the still-shuttered home of the family she worked for early in the morning to prepare a breakfast that might not be eaten until late forenoon.

There was no chance to be with her son during the day, except when she was forced to take an afternoon off to buy him shoes, or for some other absolutely necessary reason. That she was able, under these handicaps, to influence and to train him throughout his childhood and youth is evidence of an almost incredible character. Only one way could be devised for overseeing the boy she loved so much: asking the help of the neighbours who lived in the same 'yard' with them. It was necessary, though distasteful, to set up a well-organized spy system. Only in this way could

she know if he was at home when he should be in school; if he was rude or impolite or lacking in manners to any adult, white or coloured; if he had been fighting when there were no tattle-tale bruises; if he sniffled or sneezed with one of his frequent colds; if, in short, anything transpired that should be brought to the attention of an anxious mother. It did not endear the neighbours to George Lewis, but it provided her with some sort of check on his activities.

By this time Alice Zeno was in her mid-forties, and was going through a difficult, painful, and debilitating menopause. There were undoubtedly other physical disabilities, but she did not seek medical aid, asking only for strength from the God she believed in so unswervingly. She told, in her latter years, of waking in the morning, before dawn, scarcely able to get out of bed, yet somehow dressing and walking to the streetcar. Later, when she arrived at the house where she worked, she would find herself leaning against the gate before she entered, sweating with weakness and pain, praying soundlessly. George remembers vividly nights when, after she had come home, she would double up with pain, almost sinking to the floor, while he tried futilely to help her. But there is no record that she ever begged off and came home early because of illness. If God could get her to the gate, she could make it through the day. She took time off only for her son's illnesses, and this was a serious matter for she was not paid for the days she did not work.

And always, no matter how ill or weak she might be, there was a stop to be made at the church on the way to the streetcar, to pray for the child she must leave alone all day in order to provide for him.

"Watch over him, Blessed Mother, in the name of thy son, Jesus Christ, Amen," she would end her prayer, and after a while the lump in her throat would go down and she would know the peace of faith. But only for a little while, for few mothers can leave a frail child alone for from twelve to fourteen hours a day without suffering agonies of anxiety, no matter how great their faith.

"Alice is sick, mother," she once overheard the daughter of an employer say.

"Don't worry, child," she heard the mother reply. "You'll learn to take these coloured folks 'sickness' with a grain of salt. I declare, they love to complain."

Each day she left her son with five cents for a "poor boy" sandwich for lunch. Had he always bought one of these famous New Orleans specialities he would have been more than well fed, for they were huge half-loaves of French bread, crammed with meat and cheese, lettuce and sausage—enough to stay the hunger of a working man; more than enough for a small boy.

But he did not always buy them, and sometimes the nickel went for all-day suckers, and licorice, or soft drinks, or some trinket he wanted. It is probable that the pattern of irregular eating that stayed with him all his life was started then; a pattern that eventually caused doctors, not only in the United States but half-a-dozen other countries, to throw up their hands in despair at the problem of keeping him strong and well.

Beneath his outer clothing in fall and winter he wore a woollen shirt that he and his mother called "Joseph's coat." Started when he was four years old, made from a fragment of woollen blanket, each year it was added to in length and breadth. Eventually it included a piece of just about every warm woollen article Alice Zeno was able to lay her hands on. He hated it with a deadly hatred, for some of the pieces of wool were the itchy kind, and others were not, but he dared not take it off. If she had come home early unexpectedly and found him without it, retribution would have been swift and painful.

In summer he wore fresh, clean underthings every day. Alice always managed to find time to keep them washed, and most of the time she made them for him herself from pieces of flour sacking, or scraps of material her employers would give her. He was so small they did not need to be large scraps. Before he was seven she had taught him to wash them himself, and he never balked at the chore. Neatness, with George Lewis, and a passion for cleanliness, must have been born in him, regardless of the theories of modern psychologists that training is everything. Most mothers struggle endlessly with children to enforce neatness and cleanliness. Young George Lewis gloried in it. When she was 93 years old, and living with her son in Algiers, Mrs Zeno told this writer that he was making her nervous. "He's so dratted fussy," she said. "Always going around picking things up, wiping up a grain of dust. Sometimes I wish I was back in my own apartment over the river, where I could relax." But she wouldn't have left his side for all the gold and precious jewels of the Indies.

It was fortunate for Alice's peace of mind that she did not

know in those days how often he played hookey from school to go swimming or fishing in the river, or to follow the parades and band wagons around the city. Next to playing in Hopes Hall which, in the eyes of George Lewis, was a matter of prestige as well as accomplishment, playing on the back of one of the advertising band wagons came as close to what must go on in Heaven as anything he knew about. Thus must the blessed travel on celestial highways! To ride through the streets on a mule- or horse-drawn truck or wagon, singing on a horn, the brass and drums blazing forth in golden glory, meeting in fair combat with other wagons full of musicians—this must be ecstasy. He followed them for blocks,—school, chores, everything forgotten but the sound and the rhythm and the message of the music. And when the wagons met and locked wheels and settled down to grim and glorious competition he stood motionless except for the rhythmic flexing of the knees, the soft pat-pat of the hands, until one or the other of the bands emerged from the contest victorious. Nothing like this band wagon music has ever been heard outside of New Orleans, for no stage or concert hall or crowded night-club can offer the driving incentive to musical inventiveness and imagination that these bitter-end duels afforded the musicians who took part in them. Let the modernists criticise the "technique" of these musicians as compared with school- and academy-trained men; they show by so doing only their own ignorance of an art form that is in every phase of its manifestation an example of supreme individual accomplishment. Without technique, a complete and absolute mastery of their instruments, they would not have been able to last ten minutes in such a battle, for these men were harsh and jealous judges of each other's merits, and the man who substituted noise for skill found himself without jobs, shunted aside and overlooked when a musician was needed for a 'gig.'

George Lewis frequently came to grief on these forbidden excursions away from home or school. He was so small he was fair game for the white boys who, either singly or in gangs, made it their business to set upon a coloured child or group of children. Many a cut and bruise his mother found on him at the end of the day he attributed to his now almost routine fights with the boys in the neighbourhood, rather than reveal that he had been in a "rock fight" with the whites. His own aim was unerring with a rock, and while he knew better than to throw one first, he always

gave a good account of himself after the first one had sailed in his direction from the hands of a white boy.

By night the small youngster was exhausted. There had been no mother to see that he rested, no one to call him in from the streets and the constant running and playing. There was never a respite to re-charge his batteries as there would have been if Alice had been there. When sickness came it found an undersized body all too ready to receive it, an organism in which a virus or a germ could find a ideal spot to set up housekeeping.

The end of a day's work might seem an aeon to Alice, but as the shadows lengthened on St Phillip Street and the other children of the neighbourhood scampered home in answer to their mothers' calls to supper, the time that must elapse before his mother could alight from the streetcar seemed endless to her tired, lonely son.

Then he would walk slowly to the corner of Rampart and St Phillip Streets and take up what frequently became a long and frightened vigil. He might have gone to Urania and Zaier, but he was afraid that he would miss his mother when she got off the streetcar, and that she would go home and he would not be there. As a child and man George Lewis had great physical courage, but his mental life was and always has been full of fear and foreboding, and his imagination has led him into dark and disastrous situations, few of which have ever materialized.

And so he would stand and wait, not fidgeting too much, for he was too tired. Sometimes rain would drench him to the skin, other times the heat that at home made the pitch between the pine boards of their house ooze and bubble would wrap around him like a sticky blanket. The times when his mother worked late were nightmares to the boy. As the darkness grew thicker, and the night life of the French Quarter began to surge around him his mind conjured up all manner of frightful things that might have happened to her. Fear was a lump of ice in his stomach, and even when the air was hot his teeth would chatter.

Finally he would start for home, often sent on his way by a policeman or a kindly friend and, if it was winter, once home he would build a fire in the "furnish" if there was coal, so she would be able to get warm when she came in, although by that time he would be almost certain she would never come home. Then he would huddle in front of the fire until the sound of her steps sent him into tears of relief.

But if he was still on the corner when her streetcar rumbled to a stop, and her tall, spare form descended wearily, the boy would dart forward, heedless of traffic, with a Comanche-like yell of joy. "Ma! Ma! Here I am, Ma!" Alice always carried a large bag for the left-overs which she "toted" and which would be his dinner (a dinner fit for any gourmet, for had not Alice cooked it with the skill of Zaier and Urania in every mouthful?), and containing also two or three lumps of stone coal to keep them warm. Half the time the bag went skittering across the pavement as he catapulted into her. Her first words were usually sharp from love and inexpressible relief that he was there and whole.

"What you doing here, son? How many times have I told you not to wait here? Why aren't you in bed?" Then when they reached the banquette she would stop and throw an arm around the thin shoulders and rest her cheek on the kinky head. Time enough when she got home to scold or punish for the misdeeds of the day. Enough now that the saints had heard, and for a few moments her own weariness and pain were lost in gratitude.

"You been good, son?"

"How I lied sometimes," says George. "I always told her 'yes.' But I knew she'd find out everything I'd done. It didn't matter. Lots of times I'd get a licking that night, after she'd talked with the neighbours, and I knew it. It didn't matter."

All that mattered was that love and security, warmth and protection, were round him again, and that he need not face the rest of the night alone.

ten

"ANYBODY need a hatchet, a ladder, an' a nail?"

"Here, boy!"

"Yes, *m'am*!"

A ladder to reach high on the wall of a tomb in St Louis cemetery, a nail on which to hang a vase of flowers, a hatchet to hammer in the nail and clear away the undergrowth—on All Saints day the wide-smiling, thin, brown-skinned child with the "soft sell" approach would furnish all three for a few pennies.

On that day the cemeteries in New Orleans are full of people. The day before, those who can afford it have paid to have the family tombs scrubbed and whitewashed if need be, or have done it themselves, and on that all-important occasion these strange, above-ground abodes of the New Orleans dead gleam white under the flowers and wreaths. It might be spring instead of fall, and they gardens instead of graveyards.

Zaier's family needed no calendar to tell them when All Saints' day was approaching. Throughout the last week of October the constant toneless whistling of Urania warned all and sundry that she was preparing candies—pralines and *Tante Betsies* and her own special snow-white concoction—for sale at the gates of the cemetery.

When that day came Urania would be seated at the gates, her wares spread in front of her, doing a brisk business. Nearby other vendors offered peanuts and soft drinks and candy, and within the cemetery her small grandson was gleaning pennies for the pockets of his mended, carefully pressed suit. The tombs were high, and the ladder he dragged behind him often needed. He had made the ladder himself and because he did not have money to buy new nails had scavenged old and rusty ones, bent and apparently useless, and with the hatchet his Uncle Arthur had given him hammered them straight and true.

But his activities did not stop with the furnishing of the ladder, the careful placing of the nail, the hanging of the vase of flowers for his customers. When these things were done to his satisfaction —and he was meticulously careful—he would stand back and after he had thanked his patrons for his pay with a wide smile and a quick bob of the head, his eyes would travel quickly down to their shoe tops and flash as swiftly back again.

"I'd be happy to shine those shoes, m'am. Mighty dusty around here."

Where the home-made shoeshine kit came from, or how he produced it so instantaneously, was hard to figure out. It must, to his customers' bewildered eyes, have materialized from the ground. It was almost impossible to say "no." The boy was so small, so polite, so breathtakingly efficient.

When his shoe-shining chore was finished, he would rear back on thin haunches and swiftly pack away his equipment, deftly and neatly. Then he would draw a clean handkerchief from his pocket and wipe his forehead.

"Kind of warm today, m'am," he would say. "Can I carry you a glass of water before I goes away? Yes, *m'am,* jes' a minute an' I'll be back with it."

When his mother arrived home that night there would be pennies to show her, and nickels and even a few dimes. He would account to her, as she had accounted to her mother long ago, for every cent he had made, telling her how many vases of flowers he'd hung, how many pairs of shoes shined, how many glasses of water "carried" to his customers, and how much he had received for each service.

The money would help Alice with her carfare, but she always left him with a few pennies for anything he wanted for himself, a piece of candy, the ice cream he so seldom was able to have, a trinket he had wanted. *His money.*

She knew he did not always buy these luxuries but instead tucked the pennies away in a secret hiding place all his own. She was glad that he was saving his pennies, but she was concerned over his plans for their eventual use. Alice had not given up hope entirely that she could sway him from his determination to play a 'horn' some day. She tried both devious and direct approaches to the problem, extravagantly admiring the music from the violins they heard in Hopes Hall, or telling him flatly that he wasn't strong enough to blow a horn and that it would be bad for him. It is extremely doubtful that he heard a word she said in either form of persuasion.

She had been forced to admit that she was at least two-thirds defeated one day when he was seven years old. She was between jobs, and had been doing washing and ironing for several days, and for what seemed to her constantly her son had been begging her to get him a toy whistle. At last she gave in, although not completely. A quarter in those days, for the Zenos, could mean not one but several meals, but she dug into her purse and brought one out.

"If I give you this, son, will you stop at Kirby's after you carry the laundry, and buy the toy violin I saw there?"

The boy looked at the quarter with big eyes and though he knew very well the penalties for lying, answered: "Sure, ma."

He had gone to Kirby's, now a red-fronted chain five and ten-cent store, and dutifully picked up and looked at the toy violin. And then he saw on the same counter—not a toy whistle, but a flute, a real flute, such as the boys played in the little "field"

bands that marched round the neighbourhoods. Without so much as a pang of conscience he relinquished his mother's hard-earned quarter for the flute, and ran the rest of the way home.

For once she had not been able to punish him for his disobedience, though she scolded him roundly. But she could not mar that ecstatic happiness. She had never seen her son's eyes shine as they shone that day as he held his flute caressingly, stroking it with long, thin fingers. And any flickering idea of retribution she may have had vanished when he said—

"Now I can play for you when you sing, ma."

It was after that incident that the saving of the pennies began, and although Alice was not one to give up easily, she mentally stopped struggling one afternoon two years later, when they had gone to buy him shoes.

She always held his hand tightly on these shopping expeditions. He was so fast on his feet that before she knew it he would dart away, into traffic, around a corner, down the street, and when she caught up with him she would usually find him with his nose flattened against the window of a music or second-hand store, or pawn shop, anywhere there might be displayed or hidden away in a musty interior what she had begun to call "one of those damned horns."

On this particular day he had wriggled from her grasp, and she had found him staring in speechless admiration at a clarinet displayed in the window of a second-hand store. The price card propped in front of it read "$5.00."

After she had managed to drag him away from the window they had proceeded down the block in silence. Then he had spoken.

"Gee, five dollars, maw."

"Don't call me maw."

"Five *dollars,* ma."

"Don't call me ma, either. Mamma or mother."

"Five dollars, mamma. How many pennies is that?"

"Five hundred."

Awed silence for a few feet.

"Gee." More silence. "How many nickels?"

"One hundred."

More silence as the boy skipped beside her. He had to skip or half-run to keep up with her long strides, and a boy could skip with a beat. SKIP-skip-skip-skip; SKIP-skip-skip-skip; SKIP-skippety-SKIP-skip-skip. At last he said:

"That's fifty dimes."

"Yes, son, fifty dimes."

Silence.

"I got—I got—gee, ma—mamma, I got four nickels, an' 23 pennies, an' two dimes."

"That's fine, son."

"How much is it, mamma?"

"Figure it out for yourself, son."

More skipping until suddenly the boy came to a dead stop, almost pulling his mother off her feet.

"George Lewis!"

"I'm sorry, ma. Honest—I'm sorry. But, ma—mamma—wait now—ma, I got 63 cents!"

The boy started along beside her again, and then said sadly:

"I mighta had enough, ma, if it hadn't been for last year—and them times I was sick."

It was true that his opportunities for saving had been greatly curtailed, both by illness and by a year of isolation in a private school, where his mother had placed him after she had discovered he had played hookey from the public school for a straight and uninterrupted three months. The story of this black twelve-month period belongs a little later on, although it occurred when he was approximately eight years old.

The first illness had come perhaps two years before, when even the boy's excessive bounding nervous energy could not outdo the fever that sent him home alone from play to lie across the bed. When his mother arrived home that night he was sleeping, and when she wakened him she saw the glazed eyes, noted the confused mind, felt the burning hands and forehead. His throat was so sore he could not speak. She did what she could for him throughout a long night, and the next morning, when his condition grew worse, ran to fetch a doctor.

"Diphtheria," said the doctor succinctly, after examining the child. "He'll have to have constant care."

Alice was shaking with nerves and fright.

"What can I do, doctor? I have to go to work. I can't make enough if I stay home to buy his medicine. His grandmother has too much to do, her house is too crowded—I can't take him there."

"Then he must go to the hospital."

At first she fought the idea, but then knew that for his own good it must be done. Throughout long days she worked in a

trance-like fog of worry and apprehension while the boy's spirit flickered between life and death in Charity Hospital. When at last the worst was over the doctor advised her to leave him in the hospital.

"Those tonsils will give him trouble all his life. They should come out," he told her.

Alice understood the need for this very well. The children of some of her employers had survived the same operation—but they were not frail and sickly like her son, and they had been in private hospitals. Still, the care he had received during the illness had pulled him through, and she could only renew her prayers that he would survive surgery as well.

When he was declared ready to leave the hospital the doctor told her sternly that he must be watched carefully. There had been, he believed, some previous heart damage. Had the child ever, the doctor asked, complained of joint pains? Alice replied that he had, that there had been one time when for two weeks he had lain in bed with swollen, painful knees and ankles, unable even to play around the room, and that during that time there had been some fever.

"He mustn't run or play hard. And he mustn't be allowed to run up and down stairs; or even, for a while, to go up and down stairs at all. Watch him closely."

Watch him closely! Alice's smile was bitter as she carried him into the house. To watch him closely meant to give up her work, and to remain at home and take in washing meant there would not be enough money for the medicines, the warm clothes, the rent and food—or the shoes he would soon be needing.

Later in that same year she woke in the night, her son's fretful moaning in her ears. She felt his body quickly and the fever burned through his nightclothes into her hand. By the next day she knew that once again the boy was critically ill and again she called the doctor.

"Scarlet fever," said the doctor.

This time she could not face sending him to the hospital, but instead went to her employers and told them of the doctor's verdict. She knew that her absence from work to care for the child meant no pay, but she would manage somehow. All she could hope for was that they would permit her to return to work when he was well—if he should get well. They recognized immediately that here was no bid for sympathy, but genuine trouble,

and they agreed; if, they said, "you aren't away too long Alice."

It was a long battle, and Alice waged it with every atom of love and faith she had within her. The words of the doctor rang in her ears like a knell. "I believe there has been some heart damage." And, then, miraculously, the fever broke, the child's eyes lighted with a clear, natural light instead of the dull, burning glaze of fever, and one day when she was at the store he slipped from bed and spooned himself up a plate of beans from the pot on the stove and ate them ravenously. In those days the "starve a fever" theory was popular, and when she found out what he had done she raged in futile, fear-ridden anger.

The next day the doctor pronounced him out of immediate danger.

"Nourishing food in small quantities now," said the doctor. "He couldn't have anything better than ice-cream. It's nourishing, and he'll relish it."

Ice-cream! Relish it! The boy wriggled with delight under the bedclothes, then lay quiet. Shucks! There wasn't ever enough money for ice-cream even when his mother was working. There wouldn't be any at all now, after she'd had to stay home and take care of him so long.

He underestimated his mother. In the Zeno household were two heavy antique chairs given to Alice by the family her grand-mother worked for. They were beautiful chairs, and the only furniture in the place that gave it any semblance of life and beauty. They were also the only two chairs that Alice and her son had to sit on, save one rickety kitchen chair.

A white woman who lived a few doors away had always admired the chairs whenever she had come to Alice's home to ask her to do a bit of laundry, or to inquire for the sick boy. Alice, without a second thought, went to her now.

"Would you like to buy my two chairs?" asked Alice.

The woman's eyes had lighted avidly.

"Why, Alice! I never thought you'd part with them."

Alice must have known the approximate intrinsic value of the chairs. But she also knew that she could never hope to realize their worth.

"The doctor just left the house," said Alice. "He told me ice-cream would be one of the best things for my boy now that he's getting better. If you want the chairs you can have them for a dollar."

They would have been one of the bargains of the century at a lot more. Alice did not know until several years later when she saw their counterparts in an antique shop window and inquired the price, just exactly how big a bargain she was giving the woman.

"Bring them over, Alice," said her neighbour quickly. "I'll give you a dollar for them, seeing that you need it so badly."

Across the street from the Zeno home the proprietor of the grocery store and sweet shop where Alice did much of her shopping—a voluble, kindly, Italian woman,—watched with deep concern as Alice carried the chairs, one by one, along the banquette.

"Poor Mrs Zeno!" She felt certain that the sick boy had at last died. "So much trouble. So much trouble. And now she's lost the boy. But the little one had no chance. Poor Mrs Zeno!"

In a few moments Mrs Zeno was crossing the street to her shop. Her eyes were dry, and the woman thought how much better for the poor woman it would be if she would cry and not try to hold up so bravely.

When Alice entered the woman did not ask for her son. Better to let it come from the mother, God help her.

"I want ice-cream," said Mrs Zeno. "A half-pint now, and later more. The doctor said George should have it."

The woman gave a little cry of gladness. "Then he is not dead, the bambino? I saw the doctor leave—I saw you carrying the chairs—I thought he had died and you were moving. God is good!"

"I was carrying the chairs to Mrs ———" said Alice. "She paid me a dollar for them so I could get ice-cream."

"Mother of God!" The Italian woman's eyes had almost started from her head. "You sold those beautiful chairs for a dollar—for ice-cream! Alice! Alice! For shame! You would not come to me—you would not ask me? I would have given you the ice-cream for the boy. Go back quickly and get the chairs and give them their stinking dollar. Quickly! I will get the ice-cream. I do not want pay, but if you must, let it be when you can. Hurry now! Get the chairs!"

But when Alice returned she still had the dollar. "They wouldn't take it," she said. "They kept the chairs."

"Then I will not take your money—ever. Better to be a pauper than take that money. Use it for meat broth, and for coal."

And so Alice had ice-cream for her son, and enough money for medicine and to put towards the rent. But for a long time they had one chair, battered and rickety, and one only in their home.

During the periods that he was well George had not spent the entire time in play or following parades or playing hooky to swim and fish. He had absorbed from infancy the need for money, and the knowledge that the only way it was obtainable was by work. So, on his own initiative, he sought out ways and means to make money. Through the childhood years he did many things; worked after school in a cracker factory, and in another factory cracking pecans; gathered brickdust and sold it; collected old bones and scraps of metal and sold them; shined shoes, ran errands; delivered papers early on Sunday mornings, before Mass, and for a period of several months worked afternoons in a pressing shop which was run as a blind by a notorious pimp and gangster.

It would be wrong to give the impression that the boy felt unhappy about all this. He loved every minute of it. He had two definite purposes in working, to help his mother and to save money for a horn. They satisfied two fundamental characteristics of his nature, already becoming marked, the necessity to be needed, and joy in possession of things—including money—he could call "his own."

The most heart-breaking words this writer ever heard George Lewis say were spoken shortly after Alice Zeno's death in 1960, when he was torn by grief. "Nobody *needs* me now," said George.

Not all the pennies he acquired in those childhood days came from working. Some of them were largesse distributed by a handsome white man, who rode a spirited horse each morning through the streets of the area, past the school yards. He always carried a quantity of flowers and of pennies and nickels. He either came in the morning while the children were playing in the school yard before classes, white and coloured together for segregation had not yet reached the schools, or during the recess period.

As the children ran and shrieked and tumbled in play the man would toss the flowers and pennies and nickels into the school yards for them, laughing as they scrambled for them, tossing the coins directly into the hands of the smaller, less aggressive ones so that no one would get more than his share.

He was the man whose courage wrote "finis" to one of the

most shameful chapters in the history of New Orleans when he inserted in a daily paper an announcement that he would furnish a Winchester rifle free to any Negro who felt the need of it to protect himself and his home from the rioting of the whites and persecutions of the police after the Robert Charles incident.

"He was a wonderful man," said George Lewis.

Any Negro in New Orleans would answer "Amen!"

But in spite of all his other activities, the boy still found time to practise on his flute. The neighbours in the yard would hear at odd hours—early in the morning, mid-afternoon on rainy days, or late evening—the high, sweet notes of the cheap tin instrument. Had they looked through the windows of the Zeno home they would have seen a small, thin, bright-eyed boy solemnly prancing up and down the tiny room, playing march music over and over, the same tune, until it pleased him. Or they would have seen him in step with the lilting rhythms of the Schottische, or the slower, more accented beat of the waltz. But always, over and over, he would play the same tune until at last he was satisfied. At least for that day. The next day he would improve on it.

At night when it was dark they would see the glow of an oil lamp through the Zeno window, and had they looked into the window they would have seen, beyond the glow, a tired woman seated—perhaps for the first time that day—on a battered kitchen chair, her son in her lap, his thin legs dangling, as she softly sang to him a Creole lullaby. Beneath her voice was the music of the flute, low and sweet, and when the pauses came in the song the flute would fill them in with quick, darting notes until the small, tired hands could hold it no longer and the black eyes, heavy with sleep, would close, and the boy's head drop on her shoulder.

She would sit rocking him gently for a long time before she carried him to bed, for she needed now to rest.

eleven

AND now Zaier, the Senegalese woman, was in her one hundred and tenth year. She had not spoken for twenty-four months. She and her daughter, Urania, were living now on Governor Nicholas Street. They had moved there two years previously when the two sisters, sole survivors of the family to which Zaier had been sold, died, and distant relatives came and claimed the property on Treme Street. It was the only home Zaier had known since being brought to this country, and she had served loyally within it for almost a century.

During these last two years her existence was that of an infant, concerned primarily with sleep, and with the food her daughter fed to her with unremitting care. Yet each day she managed to indicate that she wanted to sit up, and each day Urania dressed her carefully, from *tignon* to slippers, and with big pillows propped her in an armchair in the kitchen. The words that she had used, before she stopped speaking entirely, were Senegalese, childhood phrases for the most part, but each morning at daybreak she had always said, as she had throughout her life, in those strange accents: "Good morning! I hope everyone is happy."

For many years she had been content. Around her were her children, her grandchildren, and her great-grandchildren. Her daughter was by her side constantly, and her son Arthur lived nearby. It had been more than fifty years since that son had crept to her side in the night, seeking comfort and refuge, believing she would hide him, and—lest he be hunted down and punished further or perhaps killed as a fugitive—she had sent him away, back to the master to whom he had been sold and who had whipped and abused him.

There had never been again an agony of heart as great as she had suffered that night. Now for nearly fifty years, whenever his love for her moved him to, he had walked into her home as a man should, head up, scarred shoulders straight.

Her own dignity was in these children she had borne, and their

children, and their children's children, the dignity of an innate knowledge of worth that could not be taken from them. They were good—the men, the women, and the children—living according to her precepts and example, carrying within them something of herself. For these reasons she was content.

In the fall, just before All Saints day, Urania called the parish priest to administer the last rites. Zaier's son was there, and Urania, and her granddaughter Alice. Outside the warm sun of a belated summer was beating on the banquette. Inside the house seemed dim and cool. The priest spoke in French, and those who had loved her knelt about her, and gave the responses for her. The tears that choked their voices were as much in tribute as in sorrow.

"Go, Christian soul, from this world; in the name of God the Father Almighty Who created thee; in the name of Jesus Christ, the Son of the Living God, Who suffered for thee . . . in the name of angels and archangels . . . in the name of thrones and dominions . . . in the name of principalities and powers . . . in the name of the holy martyrs and confessors . . . and of all God's saints."

They were words that would have been said had she been sinner or saint, monarch or servant, wife or prostitute, rich or poor, black or white, and after the priest had blessed her, he turned and blessed the others, comforting them with the assurance that she had died a good death, and that the life she had lived would bring her quickly into the sight of God. No one of them doubted his words.

On New Year's eve, with 1910 on the threshold of the world, Urania hurried to her mother's side. For two weeks Zaier had not been able to sit up, but had lain day and night in a coma-like sleep. Now Urania thought she heard her struggling to speak. She took the incredibly aged hand in her own and held it gently, as the sounds in the throat grew stronger. At last Zaier spoke, for the first time in two years, and as she did so her fingers tightened perceptibly about her daughter's. It was the word that had been on her lips so often during the eternity she had spent in a cage on the deck of a slave ship, and during the lonely, heart-breaking nights in a new and frightening country.

"Bi-a!" The word came strong and clear. Her mother's name. She never spoke again, and two weeks later slipped away from a world that had ceased to exist for her at all.

But Zaier was not to leave the world unhonoured. As did most of her people, she carried a small burial insurance policy. Many years before her death the company had stopped insuring Negroes, although those already holding policies remained covered. She was the last of their Negro policy-holders to die.

Urania sent the necessary forms to the insurance office. And there someone in authority noticed two things. The first was the unbelievable age of the insured at death, and the second was that she was the last Negro to hold a policy with their company. The principal sum was very small, and would provide for only the simplest of funerals. It was not nearly enough to make the purchase of a casket possible, but just enough to provide a simple pine coffin, of the type called by her people "pin-toe" coffins. They were given this name because, while they were wide at the top to accommodate the shoulders, they were so narrow at the foot, to conserve material, that it was necessary to fasten the two great toes of the deceased together to prevent the feet from turning sideways against the walls. This was done by means of a small piece of cloth, or gauze, and a safety pin.

Years before, when all her children had been living, they had pooled their resources and bought a cemetery vault, and the pin-toe coffin Urania ordered was to be laid in this vault.

But when instructions came from the insurance company to the funeral director they ruled out any "pin-toe" coffin for Zaier. Instead the director was ordered to provide the best his establishment could produce in the way of a casket, and of fine burial clothes. The casket was a huge, magnificent affair of expensive wood, with silver handles, lined with gleaming white satin and containing—luxury of luxuries—a white velvet pillow. The burial clothes were of finest silk, edged with lace. She had entered this country in a cage; she was leaving it as befitted a woman of her accomplishments.

The woman who had been so tall and straight looked very tiny in the big black casket. Those who came to the wake smiled gently at the peaceful face, with its fine bones, and at the snow-white hair. At last, in death, the *tignon* was gone.

During the funeral Mass the casket was closed, in accordance with the custom of the Roman Catholic church; the time for earthly classifications was past, the soul at last anonymous.

No one of her ancestors had died in this land. She was the first of her line. Only her children and grandchildren—a son, a

Book Two

"A March in the Ranks Hard-Pressed and the Road Unknown."

WALT WHITMAN

one

THE circumstances of two Mardi Gras parades in one year were almost as wearing on the excitable ten-year-old George Lewis as scarlet fever had been.

"I wasn't sure whether I'd pull him through or not," Mrs Zeno said many years later.

The first Mardi Gras parade scheduled in New Orleans in 1910 was the annual traditional celebration on Shrove Tuesday, which fell in February that year. The second was scheduled for April, and was to be staged by the Shriners as part of their national convention.

"Ma!" George was out of breath with excitement when he heard of the second. "Ma! You gonna take me to *both*?"

"If you're good, son." And then she wondered why she had said it, for she knew no matter how heinous his conduct might be she would never be able to say 'no' when he asked to be taken to the Mardi Gras parade. She had even taken him to the parade the year he was at Professor Nelson's school. Mardi Gras was the one day of the year when she did not work. She would never have been able to make her way across town, even in the early morning, through the crowded streets and blocked-off traffic, with street cars not even running; and even if she had been able to do so, there would have been little or no work, for no one stayed at

home on Mardi Gras day. Even domestic servants were freed for the day's excitement on Shrove Tuesday.

In the pre-Lenten season in New Orleans the spirit of Mardi Gras was an almost tangible thing, like an unbelievably brilliant Christmas tree ornament that one could take in one's hands and feel the warmth and tingle of its sparkle. Daily, for five days before the big parade there were other parades, of all sizes and descriptions, with every club and organization in the city, white and coloured, participating, although always separately. Gay, irresponsible, carousing crowds thronged the streets day and night, and little work was done.

Music was a more or less commonplace thing, though by no means a commonplace music, at any time in any part of New Orleans with a large Negro population. During the Mardi Gras season an outsider would have been justified in thinking that there was no other activity going on, work or pleasure, except that of "making music."

When bands weren't marching they were practising, and when they weren't practising ensemble, the individual musicians were practising solo at any time or place the fancy struck them. Through every bar and cabaret window the highly skilled, incredibly adept fingers of Negro piano players sent the syncopated, swinging, broken rhythms of ragtime into the noisy streets, or haunting, gut-grabbing, intensely moving blues chords. In the honky-tonks and dives the women sang these blues, their tones ranging from stridency to whisper, from throaty roughness to the smoothness of dark velvet, subtly slurred notes deliberately missing the half-tones, finding the quarter tones with poignant impact. Men accustomed to drive a hard bargain for their talents played for sheer love of playing then, shouldering their way through customers in a crowded bar, pushing the man at the piano aside with a "Let me at it—. Move over, son, and let a *real* man take yo' place." And there was no dearth of real men.

Certainly it would have been hard to find a coloured child in all New Orleans who wasn't tooting, drumming, blowing, whistling, marching or in some other way releasing his inherent musicality.

If he wasn't fortunate enough, as George Lewis was, to have a "store-bought" instrument, he made one for himself and home-made horns, flutes, fifes, and whistles were heard up and down the streets and in the courtyards and the alleys—anywhere a

dark-skinned child could be found. Tin cans of varying sizes, they had learned, made a fine set of drums, and many irate parents found out that chair rungs likewise made good drum-sticks.

An old inner tube, a knife, some nails, and a packing case, and a boy had a bass fiddle. The inner tube was cut in strips of varying widths, nailed taut across the packing case—and what was that strange melodic thrumming you heard from just around the corner? A small Negro ecstatically plucking his bass, coaxing not only rhythm but melody from it, with perhaps a friend by his side blowing a penny whistle or a ten-cent store flute, or—lacking anything to blow—just whistling and tapping and clapping his hands. If they couldn't march in the organized children's groups that abounded in those days they made up their own parades, and their costumes and make-shift floats showed an ingenuity the planners of the elaborate floats in the big parades could well have envied.

"There was all kinds of bands," says George Lewis. "I mean *all* kinds. Brass bands, ragtime bands, little bands, big bands, spasm bands—them's kids with washboards and washtubs and whistles and all kinds of instruments playing like five hundred—and bands from every part of town. There was what we called the 'Million Dollar Babies,' the women from the Storyville district. They'd be all dressed up in high-heeled, high-button shoes, some of them with bells on their ankles and God knows what all. They'd be playing guitars and banjoes and having them-selves a time. We called them the 'Million Dollar Babies' because they always had plenty—I mean *plenty* of money. Especially around Mardi Gras with all the tourists in town. They carried it all in their stockings, and when they hiked up their skirts or kicked up their heels you could see it. But I wouldn't have wanted to be the one who tried to touch it. Lots of them carried guns and razors, things like that. Us kids knew why they had money and who they were. Kids learn young in New Orleans. Didn't make any difference to us. They looked pretty and they made real nice music, and we knew lots of them."

In another world, the white world, the people were planning, working, and worrying, and had been planning, working, and worrying since the previous year's Mardi Gras, for this event was—and is—the focus of the whole year's social life. There are time-honoured traditions to be followed; customs based on caste

and social standing to be rigidly observed; dinners, balls, and parties to be arranged; costumes to be fitted and floats to be decorated, these last two in deepest secrecy. There is no other event comparable to it in the United States. It is like the social season in London prior to a Coronation or a Royal wedding.

"But," says George Lewis. "We was the happiest. Us kids."

During the pre-Mardi Gras season families suspended most rules of conduct as being unenforceable. Today it is different. Time has not dealt kindly with the Mardi Gras, as it has not dealt kindly with similar celebrations in other cities. An example is the annual Tournament of Roses in Pasadena, California. Both affairs have felt the encroachment, and in some aspects the complete mastery, of commercialism, so that little spontaneity remains. Even the most prideful Orleanian admits that there can never be again the unalloyed gold of enchantment and excitement of those earlier times.

"I was always a sleepy-head when night came," says George Lewis. "Except before Mardi Gras, or when the bands were playing. Most of the time I'd fall asleep before I could even get undressed and my mother would make me say my prayers first so they'd get said. But not before Mardi Gras. For nights and days my mother couldn't hardly get me in, much less to bed, I was that keyed up. And then the night before Mardi Gras, on Mardi Gras eve, I never slep' at all. Real sleep, that is. I'd lie there half-awake, all night long, and every so often I'd peep at the clock to see was it time to wake my mother up. I'd be wide awake long before day, and I'd wake her up, too, poor soul, so's we could get an early start and a good place right down front. Sometimes she'd be feeling real bad, and be needing that day to res', but I was too young to understand. Nothing mattered but seeing the parade and hearing the bands. I guess I gave my mother a mighty bad time."

Mardi Gras day, 1910, was one of the days when Mrs Zeno was feeling "real bad." She was so ill, in fact, that she knew she would not be able to take the boy to the parade. Common sense told her that from five to seven hours standing would result in collapse, and in that event her son would not only be hysterical with fear, but could just as conceivably get in as much trouble as if he had gone without her in the first place. She knew that during the parade he would remain rooted in one spot, awed into quietness except for jigging or clapping his hands to the music.

She saw him struggling against tears and, sitting on the edge of the bed, took him by thin shoulders and shook him gently.

"George Lewis," she said. "Surely a boy ten years old can go to a Mardi Gras parade just once alone and not get into trouble. You go straight to the corner. Don't go by the French market, or you'll get into it with those Italian boys who hang around waiting to jump coloured boys. Stay away from fights. You just stand on the corner there and watch. And don't you push, or squirm, or get in any one's way, or be rude. Then you come home. You hear? The minute the parade's over, *you come home*!"

His mother's words stayed with him for as long as it took the first float and the first band to sweep by, carried along on a golden wave of sound. From then on he was in a different world, with different values. When the final band and the last of the floats had vanished, George Lewis started on a dead run for the square in front of the old French Opera House, a building since destroyed by fire, where he knew some of the parade bands would be breaking up. They might, they just might, blow another number or two there. If there had been a chance they would blow even a bar the child's legs would have propelled him there with all the considerable speed of which they were capable.

Some of the bands were already there when he arrived, and the area had been roped off. He joined a group of boys from his own neighbourhood, and then, not satisfied with what could be seen through a forest of intervening legs, employed the only strategy possible. He "scrooched down and wriggled through them people's legs somehow" emerging with his head and shoulders through the ropes. Almost instantly he was hit a resounding clip on the side of the head by a white man, standing nearby. He had not seen the blow coming and yelped in surprise and hurt.

There is just as much possibility that the blow was a warning to bring him back in line and keep him out of trouble with the police as there is that it was intentionally malicious. But ten years is well past the age when a young coloured boy in the South regards any act of this nature by a white person as kindly or unintentional. Nor did his companions see it in that light, either. At the sound of his startled yelp, heard by a group of nearby white boys, the battle was on. Individually and collectively his companions protested, and the white boys moved in. Within seconds he was in the midst of a howling, fist-flailing, rock-

throwing, coloured-white fight. Police intervened, picking up and shaking both white and coloured with commendable impartiality, separating those bent on mayhem in individual fights, and ordering all of them home with dire threats of arrest. It was all a part of Mardi Gras—high excitement, high tension, high spirits and the inevitable blow-offs. They were happening, for one reason or another, all over town; not mixed racial battles, but just good old-fashioned brawls, whites and Negroes among themselves, because it was a time for brawling. Like St Patrick's Day in South Boston.

All the time Alice Zeno was patching up her son that night, a cut here, a bruise there, he talked of the parade. The fight was forgotten, only the wonder of the parade and the music remained, and he jigged and chattered like a magpie as she worked on him. Alice remained grimly silent. After she had almost exhausted her essential and much-called-upon stock of first-aid supplies, she gave him a licking. As if that made any difference. On Mardi Gras night?

A few months later, on July 5, when she applied arnica and disinfectant and plaster, she was grimly silent too, but it was a different silence. There was no punishment that night, but a tight embrace and a silent prayer of thanksgiving. It was the day after a 208-pound Negro named Jack Johnson had knocked out, in the 15th round, a 227-pound white man named Jim Jeffries, and become the first Negro heavyweight champion of the world. This did not "endanger white supremacy." This was out-and-out, intolerable proof of black supremacy, at least in one field and for the time being. The whites could not and would not accept this, and riots broke out in every part of the city, the worst since the days following the Robert Charles incident. Along the streets and through the alleys of New Orleans prowling groups of white youths sought out Negroes. These youths were, perhaps, the grandparents of the adults who, fifty years later, hurled insults and obscenities at four frightened six-year-old Negro girls as they entered a newly integrated school each day; who drove a courageous white family from the city because they dared live their belief in the brotherhood of man and let their child go to school with the Negro girls. "It is the minority who do these things!" cry the Southerners. Yet it is not minorities who elect governors and administrators pledged to perpetuate ad infinitum the spirit of the Bienville Black Code.

George Lewis had known the sting of white gibes and had never run from a rock battle until he had at least made his participation in it memorable for his tormentors. But on this day the tenor of the opposition was different. Previously the battles had been much the same as those fought on the streets of the slums of any big city; the Irish boys against the Protestants, the Italians against the Jews, one side of the block against the other, fists, bricks, and rocks the only weapons. Switch-blade knives were yet to come, and the crowds of jeering white boys had been more like a pack of excited dogs chasing the family cat for the fun of seeing it run and scamper up a tree, licking their wounds philosophically if the cat turned on them. But on July 5, 1910, the dogs had suddenly become vicious, like a pack on the hunt, extending their legs and baying in the race for a kill.

It was the first time he had ever run from a fight, but he was fleeing a new terror, filled with a new spirit-scalding fear. He almost literally flew through the streets, through his own gate and into the courtyard. The yard was deserted. The other occupants had heard the ominous howling of the little boy's pursuers in the distance, the thudding feet, and knew, as their people had known for generations, the meaning of the sounds. Every door and window was tightly closed and locked.

Once inside his own house, the door locked behind him and the bureau pushed against it, he found himself trembling too violently to do anything for a few moments. Then, hands still shaking, he washed the blood from his face and head so his mother wouldn't be too worried when she came home. More than one of the rocks and bricks that had followed him in flight had found their mark.

So it was that Alice Zeno held him close that night, with no word of reproof for his bruises.

The second Mardi-Gras parade in April was not preceded by as many days of excitement and preparation as the first one had been, but there was still enough to keep a small boy in a state of continual bliss. The streets were gay with bunting and signs reading "Glad you came, Shriners!" George had not the vaguest idea what a Shriner was, but he, too, was glad they came, with their bright uniforms; gay, baggy, Oriental trousers and fancy hats, and, most of all, their bands. When the big day came it was evident the Shriners had planned long and well for their parade

to offer substantial competition to New Orleans' own annual spectacle. But until that day arrived, George Lewis was, while continually blissful, none the less apprehensive. His mother had said that, as further punishment for his disobedience at the earlier parade, she would not permit him to go.

"And I wasn't going to, either," said Mrs Zeno, fifty years later. "But I guess I spoiled him. He was the only one God left me, and there was so little I could do for him. It seemed a mighty small thing to do to bring a child that much happiness. Of course I took him. And bought him a balloon and a fancy cane and candy too."

But all of the events in the year 1910 were of only passing importance to Mrs Zeno compared to the significance of the one toward which all her thoughts and most worried planning had been directed since her son's baptism; his first communion. It would be, in her view, the major event of his life, the attainment of spiritual majority, his formal dedication to her faith and acceptance by her Saviour as one of His own.

For once her son would wear, cost what it might in sacrifice, new clothes, clothes that had never been worn before by another child, fresh from the store or from her needle, sewn from new cloth. His shoes would look as fine as those of any boy, white or coloured, in his communion class, his suit and linen be as fresh and new.

When extra pennies and extra nickels meant extra food and warmth and transportation to work, the acquisition of a completely new wardrobe suitable for first communion was not a simple problem.

There were many who were willing to help Alice within the limits of their own scanty means, but her greatest help came as the direct result of her own warm love of humanity. Near the Zenos at that time there lived a woman known as Miz Mary Jackson. Miz Jackson did not live in a house, or even in a shack in the back of a courtyard, but in a cistern. True, it was a large cistern, but it was damp, there was no ventilation, snails crawled along its inner walls, and it definitely did not smell good. In it were a bed, a table, and a stove on which Miz Jackson cooked the small amounts of food that were given to her, or that she could scavenge from the ground around the stalls at the French Market. She had lived in this fashion ever since twenty years of devoted

companionship had ended with the death of her husband, yet no one seemed able to remember just when she had first crept into the cistern and taken up residence there. They knew it had been a long time.

"It's not good just to keep on giving that poor woman food," said Mrs Zeno to her son. "She needs something to think about. Some interest in life. Grief's a cold companion. Suppose she dies? Who'll bury her? A pauper's funeral, that's all she can expect."

And Alice moved into the situation. By dint of scraping and saving she managed to make the initial payment for Miz Jackson's membership in one of the many benevolent associations organized and run by the Negroes. Thrust upon themselves and their own resources and initiative, the Negroes had, for many years, been active in forming lodge groups and benevolent societies, affiliating through these groups with insurance companies for the payment of medical bills, sick benefits, and funeral expenses (including parades) for their members. Branches for young people were established by the larger groups, and George Lewis, for example, was a proud member of the Young Veterans Benevolent Association, marching proudly in bowler hat and knee pants on the occasions of their parades. Picnics, dances, parties, luncheons, parades, all were sponsored by these groups.

As soon as Mrs Zeno had secured Miz Jackson's membership in one of these organizations, a delegation of its members presented itself at the cistern. They paid no attention to the damp, windowless walls of this eerie dwelling place, or the snails, or the damp odour of mould. It might have been any home in which they sat, ranged in a row on the bed, while the old lady, half-suspicious and more than half-frightened, sat in the lone chair. They invited her to one of their luncheons at a nearby church. "We each brings something we cooks ourse'f" they told her. "Miz Zeno says you fix mighty fine co'n bread."

Stunned by the attention, warmed at being regarded as a human being for the first time in years, unable to find words or reason for refusal, Miz Jackson agreed. The night before the luncheon Mrs Zeno 'just happened' to be cleaning out some boxes, and 'just happened' on a dress she couldn't wear, and 'just happened' to think of Miz Jackson.

The members of the association didn't stop with the gesture of a luncheon invitation. One of the women found her a little work to do. She moved from the cistern to a small room in the

neighbourhood. She was elected eventually to the board of directors of the association, and then appointed secretary. She found more work to do. At the time she died, a few months before George Lewis's first communion, she was president of the society.

The insurance policy which she carried as a result of her membership provided a small additional sum to be paid to a beneficiary after funeral expenses were taken care of. The beneficiary of Miz Mary Jackson's policy was Alice Zeno.

It came as a complete surprise to Alice. She frequently used the incident as evidence that the saints had open ears for prayers.

It did not pay the entire cost of the first communion by any means, for Alice Zeno, forced all her life to be so painstakingly careful with the expenditure of even a penny, had no intention of stinting on this occasion. Henry Zeno, soon to undergo major surgery for the kidney and bladder condition that periodically reduced him to semi-invalidism, managed to contribute a few dollars. Urania, despite heavy demands on her pocket-book because of the various nieces, nephews and grandchildren now in her care, managed a few more dollars. Alice's employers, the Judge Harry Renshaws, gave her extra money and a new prayer book for her son. Still it was necessary for Alice once again to borrow from a loan company. It was only ten dollars but the interest was usurious, and she dreaded the weeks of sacrifice it would entail. She did not doubt, however, that God would help her, for had He not already proven His interest in her son's first communion by guiding the woman in the cistern to name her as beneficiary? Without Miz Jackson's posthumous contribution she could not have made it at all.

At last the wardrobe was assembled. Each boy in the class was to wear the same outfit: black patent-leather shoes, black stockings, straight black knee pants, white shirt, white tie, and sailor hat. The oil lamp burned late every night while her small son slept, and Alice Zeno worked with smarting, strained eyes on the fine white shirt, and the underclothes made for once from good material instead of flour sacking. She and her son went together to the store to buy the shoes, the long stockings, and the sailor hat.

George maintained a discreet silence during the picking out and trying on of the hat. He knew that if it was humanly possible to avoid his mother's eyes he would not wear it, not even in the parade to the church. Alice knew this, too, and knew that it was

not going to be humanly possible to avoid her eyes, and that whatever the cost to him he was going to wear the hat. He did.

The item of his costume, though, that swelled his small chest with the greatest pride, was the pair of patent-leather shoes. His feet were not easy to fit, long, narrow out of proportion even to their length, with a high instep not usually found among his people. Cheap shoes were always, throughout his life, to cause him agonizing discomfort, but no amount of discomfort was too great a price for the pleasure of wearing the black patent-leather shoes they bought that day. They were cheap, but they were the finest-looking shoes he had ever had, a pair bought for once with some other thought in mind than practicality. The heels were of stacked cardboard and tended to fall apart when wet. He was inordinately proud of the shoes, rubbing the uppers with vaseline constantly to prevent the inevitable cracking, keeping them polished and gleaming, wearing them each Sunday when he served as altar boy; their squeak, as he came solemnly down the aisle, lost to his ears in the glimpses he caught of their fascinating twinkle beneath his robe.

When the day arrived Alice was exhausted and her son in a transport of delight at all-new clothes, his new position as a person of importance and the centre of attraction—and patent-leather shoes. Yet the significance of the occasion was not lost on him. The Alice Zenos of this world, their own beings powered by the dynamo of faith, seem to have the ability to transmit that power to others. The faith that she passed on to her son was the faith that had been passed on to her by Zaier and Urania, a hard, unrelenting faith that had kept her alive and dared her strength to fail in the face of illness, poverty, hunger, heartbreak, and despair. It was a faith in a God who was just, but mighty in wrath if displeased, but whose love for His children was an everlasting thing. The God in Whom she believed had no ears for selfish supplication, but demanded that His children seek strength to bear their burdens, not release from those burdens. He was a God who asked that He be glorified in all their labours, and who granted them rest only when those labours were done.

Yet it was a gentle faith, too, that she gave to her son. She made the man she called "my Jesus" as real to the boy as He was to her. When she talked to the boy of Jesus she brought Him into their room as infant, child, and man. He was not some allegorical figure dressed in long robes, but "God's son," as one might say

"Mr Smith's son." George remembers vaguely that during his childhood, before the concept of time was clear and a thousand years ago was any time prior to the week before last, he had thought of Jesus as a contemporary of his great-grandmother's.

And, as was to be expected, during the days before his first communion, she kept an extra watchful eye on him for any of the attitudes which she had always rebuked with all the sternness at her command—self-pride, vanity, or lack of proper humility. It was not the humility of subservience that she tried to inculcate in her son, for she loathed that with the same loathing she had for self-pride, but the true humility of the spirit that credits God before self.

The parents of other children in St Catherine's parish that May were planning for the same event, and many of them were making additional plans for the traditional communion party to follow the ceremony. At these parties the children blessed with economically stable parents served sandwiches and cakes, and, in the really prosperous homes, even ice cream. The day before his first communion George asked:

"Ma, what we goin' to have at my party?"

"Your party, son? What party?"

"You know, ma, my communion party. I asked lots of the kids to come over after—"

"Son, you didn't! I never said anything about a communion party. You know mother hasn't got the money, with all this expense, or the time—"

"Aw, ma! You did! Honest, you did. Last week you said 'maybe we can have one.' Gee, ma, I never had a party—"

George Lewis told of it years later. "My mamma cried that day. I know now why she was crying. I know now what it's like to have a young 'un want something you don't have the money to give. It's a mighty hurtin' thing, that is. And I began to know a little bit about it that day, the day I made first communion. I began to realize a little about all my mother had done for me. It hurted me so that day to see her cry, when she'd been so happy over my new clothes and all. I don't even like to talk about it, not even today I don't."

Alice Zeno prayed again that day, this time: "Let my son have a party and forgive me for asking this, but he wants it so much. Let him just this once have something of the pleasures other children have."

Then, believing firmly that the Lord helps those who help themselves, Alice set about arranging for the party. First she went to her mother and laid her problems on Urania's broad shoulders.

"Party!" cried Urania, in quick, excited Creole. "That baby wants a party? He's going to have one. The best party in all New Orleans."

It may not have been the best but it served, and George Lewis took to his first-time role as host like a veteran. Urania brought plates heaped high with pralines, and *Tante Betsies*, and cookies and Alice found time to bake a top-of-the-stove cake, and Urania made a frosting fit for a Royal wedding. There was home-made lemonade, and the neighbours rushed in with extra chairs, and the tiny room became so crowded with laughing children they spilled over into the courtyard. Alice forgot her tiredness and played in the yard with them like a child herself, yanking her son inside abruptly when she found he'd forgotten to change his underwear when he put on his playclothes, sending him back out with an affectionate spank on his small behind, saying to herself: "Thank you, God, for everything."

"My mother was a mighty happy woman that night," said George Lewis. "I never saw her happier. Not even when I showed her all the stories and pictures of the things that happened to me over the water, and the crowds and all, was she happy like she was the day I made first communion."

two

"Fo' dolla's; fo' dolla's an' two-bits; fo' dolla's an' fo'ty cents; fo' dolla's an' sixty cents; fo' dolla's an' eighty cents, an' two more dimes—five dolla's!"

The money lay in a pile before him on the table; a pile of unbought candies and all-day suckers and licorice whips and ice

cream for which his mouth had watered; and "poor boy" sandwiches which his growing frame had needed; a pile that imprisoned in the dull glitter of its dirty coins all that the boy who had just counted it asked of life. Last night he had added two dimes and counted it; this morning, almost unbelieving, fearful he may have made a mistake, he counted it again.

Five dollars.

The horn in the window of the pawn shop, a different horn and a different window from those of last year, had been marked five dollars. It had been in the window a long time, and for several days George Lewis had been afraid to check the window again, unable to face the possibility that it might be gone. He knew about paying deposits on things, but the seeds of distrust had already been sown, and he dared not part with any of the coins he had so laboriously saved, for which he had worked so hard, albeit willingly. Suppose the man kept the money? Suppose when he went back with the rest of it the man said: "Run along, boy. I don't know anything about that piece of paper you got that says you paid me three dollars." Suppose—suppose—suppose.

No! He would get the horn when he had all the money, and he would keep the money until he had the horn.

He wrapped the coins carefully in a piece of clean white paper, and started out the door. In the yard he saw their neighbour, Miz Todd. Snoopy ol' bat. He ducked back in the house and grabbed his cap, a small, short-billed cap like those known today as "Ivy League." Once in the yard he doffed it politely to Miz Todd.

"Mornin' Miz Todd, m'am. Did you res' well last night?"

"Mornin' son. Thank you. Passably. Passably. You off to school?"

"No, ma'am. Today's Saturday."

"Sure is, at that. I clean forgot. All dressed up this mawnin' ain't you?"

"Yes, m'am. Goin' to the store. Goin' to buy me a horn."

"Lawd! Lawd! What's your poor ma goin' to say?"

"My *mother* knows about it, Miz Todd."

He was through the gate now. Snoopy ol' bat. If he'd had a dime for every hiding she'd gotten him he'd of had his horn a couple of years ago. Got him a spanking one morning when his mother was home— not a real licking, but a right smart spanking just because he forgot to tip his cap to her and she told his mother. Told her before he could even get to the corner and his

mother had come to the gate and called him back and brought him inside and spanked him, and made him go out again and tip his cap right, and bob his head right, and say "Good morning" and ask the ol' bat did she res' well last night. But he never forgot to tip his hat and say "good morning" again, not ever, to anyone.

She was out of his thoughts before he reached the corner. The hand in his pocket held the money tightly, and he was walking slowly, for the excitement and importance of the journey had a sobering effect. He didn't even whistle. His father was working on the old lake boat *Camellia* then, as a cook, or he would have stopped by and asked him to come with him. His father would have understood that a boy needs to share importance.

The child walking down the banquette was still small for his years, which were ten. He was thin, straight as an arrow, and something of the future was already evident. The warm, mellow, glowing patina of gentleness that was eventually to reach across footlights and enmesh the affections of thousands far more securely than the practised showmanship of his contemporaries was already indicated. Those who had known his grandfather Zeno, that small and gentle man, were already calling him the "spit'n image" of him, and he was to resemble him more and more as the years went on.

The child was anything but robust, but what he lacked in ruggedness he made up for in restless, driving, impatient, nervous energy, an energy that gave the small body no rest, but flogged it on mercilessly. He was cat-quick in his movements.The shyness that he displayed was not the agonizing shyness of self-centredness, but rather the shyness of sensitivity, of fear of being hurt or hurting. Even at ten he had an innate empathy with people, the ability to feel their pain, and an instinctive shrinking from inflicting pain on any living thing. His mother had stressed the need to be kind to all people, but she had no need to, for kindness was a part of him.

The temper that had the power to make him physically ill was still close to the surface, and it was to be a long time before it would be placed more or less under control, a control that grew gradually from the pressures of the society in which he lived; it was a temper which would need, as the years went on, to be sublimated, yet which through all his life was to seethe and writhe frequently in bonds of politeness, acquiescence, and conformity, bonds necessary if one was to live in a world in

which the means of survival differed according to the colour of one's skin.

His manners were as nearly perfect as one could expect from a ten-year-old. He rose when his elders, or a woman, entered the room; he doffed his cap when spoken to; he called all women "m'am" or "Miz," he used a knife and fork as he should, and said "please" and "thank you" and he did not reserve these manners for any one class but was taught and learned—sometimes with the aid of a switch—to show them toward every human being, white or coloured.

One of his mother's great concerns was with his speech. Brought up in a French- and Creole-speaking family, thrown all day with schoolmates and playmates who spoke the idiomatic, highly expressive speech of the Louisiana Negro, taught by teachers who cared little for results, and without the daily, hourly example of his mother's excellent speech in his ears, his own became a mixture. Alice did the best she could, but it was impossible to undo in a few hours in the evening and morning, or an occasional day, habits acquired in school and at play. Certain niceties of expression he adhered to throughout his life. He never "got mad" but was always "angry."

He read avidly and understood what he read, and if he translated some of the words phonetically, it was not because he did not absorb the meaning of the subject matter. The letter 'r' tended to get lost at the end of some words, and always in 'George,' and sometimes when it preceded a consonant; final 'd's' and 't's' vanished at times; final 'g's' were sometimes there, sometimes not. Collective nouns were made doubly sure in meaning by the addition of 's,' as in 'mens,' and a verb remaining unchanged in the past tense usually had 'ed' added just to be on the safe side.

He spoke well in both French and Creole, but could not read in either language, for Creole is a patois, and French was not taught in the schools which he attended. Lack of use deprived him of the ability to speak French with any fluency in later years, but an incident in Paris in 1957 proved that this ability was not completely lost but merely dormant. The incident must still be remembered by the Parisian taxicab driver responsible for it. The driver's display of surly insolence and contempt for non-French-speaking foreigners had gone on just a little too long, and he suddenly found himself the target of a barrage of rapid-fire, scalding French from his soft-spoken, quiet, middle-aged passen-

ger. The driver shot off like a bullet, making a wide U-turn in one of Paris's busiest streets, ears scarlet, waving his arms like one demented.

When asked if he had sworn at the luckless man, George replied that he had not. "I don't know what all I did say," George stated. "I know I didn't swear. And I do know I told him to mind his manners."

But Paris was just a spot on the map in a far-off country to George Lewis as he walked the sixteen blocks to Uncle Dave's pawnshop at South Rampart and Poydras Streets in New Orleans's third ward that morning in 1910. As he rounded the corner his eyes sought the window, heart thumping in apprehension and then, for a moment, stopping. The horn was gone. He pressed his nose to the glass, the contents of the window blurring. Then he went in slowly, fearfully, and a bell overhead announced his arrival. He tipped his cap respectfully to the man who came from the rear of the store.

"G-g-good mornin', sir."

"Good morning, boy. What can I do for you?"

"That horn, sir. The clarinet. The one that used to be in the window. You got any more like it, please, sir?"

"Nope. But I've still got that one. Brought it in a couple of days ago. It's marked down. Fine horn, that one. Fine wood, good tone. Only $4.50 now, boy."

Only four-fifty! The long, thin fingers tightened on the paper-wrapped coins. He had five dollars!

"You *sure*—only four-fifty?"

"That's right."

The hand came out of the pocket and the counting process began. "Fo' dolla's, fo' dolla's two-bits, fo' dolla's thu'ty five cents, fo' dolla's fo'ty cents, fo' dolla's fifty cents."

"Sold!" The man reached for the roll of brown wrapping paper.

"Wait—jus' a minute, please, sir. You got a case I could buy so's I could keep it nice? For fifty cents?"

"Case—case—let's see. Guess I have, boy. Nice case, and a brush to keep it clean, too. Your daddy play clarinet?

"No, sir."

"Brother?"

"No, sir. It's for me.

"For you!" The man's laugh filled the little shop. "For God's

sake! Little bit of a thing like you. Boy, that clarinet's almost as big as you are!"

George Lewis was becoming impatient. Heaven was really close now, and he didn't like all this chit-chat at the gate.

"Please, sir, the case?"

"Here you are—case, horn, brush, and some extra reeds for good luck. And don't you forget to use that brush. Never let that horn get fouled up inside—keep it sweet and clean—"

"Yes, *sir*. Thank you, sir—"

He was outside at last. The horn was in his hand. His horn. His own clarinet. He was carrying his own horn down the street, and the case was knocking against his leg every now and then. But it seemed a long way off, and he brought it up and tucked it under his arm, hugging it close. He kept a sharp eye out as he walked the sixteen blocks to his house. If there were any white kids around and they were looking for trouble, he'd run—run like fire, no matter what they called him. He'd walk slow so as not to attract attention. His steps quickened, though, as he neared St Phillip Street, and became a jog-trot by the time he reached the courtyard, the case clutched to his chest by now.

He wasn't at the corner of Rampart and St Phillip Streets that night when Alice Zeno got off the street car. She hadn't expected him to be. When she walked into their little room it was cold, although there was coal for a fire. The oil lamp was glowing, and in its light, on the bed, lay her son's new, second-hand clarinet. Every key sparkled. Its graceful black length shone with polishing. The boy was sitting beside it, looking at it, not handling it, and as she crossed the room he picked it up and cradled it in thin arms. He spoke in a half-whisper.

"Look, maw. Look. Ain't—isn't it the most beautifullest one you ever saw?"

She drew him close.

"Yes, dear." Then automatically. "Not beautifullest. Beautiful. Can you play it, son?"

"We-ell. I can get some notes on it. But, gee, maw, this thing's *hard* to play. I'm gonna —going to have to do an awful big lot of practisin', maw."

"Maybe it's lucky for me I'm gone all day." She looked at him closely. "You eat any lunch, George Lewis? You get your sandwich?"

"Lunch?" He looked puzzled for a minute, then broke into

peals of laughter. "Lunch! Gee, ma, I forgot all about it! You got something good there? I'm starved!"

She got up three times that night and forced him back to bed, waiting patiently each time while he carefully ran the brush through the horn, dismantled the instrument and packed it in the case. The third time she brought him into her bed, and fastened a grim hand on the waistband of his pyjamas, and at last he slept.

The boy had not listened to the music on the streets always with inarticulate awe. Never able to push himself forward in ordinary situations, thoroughly steeped in the "seen but not heard" tradition as far as adults were concerned, when it came to music the urge to learn was stronger than any training. There were few clarinettists who played in the parades or on the wagons who had not at some time heard a small, soft-spoken boy say: "Excuse me, please, sir. Could I look at your horn close?" And who hadn't found himself explaining, while he waited for a parade to start, or to climb aboard a wagon, come of the intricacies of the clarinet to the eager child. The boy learned how the musicians tuned their horns, and how they fingered them, and kept them clean, and he never forgot so much as a syllable of what he was told. He didn't worry about learning the notes. He had supreme self-confidence that once he had a horn of his own that would be simple. Even at that age, just from listening, he sensed the manner in which a melody was transposed from one key to another, and he had the great gift granted to so many of his people—an almost perfect musical memory.

But the greatest gift that he possessed was the ability to discipline himself. It was a gift which, if possessed by all embryo musicians, would gladden the hearts and make light the task of thousands of music teachers. The boy showed himself no mercy, and was more intolerant of his own quickly recognized mistakes than the harshest instructor would have been. There was no one to stand over him and force him to practise; no one to point out his errors; no one to check on his progress. He was utterly and completely alone, the sole judge of every note and phrase that came from his horn.

He was well aware, even at that age, that before he could make real his dream of playing the kind of music he heard on the balcony of Hopes Hall and in the parades and from the band wagons, he must master every key, every valve, and every nuance and phrase of his horn; that he must learn what he could do with

it and what he could say with it, and that then he must learn to make it do and say what he wanted it to. He could, he knew, learn in a few weeks time, or even days, to play simple tunes. But he also knew, with the unerring instinct of the true artist, that if he did that he would still be playing a ten cent store flute; a long, black, complicated one, but still a ten cent store flute.

He knew that the instrument he held in his hands and between his lips must become as much a part of him as his own breath, as responsive as his own whistling; that the co-ordination between ear and mind and heart and fingers and breathing must be instantaneous and perfect. The time must come—and would come —when if he "thought" a note or "felt" a tone his fingers and his breath would bring it alive without conscious effort.

The exacting standards of the established leaders and musicians were well known to him. He had seen musicians, seeking to "sit in" on a wagon, stopped abruptly by the leader who would say: "Think you kin play that thing you got there? Don't git up here if you can't." Many of the leaders were harsh and intolerant, and none of the musicians wanted a mediocre player in their ranks. In later years George Lewis stated that many promising young players, who might have gone a long way professionally, were frightened and discouraged by a number of the leaders of those days.

"When I was just a kid I'd hear them," said George. "Some of them would give a young musician a bad time. Me, I couldn't hurt another musician like that ever, and I knew I was too thin-skinned to take that kind of treatment."

So, aware of a painful sensitivity that was almost a handicap, the boy made up his mind that he would never risk the contempt or displeasure of a leader, never seek to play with any band until he could answer the question: "Think you kin play that thing you got there?" with a confident: "Yes."

He did not practise an hour or two at a time when he was at home, but all the time. At first his lips blistered, and the muscles of his cheeks ached, and his arms ached, and his fingers became sore, but he did not stop. He never missed a chance to hear a parade or follow a wagon, and when he got home he practised the runs and the tunes he heard. He was never satisfied, just as he had never been satisfied with his own playing on the flute. Sometimes the ten-year-old would sob from sheer tiredness and frustration and anger at himself, when the notes wouldn't come

right, when the tone came out sour. Still he did not stop. Gradually the muscles of the young lips hardened and strengthened until what musicians call the "embouchure" became so firm and tough that even in later years it did not weaken from lack of use, as most musicians' do, when he was forced to stop playing at times for the only reason he recognized as valid, illness—though he seldom acknowledged that unless helpless. And, as the small, delicately boned hands grew, the right thumb, which supported the clarinet, broadened until, when he was an adult, it was almost twice the breadth of the left thumb.

At first, quite sensibly, he was afraid to take the horn apart, but as his knowledge of it grew he carefully dismantled it, learning the function of every spring and part. He learned why and when the cork must be dampened, and discovered the wondrous effectiveness of elastic bands when springs were weak or broken and has never, since those childhood days, left home to play without a small bundle of them in his clarinet case. He still saved nickels and dimes and pennies, carefully and with much sacrifice, and then spent them unstintingly on reeds or whatever he might need for his horn. No man ever had a mistress more demanding, or served that mistress more slavishly.

Today the music which George Lewis and his fellow musicians played, and many of them still play, has become a shuttlecock flipped back and forth by a vast multitude of academic writers, reviewers, and critics whose knowledge of the lives and hearts of these men, and of New Orleans, is as remote as their knowledge of the life on Mars. The music is patronized by this one, extravagantly praised by that one, contemptuously derided as 'lacking in technique' or 'primitive' by yet another; each of them apparently intent to the point of desperation on impressing each other, and a supposedly ignorant public, in a display of intellectual and literary pyrotechnics that has left the music so far behind it seems at times but a faint and lovely echo, sounding down the decades. Then, suddenly, in a concert hall in New York, Paris, Berlin, London, or on a nightclub stand, or in a funeral parade in New Orleans, it bursts into vital life, proclaiming all over again its truth and beauty and validity.

Because he learned a hard and lonely way, not even George Lewis's most supercilious critics have ever been able to call him a copyist. He tried then, as a child in a shabby French Quarter room, to make his beloved horn an expression of himself, and

today plays with the same intent. No other man's hand or influence is in his playing, there is only the over-all influence of the music of his people in New Orleans. Within that frame of reference it is uniquely his own.

In London, in 1959, a young Lewis fan came up to me after a concert and asked with almost desperate pleading if he could talk with George Lewis for a few minutes. "I just want to ask Mr Lewis a few questions,' he said. "I'll try not to bother him, and I promise I won't take long."

He was a student at a conservatory, with years of clarinet study behind him. He wanted to ask George Lewis, he said, how he got his tone, and what the secret was of his technique, and as we edged our way through the crowd to the dressing-room I recall saying: "Remember, George Lewis has about forty years of playing in his favour. Be patient."

He shook his head. "I don't know," he said almost tearfully. "I just don't know. Sometimes, actually, after I hear a Lewis record I want to throw my horn out of the window. I just feel so darned —so darned discouraged."

When we had finally fought through to George, I took out a notebook and pen and, wedged against the wall, elbowed and bumped by the crowd, did my best to take down what George Lewis said to the almost tearful young man. I knew that when he was talking he was remembering the weeks and months and years of lonely, fruitful practice in a succession of tiny French Quarter rooms.

"You got to know your horn, son," said George Lewis. "Don't be in too big a hurry. You can't learn it quick. You got to know it like a baby knows its mamma's face. It takes time. And you can't do it just taking lessons. You got to play that horn just for yourself, for hours and hours and years. You got to learn to make it *say* what you want it to. You got to learn to make it talk, just like you learned to talk. I never been much of a talker, not me. But my horn talks for me. There's no one can teach you that. You got to learn it for yourself. And there's something else you got to remember. Don't try to play like George Lewis. Try to play like *you*."

"But," said the young man engagingly. "I want to *sound* like George Lewis!"

Which is what a little boy in New Orleans, 50 years ago, practising to exhaustion, being forced to bed at night by a tired

mother who needed rest, sometimes crying at his own childish ineptness, but never permitting himself to stop, wanted to sound like too.

three

THE boy pushing the crab net through the wet, dank reeds at the bayou's edge in the half light of dawn was frowning so hard in concentration he looked like a small and worried gnome. George Lewis never did anything by halves, and certainly not anything as important as crab-netting.

There was a double incentive to do the jobs of crabbing, or shrimping, or hunting or fishing, properly, for done right they would bring him the warm happiness of seeing his father's slow, gentle smile of approval, and hearing his drawling, soft words of commendation. The child's desire to please was intense, and praise from those he loved was worth any amount of effort.

The new life in Mandeville his father introduced him to when he was just past ten was markedly different from the only life he had known previously on the cobblestoned streets of the French Quarter. The water that soaked him to mid-calf now was lake or bayou water, not stagnant gutter standings; the tiredness that came after a morning's hunting or fishing by his father's side was a different tiredness from the half-fretful, keyed-up exhaustion that came at the end of a day of running errands, shining shoes, selling scrap, delivering groceries, or playing stick-ball or baseball on the streets with a mob of noisy youngsters.

The companionship between father and son was a warm, close thing, completely free of self-consciousness. They could talk companionably or remain silent together for hours on end. "We were friends," says George.

Although Henry Zeno had not yet moved back permanently to his old home in Mandeville, he was spending more and more time on that side of the lake, never lacking for work when he was

well enough to do it. At first the boy's visits with his father were only overnight, or for a few days, but he counted the hours between them. Henry's sister, Hortense, still lived in the little cabin Grandfather Zeno had shared with his Indian wife and brood of growing children. Hortense's own family had reached eight before her husband's death, and Henry had pitched in and helped her enlarge the little house. She always managed to find room somewhere for her brother and his son.

Alice did not object too strenuously to her son's spending this time with his father. Whatever her own feelings about Henry might be, she wanted his son to love and respect him, and she knew that this son was the lodestar of his existence. Return to Henry she would not, though he pleaded with her to do so constantly, but she was too big a woman to deny him the companionship of his son, or deny her son the love of his father.

Besides, during those days Alice Zeno had a dream, not a sleeping dream but a waking dream, one that she knew would never come true. Actually, she was a little ashamed of it as bordering on the sinful. It was that she and her son were on a long vacation. A trip was involved in this vacation, and long days of summer sun and idleness. Longing for idleness in Alice's code was almost as sinful as longing for the lusts of the flesh, and she never, never mentioned it in her prayers, for she respected what she knew must be the busy-ness of God, and asked only for essentials: strength for herself, health and sustenance for her son. So she tried to shut the dream away, locked in a closed compartment of her mind, but sometimes as she stood in the rear of a streetcar at the start of a day or at its exhausted end, it would leap from its hiding place and take over her thoughts. Then she would grimly grasp the dream and bundle it off again in all its wonderful happiness. "A long vacation, Alice Zeno!" she would admonish herself. "Shame! Be thankful if the good Lord gives you just a day off to rest in bed!" If she knew in her heart that a vacation was definitely out of reach for one in her position, she could at least make that dream come partially true by permitting her son long days of happiness with his father in the woods and by the bayous around Mandeville.

In 1911 Henry was rushed to Charity Hospital for emergency surgery, and the short trips to Mandeville stopped temporarily. When he had recovered sufficiently to return to work, he found a job in Mandeville with a family he had known for years, and who

were willing to permit him to have his son with him whenever he wanted.

While his father worked the boy found odd jobs for dimes and nickels. There was still need of them at home in New Orleans. In addition he never knew when he might need new reeds or something for his horn.

Right next to his Aunt Hortense's cabin was St Mary's Hall where dances and parties were held, and when he stood on the cabin's little porch, or inside by the window when the weather was bad, the music was as clear as it had been from Hopes Hall on St Phillip Street. And always there were parades and band wagons, the sound of music, to follow.

There was plenty of time for father and son to be together. In one respect Henry resembled a mule more than anything else. When he had done all the work he considered it fair to require of him, he would stop and nothing would move him to labour further. If it was a job of painting, he would start as soon as it was light enough to see, frequently with his son helping him. When the sun arrived at a certain spot in the sky, in mid-morning, he would carefully clean his brushes, put them away, sling his ladder over his shoulder, say: "Come on, son," and start away.

"Sometimes I'd want to keep on," said George. "I'd say, 'but, look, pappa, you only got a little bit to go." And he'd say 'nev' mind about that, son. Do it tomorrow. Sun's too high now.' Then he'd start off down the road and I'd have to go trailing after him. But he'd done more in that fo' or five hours than most men could do in ten, and 'way more than two men would of done. He just figured it wasn't how long he worked that counted, but how much he could do and do right—and he did it."

Henry taught his son to swim Indian-fashion, as his mother had taught him, silently and swiftly. He taught him the lore of the lake and the bayous and the woods, and made a huntsman and fisherman of him. The boy was an apt pupil, and seemed to absorb the lessons through the very pores of his skin, They spent long hours together netting crabs; the boy learned how to make casting nets for shrimps, and lower them into the water, bringing them up heavy with the catch. He learned how to bait and cast for trout, bass, sheephead, mullet, red fish, flounder, and how to catch catfish, although "the lake cat wasn't much good for eatin'. River cat's better."

He learned to recognize and fear the snakes of the region,

water moccasins, cotton mouths, rattlers; learned the strange human-like mating habits of the alligators, and became deadly quick and accurate with a rifle. At the end of the day he would walk home beside his father, a squirrel or rabbit, or perhaps both, that he had shot himself hanging over his shoulder, tranquilly discussing the best ways of cooking the day's bag. Henry knew them all, and few could equal him in front of a stove or wood fire. Possum they also caught, and George " 'most died of fright" one day when one he had thought dead came to life as he was carrying it home. Nor would he, with the ingrained fastidiousness that ruled his entire life, ever eat possum after he became aware of certain of its peculiar personal habits.

"After I seen that? You couldn't *pay* me to eat one of 'em."

At night replete, tired, but not exhausted as he had been in the city, the boy would bring out his horn and practise again. Henry's eyes would be warm with love and pride as he listened, helping the boy out by supplying home-made rhythm with whatever was handy. Now the tone was fuller, rounder, the notes coming more quickly and surely, and there would be sudden, slashing phrases away from the strain of the melody. Now and then he would get lost and have to grope his way back, but he seemed to know what path to take and always wound up—sometimes to his own surprise—on the home tone.

School had by now been almost abandoned. Mrs Zeno was too wise a woman not to realize that in this respect she was helpless. If she ever sensed that perhaps the years he had spent in Professor Nelson's school had spelled 'finis' to his career as a scholar, she did not reveal it.

Certainly, in her desperate longing to have her son acquire an education, she had done what seemed to her to be best. For three consecutive months, when he was eight years old, he had played hookey every day, avoiding by ruse and guile the eyes of the neighbours. True, before this he had played hookey occasionally, sometimes being picked up by a truant officer and taken to the Waifs' Home, there to wait with considerable trepidation for his mother to come for him that night. But when she discovered by sheer chance that her son had not attended a class in three months but instead had hidden his books under a bridge and headed for the river to swim and fish, she knew the time had come for drastic action. Corporal punishment, quickly forgotten, was not the answer.

The following morning she dressed him carefully and holding him tightly by the hand took him to the private school of Professor Nelson. Some parents in those days, unschooled in modern psychology, might say "the bogy man'll get you—" but many New Orleans parents said: "I'll put you in Professor Nelson's school" with much the same effect on the child. Although he was well qualified from a scholastic standpoint to conduct a school, Professor Nelson was tragically unqualified from the human standpoint to deal with children. He had no conception of the mind of a child, the needs of a child, or what a child's reactions might be to the restrictive discipline he imposed on his pupils. Both white and coloured children attended the school, which was in session twelve months of the year.

Professor Nelson was a tall, medium dark Negro, heavily built but well-proportioned, who invariably carried a large cigar and wore custom-made clothes of impeccable tailoring. His school and home were on the same property, the school occupying a large, single-roomed structure built on at the rear of the residence, at right angles to it.

Her heart heavy with the knowledge of what she was about to do, Mrs Zeno stood before this august individual, her frightened son's hand caught tightly in her own, and said:

"Professor Nelson, I want you to take my boy and look after him like you would your own. He's got no father at home, and I have to work all day. He's a good boy and never lies or steals, and he's smart and learns quickly. But he's mischievous, and he plays hookey. How much will it cost?"

Then after George had been peremptorily ordered to a seat in the far corner of the room they discussed finances.

Tuition would be $1.50 a month. But she wanted her son to remain there all day and not to leave the premises until she picked him up at night. He would have to have lunch, she told the professor. That would cost $1.50 more, she was told, and there would be an additional charge of 50 cents for coal to keep the room warm in winter, inasmuch as he would have to keep the fire going all day under those circumstances. In summer the same charge would be made for ice. All told, in order to make certain that George would not run the streets instead of learning, so that he could become as good a man as the next, it would cost Mrs Zeno $4.00 a month. She was paying $4.00 a month for the tiny rat-infested semi-apartment in which they lived, and a small

sum monthly for burial insurance for each of them. And she was making $12.00 a month and paying her own carfare.

It was evident, when she added up her accounts payable and balanced them against those receivable, that little niceties like food might have to be neglected. During that period it was the good St Jude who became well acquainted with the name of George Lewis, the saint upon whose shoulders falls the responsibility of helping mortals make impossible things possible. Alice gave him no chance to forget or overlook her case, and with anxious faith proceeded to enter her son in Professor Nelson's school.

She rounded up, with Urania's help, additional work to do at home, and the daughter of her employers, first swearing her to secrecy, gave her an additional two dollars a month from her own allowance. With the help of St Jude, Alice said, she made it.

It requires the pen of a Dickens to do full justice to the school of Professor Nelson in which the active, highly-strung, sensitive George Lewis was to spend the most miserable year of his life. As one entered the gate of the yard one saw a pump, and directly beneath its spigot hung a lithe rattan switch. The spigot dripped constantly, keeping the switch damp, pliable, and therefore more effective. It was the first thing a pupil's eyes fell on as he walked through the gate. The next thing he saw was the tall, stern figure of Professor Nelson, and standing beside him his wife and two daughters. It was required that the pupil advance, take off his hat if a boy or curtsy if a girl, and say "Good morning, Professor Nelson; good morning, Miz Nelson; good morning, Miss Josephine; good morning, Miss Nita."

This accomplished, the pupils were required to advance and hold out their hands, which were carefully inspected for cleanliness, the boys' sleeves pushed back to the elbow; then they were required to show their teeth, which were duly inspected, as was the area behind the ears and the back of the neck. Shoes were then looked at, and if not properly polished the culprit was either given additional work to do, sent home to shine them, or received a reminder from the wet rattan switch. This inspection did not worry George in the least, for he had never needed much supervision in the matter of neatness and cleanliness. A problem child in many ways, he was a model child in this respect. But it was the only phase of his life at Professor Nelson's that was simple for him.

The pupils sat on long benches with individual desks before them. Talking in class brought instant punishment, as did the passing of notes. There was no recess or break for play and exercise. In mid-morning they were permitted ten minutes to walk around the room and talk—no playing or rough-housing; and again in mid-afternoon. At noon those who had paid for them were served hot lunches at their desks, while the others ate lunches brought from home. The classes were never dismissed in a body, but as closing time approached Professor Nelson would dismiss each child separately, five or ten minutes apart, so there could be no group mischief on the way home. At last the schoolroom would be empty, except for George Lewis, alone at his desk. If the day was fair the professor would tell George he could go out in the yard. If it was raining he would remain in the schoolroom. There was no recreation provided, no outlet for his energies, no effort to make constructive use of this time. The boy had from then until his mother came for him at night to amuse himself as best he could.

George had shown when even younger than eight a real ability to draw and sketch. His mind was quick and grasped essentials, and in geography class, for example, while the rest of the class was laboriously learning the details of the people and products of Alaska, George would be sketching in the margin of his book his idea of what an Eskimo looked like. He was also exceptionally deft and skilled with his hands, whittling and carving all manner of things from odd scraps of wood. Yet no effort was made to encourage these activities, or to cultivate the talent.

That, under these conditions, his attention to his lessons was something less than complete, is not surprising.

Only once during that year did he escape from the confines of the school. He had been sitting beneath a tree in the yard whittling when a venturesome and curious ant found its way into his ear. Anyone who has experienced this sensation knows that the child ran shrieking into the house, dancing with discomfort and fear. He was dismissed summarily as a malingerer, dreaming this up as an excuse for freedom.

As straight as the flight of an arrow, and almost as fast, the boy, after climbing the fence like a cat, raced through the streets, sobbing, to his grandmother's house. Urania soothed him, waited until he had calmed down a bit, and then gently syringed the ear with warm oil, to George's relief and the ant's destruction.

Then, not daring to look too closely at the begging eyes and tear-stained face, she took his hand gently and led him back to Professor Nelson's school. George never heard what his grandmother said to that stern and cold man, but for a few days life was a little easier for him.

After he and his mother arrived home at night he was never permitted to leave the house unless she was with him. During the excitement of the pre-Mardi Gras season he remained in the house, hearing but never participating in its gaiety. But on the day of the Mardi Gras parade she took him to see it, buying him candy, and balloons, and trinkets from the street vendors, warmed by his happiness, keeping a firm grip on herself to prevent weakening in her resolve that he must learn, and now while he was young, the importance of both education and obedience.

But it is worth noting that during that year he did not have a sick day, and that the thin body and arms and legs plumped out as a result of the régime of regular hot lunches and regular hours. The young body caught its breath that year, though the young mind conceived an intense and lasting hatred of confinement—and formal teaching.

Alice also improved in health, for there was no constant tension of worry over her son; when the semi-tropical rains drenched the city she knew he would not be playing in the streets oblivious to it, with bronchitis a dead certainty for the next day. On cold damp nights when she had to work late it was not with half her mind and all of her heart on a cold, windy street corner, and the tired, shivering little boy who must be waiting for her there.

When at last the year ended he returned to public school, but it was a dreaded thing each day. He still played hookey, although not as often, and Alice seemed to realize that, deep as her desire was to get him as good an education as possible, she would have to trust to God to bring it to him, as hers had come, through other means than years of school. She knew from her own experience what could be gained from reading, and whenever there was time she shared with him what she had gained in knowledge.

The latter part of 1910 Alice and her son moved into the same courtyard in which Urania was living, but the move did not improve their conditions materially; nor did a subsequent move a few months later. There were still the rats, the lack of plumbing, the cracks in the walls, the primitive stoves to contend with, but at least she had greater peace of mind than she had known in

years. Days when she was gone the boy's grandmother was there to keep an eye on him. There were shared meals and companionship, shared expenses, and a lessening of the work load at home.

When Henry came to the house and asked to take his son to Mandeville Alice swallowed her bitterness and consented, and watched them leave together. Something of what her adamantine attitude toward her husband cost her emotionally may be indicated by the words she was to say to her son many times in the years to come. Whenever he returned home from a trip and unpacked the clippings and press photographs, and told her the stories of his success, she would say: "If only your father could have lived to know about this. How proud he would have been. I hope he knows."

George's hours of practice on his horn continued unabated, as they had been on St Phillip Street. Eventually he realized that he needed more than solo practice; that he must play it now with other instruments; must answer the trumpet and speak to the trombone, and feel the rhythm behind him and through him of the drums and the tuba and the bass. He needed to answer "Amen" to the band and speak his piece on his horn and hear the band's answering "Amen." He needed to feel the swelling surge of the golden tide of an ensemble riding out a number, each wave of sound resolving into one vast breaker of concluding harmony. The music he played was a communal music, a music of separate voices, each speaking in its own way, calling and responding as the tribal group music had in the country where its roots lay. Even the saddest of blues, bespeaking centuries of tragedy and heartbreak, needed the rhythmic comfort, the soft crying, sudden shouting, of other voices to interpolate "We hear you. We *hear* you."

So he roamed the streets of Mandeville and New Orleans, horn in hand, seeking other groups of young musicians who were learning as he was; following the parades and standing outside the halls, sometimes keeping his horn to his lips and playing so softly no one could hear, but playing with them, answering them, telling his story in a language that was fast becoming easier to him than speech.

In Mandeville he sat in with a group of young players when they rehearsed, all of them older than he, but none of them past eighteen. At first they tolerated him because he was so small and anxious; later, because he played so well with them, they sought

him out when they wanted to practise or just play for the joy of playing and talking in a language so uniquely their own.

When he was playing with them he felt confident, but when he returned home doubts came, and he would remember the mistakes he had made and so, as long as his long-suffering relatives would let him, he would "run down" the numbers over and over.

He did not grow much between 11 and 17, and at 14 was far smaller than most boys of his age. Perhaps through the years he had run too fast, worked too long, played too hard; whatever the cause, at fourteen he appeared not more than eleven.

In the middle of March in 1914 Henry Zeno sought out his son in New Orleans and asked him if he would like to come to Mandeville that week.

"Sure, pappa. Sure. When you want to leave?"

"On the eighteenth," said Henry. "Want to do a little work?"

"You know I do. What you want me to do?"

"We-ell, son, it's not exactly me that wants it. It's the boys you been playin' with. The Black Eagles, I guess you call yo'selfs?"

"That's right." Proudly. "The Black Eagles. What they want, pappa?"

"They take it mighty kindly if you'd play a dance with 'em on St Joseph's night, the nineteenth in St Mary's Hall."

"Play! Honest, pappa, honest?" He almost forgot he was fourteen years old and had been wearing long pants for more than a year, and came close to jumping up and down.

"Yup. I told 'em that maybe you might be willin' to play with 'em. That is, if you didn't have nothin' better to do."

The boy was stunned. "They want me to really play, pappa? Not just practise? Play for real?"

"Play for real. Hard work, son." Henry was as close to grinning as he ever came. "Got to play in the afternoon and at night."

"Where they playin' in the afternoon?" The child still couldn't believe what he was hearing.

"On a wagon. You know, advertising the dance. They got a mule and a wagon all lined up, goin' all over town with it."

A wagon. A band wagon. And he would be playing on it. For a minute he thought he was going to be sick.

"Can I go over a couple of days ahead, pappa? So's to talk to them and practise—and all. A *wagon*."

"Hold up there, boy. Don't you want to know how much they payin' you?"

"Paying me! You mean I'm gonna get paid? Really paid?"

"Really paid. Real money, son. Two dollars. Sure you wouldn't rather go fishin'?"

When his mother came home that night she heard the clarinet a block away.

"Good Lord, boy, what're you playing so loud for?"

"Ma you won't believe me, ma, but it's true. It's true. I'm going to play on St Joseph's day. Play music at a dance with a band. And in the afternoon I'm going to play on a wagon. A real wagon, ma!"

"It's fine, George, it's fine. But I still think all this blowing's too hard for you. Look at you. Thin as a rail—"

"And I'm going to get paid, ma. Listen, ma. Paid. Two dolla's. For playing."

"St Joseph's Day, you say, son? See what happens when you pray? I told you St Joseph would help you. Don't forget to thank him, son."

When he went to Mandeville two days before the dance there was a haze of unreality over everything. He tried to stand tall, and talk business-like while the others towered over him, and they planned what they'd play, and practised. As he practised he seemed to be playing clearer, stronger than ever before. "I may be small," his horn said for him. "But hear me! Hear me! I got a song to sing tonight!"

The day of the engagement he was like an actor with opening night nerves. He put on three different pairs of socks before finally deciding which to wear. By now he was earning enough money to buy his own shoes, and he polished the comparatively new pair he was wearing until each shoe shone like a mirror.

He wasn't exactly shaking when he climbed on the gaily decorated wagon that was strung with coloured paper and big signs telling about the dance that night, but he was probably the most nervous fourteen-year-old in the state of Louisiana. Everywhere the doors of houses were open, and the feasts of St Joseph, spread out on lavishly decorated tables, could be seen as they drove by. The people came to the doors and waved and clapped their hands, and some of them followed the wagon, with the children running close beside it. "I never felt so big in all my life as when I said to one little kid who got too close, 'get back from

there, son, or you'll get hurt.' Lord knows how many times someone had said it to me," said George.

That night St Mary's Hall was crowded and the boy's nervousness, temporarily overcome by the excitement of the wagon trip, returned in full force. Yet he played loud and strong, and when he made a mistake forced himself to keep on playing, and to play better for having made it. The biographical sketch of Lewis published in a book of such sketches in the nineteen-fifties which said the band knew "only two numbers" was wrong by a whole night full of different numbers. They played blues, waltzes, schottisches, marches, and the music that was none of those they called "ragtime."

"But we didn't play it fast in those days. Not like they make us play it now. No, indeed. We played 'Tiger Rag' that night, about three times I guess, because the folks kept asking for it. After we got going I didn't feel so nervous. And I was mighty proud."

Before he left for Mandeville he kissed his mother good-bye, as he always did. It was then she did something for the first time she was to do each time he left her, throughout his life, to play his music, whether it was in a parade, a New Orleans bistro, or the concert halls of the great cities of the United States and Europe. She laid long, graceful, black fingers on his forehead, and said:

"Offer your music to God, son, and ask Him for help. Before you get up to play, son, say 'all for Thee, Jesus.' God bless you."

There have been many who have derided this faith; who have even said to the writer: "Surely you can't think—" and left the sentence unfinished. It seems a senseless thing, to deride a man's faith. One may not believe in the least in the object of that faith, but the faith itself is as real as the sun and the moon and the stars and the seasons, and as sustaining to its possessor as the breath of life.

Alice Zeno's son will tell you he has never forgotten her words, or lost the faith she gave him, no matter how deep his trouble and despair. No matter where he has played there has been a split second before the parade falls in line, the men climb on the wagon, the band leaves the Jim Crow backroom seclusion forced on them in New Orleans clubs, or the curtains part before an audience of waiting thousands in a big concert hall, when George Lewis raises his horn almost imperceptibly, pauses for the space of a breath, and then steps forward to play.

"But no one ever prayed harder," grins George, "than that spindly little kid when he climbed up there on that wagon and blew his first note on his first job. Guess no one was ever happier, either, if it comes to that."

four

MANDEVILLE, Ponchatoula, Bogalusa, Rayne, Slidell, Bay St Louis, Pass St Charles, Gretna, the dark hinterlands of Alabama and Mississippi, in the little towns and way stations that sound like Pullman cars, at picnics and fish frys and dances, on wagons and on foot the Black Eagles made themselves felt, horns shouting, singing, wailing, drums driving, strings driving.

They weren't the greatest band in all the South by any means, and they were one of the youngest, but they were good enough to set the people dancing, to bring them out to clap and stomp and wail "Lawd! Lawd!"; good enough to be asked back, good enough to be called on to play over the lake in New Orleans at yard parties and dances.

There was never any question, after that St Joseph's night dance, who would be their clarinettist. Nor can there be much question but that the two years George Lewis spent with the Black Eagles set the pattern of his playing throughout his life. The "ceaseless inventiveness" of the Lewis playing to which Rudi Blesh and others have referred was given its first impetus then, and that impetus has never been lost. In the early days, when the critics and the academicians and the—God help us—musicologists first condescended to notice this music, some of them referred to it as the "nothing to lose" school of music. This, far more than their learned analysis, reached its heart. The Negro had nothing to lose. There was no progress beyond a certain point possible for him in the South, proscribed as he was by the "thus far and

no farther" policy of the white governing class. Few of them could look forward to anything even resembling economic security; the withholding of proper educations had taken care of that. Only a limited number of them could hope for anything but the lowest form of manual labour, performed for the lowest possible rate of pay. At that time he had little hope of legal equality, and his status in the courts was indeed dubious. George Lewis's cousin, fourteen year old son of his Aunt Hortense, was shot wantonly and in cold blood, without cause, by a white boy, yet none of the Negro eyewitnesses dared testify against the murderer. All around him, and frequently in his own family, the Negro saw the unmistakeable evidence that throughout the decades the white man had not hesitated to make free with the Negro woman, yet he knew the unspeakable fate that awaited him if he was even suspected of speaking in a familiar tone to a white woman. He saw sorrow, heartbreak, illness, inhuman working conditions, all leave their brand on those he loved simply because these things were the lot of his people. He accepted the patronage of the "kind" whites with a beaming smile, and went home to curse the rats that infested his home and threatened his children, and kept locked within him the thoughts behind the smile.

There was, indeed, nothing to lose.

And so it was with the music. There was nothing to lose by playing as you wanted to play, certainly not prestige. There was no one to criticise except other musicians, and their judgments were harsher, their standards more exacting, than any professional critic's could ever be. It did not matter what the rest of the world thought; in fact, they gave no thought to the rest of the world, for no one but themselves would ever hear them to any extent, or, hearing, care. They played for each other, to each other, and for their own people and they needed no interpreters from outer space to tell them if it was good or bad.

After that first nerve-shattering March 19, in 1914, George Lewis's nervousness gradually subsided, giving way instead to a slowly growing confidence as his horn became clearer, his message more exact, yet which never took over completely. He still played long hours by himself until each note and phrase was to become a reflex of his thoughts and feelings. On several occasions he was given the opportunity to learn to read by older musicians who, hearing the boy, knew what lay within him.

"I tried," says George. "I could have learned. A lot of the musicians who bragged all through the years that they could 'read' only knew the notes. Real reading and knowing A from B-flat on the staff's two different things. But when I tried it got in my way. The notes there, like in a blues or in a march, they weren't my notes, they was the way some other man felt about something. I heard what I wanted to play in my mind, and how I felt, and when I tried to play another man's music it sounded dead and cold. So I continued on the way I was going and the folks seem to like it. There's a lot more you can do with your own self, your own feelings, if you speak your own piece."

And the undersized youngster, standing on the wagons, playing in the courtyards and dance halls, spoke his piece through those years with more and more conviction. Each time he raised his horn to his lips the liquid, silver tones flowed more easily, stronger, broader; and more and more often the other boys in the band stood back, giving him support, saying "Amen" with their instruments in the right places; holding him up with sure, unobtrusive rhythm, while his horn said to them and to the people: "Stand back! I got a song to sing tonight, man! I got a story to tell tonight! Hear me!"

When he was not playing himself or working at some job he listened, and listening learned, from men like Alphonse Picou, George Baquet, Charley McCurtis—"he sure helped me a lot when I was young"—' Jimmy Noone, Johnny Dodds, King Oliver, Frankie Dusen, Roy Palmer—"there never was a greater trombone player than Roy"—, Ezeb Landred, Baby Dodds, Billy Marrero, Oke Gaspard, Lorenzo Tio, Jr., Willie Cornish, Kid Rena, Chris Kelly, and Buddy Petit, and the latter three were to seek him out to play with their bands within a few years. He learned from every instrument and every group, not from clarinettists alone, for as much as any New Orleans musician who ever lived, George Lewis believed in ensemble playing, with each man contributing, no man starring unless and until his message became so urgent, his instrument so insistent, that his fellows must perforce 'take down' to let him tell his story.

The jealousy shown by many leaders toward their men—a situation particularly noticeable in the groups that George heard after he left New Orleans—was always a puzzle to him. He was never able to divorce the leader from the ensemble, and in his own bands, starting with his first little group in 1923, he brought

the individual members forward as much as he could without violating his concepts of what the music should be. When they had a piece to speak he let them speak it, and when the crowds applauded he smiled and was happy.

Many times the writer has heard George Lewis say, in effect, after a particularly fine performance by some member of his band: "You hear Jim tonight (or Drag or Joe or one of the others)? He sure was laying it down. Never heard him sound so good and them folks loved it. If they'd all play like that all the time I wouldn't have no worries."

But during the hey-day of the music in New Orleans this jealousy was not noticeable among the really great leaders. They might be—and were—jealous of material success, for they lived in a dog-eat-dog world and could not afford to show too much consideration, even to each other, but it did not interfere with their music. A good leader usually picked the best men he could find, and never made the mistake of seeking mediocrity in order to provide contrast for his own superior talents.

There was nothing particularly noble or commendably self-effacing in the Lewis attitude toward a leader's role. It was an attitude that grew out of the music which he played, music that thrived on the give-and-take of individual expression within the group itself.

The men who were so soon to take the music out of New Orleans, into the west and midwest by way of San Francisco and Chicago and then into New York, were playing around him, and he heard them all. Most of them, except Louis Armstrong, were older than he; Kid Ory, Jimmy Noone, King Oliver, the Dodds brothers, Mutt Carey, and Freddy Keppard, heir to Buddy Bolden's crown. These, and others, were to leave New Orleans to find fame but—with few exceptions—not fortune, in other parts of the country and the world.

The stories of New Orleans and its music, as told by these musicians, have necessarily ended, as far as the New Orleans phase was concerned, sometime during the period between 1915 and 1925. As a result there is a wide-spread impression that the exodus of a few musicians left that city without its music; that as ragtime became known as "jass" and then "jazz" and then moved north, there was a vacuum in the Crescent City as far as its traditional music was concerned. Yet the golden era of New Orleans music extended many years beyond that. "Some of the

greatest of all the mens who played the music never left New Orleans." This statement I have heard made by not one but a score of those who stayed behind.

Because the classic music of the Negro, which was damned so young by the word "jazz," was erroneously considered by those who knew little about it to be "whorehouse" music, statements were made that with the closing of the "district" the music died out. The truth is that it scarcely felt the change. It had always been played in the cabarets and dives of the district; many of these remained in their old locations, others merely moved to another. There were still parades, picnics, fish frys, Labour Day and Fourth of July celebrations, dances, riverboats and funerals. It will come as a disappointment to a certain patronizing type of student of the music to learn that very little of it was ever played in whorehouses. Musicians were employed by the madams, and piano players were always in demand, but the Negro band was not. The music was more apt to be that of piano, banjo, and guitar, and, sometimes, violin. The music that the great New Orleans musicians were playing in those days, and continued to play, would have been a mighty distracting thing in a whorehouse.

Freddy Keppard, the trumpeter on whose shoulders the mantle of Buddy Bolden fitted naturally, and who was at times a hard man to play for because of his dedication to the principles of his music, was perhaps the wisest and most discerning of those early players. Keppard refused practically all offers to record, to the despair of latter-day collectors. He apparently sensed what the future would bring forth, and wanted no part in contributing to it. It was Keppard's expressed prophecy that the commercial record companies would do exactly what they did: record the gold, make imitations of it in inferior metal, and sell the imitations to a jazz-crazy public for more-than-tidy profits. There are only a few records extant on which this trumpeter can be heard, a man who sensed so well the need to guard his music from the depredations of mediocre white copyists and commercial exploiters.

George Lewis, playing in that second decade of the twentieth century, heard stories of this one and that one going "up no'th" and for the life of him couldn't see why, when the music was in New Orleans and there would be no one to play it with there except the few home town boys who had gone with you or followed you.

He did not hanker for far places in those days, and even less a few years later when one by one the stories came back of the musicians who had gone north and fared badly. Here in New Orleans was the music, here were the people, his people, who knew its language, who carried around in their hearts the memories he carried, who heard what he said when his horn took fire, who could laugh with it at a shared and secret joke, or cry with it at a shared and secret sorrow.

A few of the dates he played in those days were for white people, and he sensed the difference in the audience. When he played for his own people he sensed what they were hearing; when he played for white people he sensed what they were not hearing. The white people did not want them to play the blues. They were disquieted by them, wanting never to think of the Negroes, whom they delighted and still delight to call "our people"—to the secret contemptuous amusement of the Negro—as ever sad or sorry, tormented or lost. Never wanting to hear a small, thin adolescent playing a blues solo on his clarinet with the sound of his mother's weeping in his heart; crying "no, no! rag it up!" to a trumpeter wailing a blues, the scar on his head hiding a steel plate, the result of a wanton attack by a white gang.

These people, he felt sure, would be found to a painful degree in the "no'th," and he found hard to believe the stories that it was there, far more than at home, that the musicians were finding white acceptance and understanding of the music.

For the white audiences in New Orleans they played as best they could, in the manner they thought would be pleasing. Numbers of writers have mentioned, in phrases varying only in wordage, of the Negroes' "almost pitiful desire to please the white man," without going any further into the matter, perhaps because they were not able to. It is true, but this desire to please the white man is not from love, but for the simple reason that in his pale hands lies their economic salvation, the power to make their road rougher than it already is, or to remove a few of the hazards. No praise from a white man ever meant as much to a New Orleans musician as praise from a fellow Negro musician. But the approval of the white man of anything he did, whether it was making music or cleaning out a sewer, could mean money in the pocket, coal in the scuttle, milk for the babies, and shoes on the feet. What did it matter if the message of his music was lost? The message of his ancestors who sang and drummed and danced

in Congo Square also had been lost to those who stood on the outer edges. And completely lost to the master was the message in the songs of the Negroes in the fields, and in the cabins of the slave quarters.

A little less than a year before George Lewis played his first professional date in Mandeville his grandmother, Urania, died. She was ill less than a week with a "pain in her side" which grew worse, then better, but she never recovered, and died after a six-day illness. Her brother, Arthur, who had been taken away from his mother, Zaier, and sold as a boy, had died a few months before. And so, in the space of six months, the pine coffins of her son and daughter were placed with Zaier's magnificent black one in the family vault. The vault was full now.

Alice's grief and loneliness were almost more than she could bear. She remained for a few months at the Prier Street home she and her son and Urania had shared, then fled its associations and moved to a place on St Claude and Esplanade Streets. She found there the same unpleasant physical discomforts and dangers to combat, but she did not see Urania's comforting, strong presence wherever she turned.

It was a comfort to her that her son was fast approaching manhood. She prayed that he might become healthier than he was, and she continued to blame that "damned horn" for much of his frailness, but she was proud of the manner in which he was making a way for himself, proud that she had to hold him in check to keep him from working too hard, while never letting him forget that work was the one form of salvation on this earth.

Unlike many mothers whose whole existences are focussed on their sons, Alice Zeno made no effort to hold him back from life. She knew what hazards lay ahead for him, the dragons that may have been in Urania's subconscious when she said "call him George" the morning of his birth, and she knew that he must develop his own defences against them. She did not baby him, nor was she over-protective, but she was always there, like an oasis in the desert, the earth on which the warrior throws himself to gather strength.

Other things besides music were bound to preoccupy the mind of an adolescent boy. Girls began to be important, and when he was fourteen he found out how important. Henry Zeno, from whom his son kept little, only smiled and shook his head in wonderment, remembering his own celibate youth, and warned

him tolerantly that girls meant trouble. Inclined to doubt his father's pessimism at first, when he was sixteen George Lewis found out that father knew best, after all.

Mrs Zeno, when informed of the situation in which a neighbour girl found herself, sat down and talked to her son sternly.

"You will do the right thing, George Lewis," she said.

"What you mean, ma?"

"I mean, son, that you'll go over there now—tonight—and you'll make arrangements to marry her. You're a man now. Act like one."

George did not protest. It didn't seem such a bad idea. Obviously, he liked the girl very much. He was to attain, as he grew older, a reputation for conquest that many of his colleagues envied, but he was always to show the same discrimination and selectivity he displayed in other facets of his personality. The strong opposition Mrs Zeno expected from her son did not materialize.

Instead it came from another quarter, the girl's grandmother. This worthy lady, with whom the girl lived, flatly refused to hear of any such alliance. "My granddaughter will be all right," she said. "A lot better off than she would be married to a street musician. None of 'em ever come to any good, and there won't be one in this family unless it's over my dead body."

A short time later her granddaughter married another man, much older than George, who, after a year, went away one afternoon and was never seen again.

During this period George worked constantly during the day, playing nights. Every Sunday he played at picnics or fish-frys. He joined Leonard Parker's band when he was sixteen, when, for one reason or another, the ranks of the Black Eagles were thinning. He found that indoor work resulted in illness, and during most of the year, when he was employed doing inside manual work in a bakery, he never felt well.

In 1917 another incident involving a girl, although without the same troubling results, suddenly brought him a vast discontent with his surroundings. A number of his friends had gone to Muscle Shoals in Alabama, to work on the government project there, the site of what was to become one of the hottest political potatoes of depression days. This, he decided, would be worth trying, and carrying his horn in one hand and a cheap suitcase in the other, set forth.

Until then he had held a vast variety of jobs, but the hardest manual labour he had done had been the work in the bakery, which had not required great strength. At Muscle Shoals he learned what the white man means when he says "we never give the niggers the walkin' jobs." Although obviously too small for that type of job he was put to work pushing a "Georgia buggy," a sort of out-sized wheelbarrow loaded with gravel or cement. It "liked to killed me" but he never slackened or slowed down; instead, driven perhaps by the very fact of his own comparative weakness, he tried to outdo every other man on the project. He learned then something that almost cost him his life in later years—that there is always another ounce of spirit to call on when your body tells you you can't go any further. It was then, when his boy's body, frailer than most, attempted to adjust itself to work far beyond its capacity, that the gradual process of destruction began which was to bring him in middle life so close to death at times that only the faith that was in him pulled him through. There were many George Lewises in the South whose dark skins did not necessarily mean strong bodies, who might have rounded out normal life spans had they not been needed for the "heavy, dirty jobs" the white man would not deign to perform. There is a saying that the Negroes quote among themselves and attribute to the white boss: "Kill a mule, buy another; kill a nigger, get another."

He had, of course, brought his horn with him but there was little time to play, though he entertained his barracks mates with it at night. Working there then, although they never met, was a man whose path would cross George's many years later, first in San Francisco and then in England and Europe, a folk singer named Jesse Fuller, to whom recognition came late in life, when he was working a jack hammer on the streets of Oakland, California, in the mid-nineteen-fifties.

But if Muscle Shoals did nothing else for George Lewis, it brought him the final fist fight of his battle-fraught career. He does not recall exactly what started it, except that it was a remark he took as a slur on his size and ability to do as much work as the next man. The man who made it was easily twice his weight, and well over six feet tall, with ham-like fists and powerful muscles.

"Take it back," said George.

"Well, Lawd, Lawd, look who's talkin'," grinned the other, fists on hips.

The fight was on.

George says his first swing didn't come within six inches of the man's jaw, and the next thing he knew he was flying through the air in the barracks, landing across a cot. He bounced back like a rubber ball, connecting this time, hurting his hand. Then he found himself sailing across the room again, this time landing on the floor. Again he bounced back.

"And you know something?" said George. "I didn't have sense enough to realize that man hadn't hit me a lick yet. I just kept comin' back and comin' back. He could of killed me without even getting out of breath. I don't know how many times I tried to get at him, I was that angry. Each time I'd find myself sailing thro the air. It was getting mighty tiresome."

Finally his opponent—if in such a one-sided affair one can be said to have an opponent—picked up the still fighting young man, and held him, feet dangling and kicking, and shook him gently.

"You is, without a doubt, the feistiest, cockiest, little son-of-a-gun I ever met up with in all my life," said the man. He did not swear, because he wanted the fight to end. "You gonna git hurt one of these days, little man. You better sign the pledge right now—no mo' fightin'. Ain't everybody gonna be this good to you."

Suddenly the fire went out of George Lewis. He was tired, battered, and saw himself as he must appear to the other, a little ridiculous, completely helpless, licked before he even began. He grew up a little in those few moments, and never fought again except to defend himself against physical attack. He loathed and feared all forms of weapons other than his fists or a handy rock: the knives, guns, brass knuckles, and other paraphernalia a man who is physically weak will frequently fall back on. He was to carry a gun only once, and then only to protect himself from a threatened attack. He never used it, and when the need for it was past he sold it. The experience in Muscle Shoals did not eliminate his temper, but it awakened him for the first time to its real potentials of danger.

A notice from his draft board brought him back to New Orleans. After registering he went to the Navy recruiting office in an attempt to enlist. When he presented his 118 pounds and

asked to be signed up they did not examine him, merely weighed him. Go back, they told him, and gain seven pounds; then, if you're all right otherwise, you can join up.

He did as they advised him, stuffing himself with rice and potatoes and sweets and in a few weeks, detecting a slight tightness in his clothing, returned to the recruiting office. One hundred and twenty one pounds. Again he was sent back home and again he tried valiantly to put on weight. The next time he presented himself his weight was 123 pounds. He could get it no higher, and on the advice of the doctors gave up trying.

But in a sense he served, for there must today be veterans of World War I living in New Orleans who recall the music of the bands that escorted them, as draftees, to the station when they were shipped out to training camps. Each outgoing group of rookies was sent on its way by the music of its city, and George Lewis played in most of the bands that furnished that music. Sometimes it would be as often as twice a day. Usually he was with the Leonard Parker band, but there were other groups, their names lost now as far as memory is concerned, remembered only in a continuum of music and marching.

The adolescent years were a kaleidoscope of experiences, each blending with the next. There was deep satisfaction in them, too, for at last he was able in some small measure to share with his mother the burden she had carried so long, and he welcomed the sharing.

When George was sixteen his father stopped hinting and came out flatly and asked for his support in changing Alice's mind about returning to him.

"I know my daddy would have given me anything he could, any time. But this time I knew he was hoping I'd try and do something to get him and my mother back together again. And that's how I got my first brand new horn. I mean a brand new one from a music store, not a second-hand one. I'm not sure now but I think it was a Harry Peddler. Took me to a store one afternoon, without telling me a thing, and bought it for me. I was sure proud, but I couldn't do what he wanted. I couldn't change my mother's mind."

If the young George Lewis escaped, as he did, the hardening and toughening of character that came to so many of his people as they grew older; if, later on, he was a more understanding and gentle leader than most; much of it must be attributed to the two

people who loved him so single-heartedly. Insecure as he was, in common with all his people; facing a future that ended at the blank wall of "thus far and no farther," he nevertheless knew in his youth the incalculable boon of emotional security, of knowing that whatever might come to him in the way of struggle, and he could expect little else, the love of the only two people in the world he really cared for would be the battlement from which he could fight.

five

"YOU crazy, Willie? What you mean bringin' a kid like that to join up with a man's band?"

"You ain't heard him play," said Willie Parker to Willie Cornish, ex-Buddy Bolden sideman, and now a member of the Eureka Band.

"Sho I've heard him. He can play good. But he ain't nothin' but a kid, Willie."

George Lewis standing back quietly, as he usually did, spoke up softly.

"I'm nineteen."

"Lawd! Lawd!" Another of the bandsmen spoke up. "Don't look more'n fifteen. This is man's work, son."

The boy turned to walk away. Willie Parker's hand on his shoulder stopped him, held him.

"Tell you what I'll do, men," said Willie. "Y'all know the kid can play good. We couldn't do no better if we was to try for the nex' month. He plays with us tonight. We gotta have someone. Then if he don't suit you, we don't pay him. And," said Willie grandly, tapping himself on the chest, "we don't pay me, neither."

Willie Parker is well past eighty now, as this is written, more than twenty years older than George Lewis. But he remembers as "good as though it was yesterday" that after that first engagement the men in the Eureka Band came to him and said:

"Think we can get the kid to play again, Willie?"

Willie, still smarting at the implied slurs on his judgment a few hours before, replied: "I dunno. You was mighty skeery 'bout takin' him on. Have to talk it over with him. He's pretty much in demand. I'll see if it can be arranged."

Willie knew, if they didn't, that it could "be arranged"; that the boy would be walking on air for days afterwards if he was taken on regularly by the band. There was never any further question about it after that first engagement. He played with them for two years, regularly, whenever they had a playing date.

When they were hesitant about hiring a young man who "wasn't nothing but a kid" he could have spoken up and told them, if he'd wanted to, that he was a grown man now, with a grown man's responsibilities and cares—that he had been married almost a year, and was the proud-to-bursting father of a daughter just a few weeks old. "But I was never one to brag," says George, gently.

He married when he was eighteen years old, a girl named Emma Johnson whom he had met at a dance. His mother was not too surprised, nor was she greatly upset. She did not like to think of so young a boy shouldering the responsibilities of a wife and family, but she felt it might be better than the aimlessness of being single. He had been able to support himself for a long time now, and to help her also; but she knew she could manage alone. Had she not managed, on practically nothing, when he had been a child, and had needed clothes, and medicine and care? She knew Emma, and liked the sturdy, strongly-built young woman with the long, straight black hair like her husband Henry's, and the reddish skin, like his, too. She felt none of the jealousy and resentment many women feel toward a daughter-in-law, especially if she is the wife of their only son. Rather, she welcomed her in all sincerity into the family as the daughter she had never reared. She knew instinctively that she would be called upon to help the young couple. Her shoulders had borne so heavy a burden for so long that to have no weight to carry at all would have given her a feeling of utter aloneness, the lost feeling of not being needed.

"I suppose," said Alice, when her son told her he planned to marry, "you're expecting a baby?"

"Well, pretty quick," he replied.

"Think you can support a wife and baby, son?"

"Sure, ma. Ain't—aren't I working every day at that cleaning place? Don't I play fo'—five nights a week? We're going to rent a room from her aunt. It's just practically around the corner."

Alice said only: "I'll miss you, son."

"No, you won't ma. I'll see you every day. You wait and see. Every day. Ma, I couldn't not do that. I couldn't not see you every day."

It was a promise made by an 18-year-old that could so easily —and forgivably—have been broken. It never was. For forty-two years there was no day when George Lewis was in New Orleans and able to walk that he did not see his mother. Throughout the years she looked for him, and was never disappointed, and each day or night they would sit for a while across a table from each other, and drink coffee, and he would tell her what he had been doing, and what he was planning to do, and what he was thinking and feeling. He might have to waken her late at night or early in the morning on his way home from playing; but sick or well, drinking or sober, sooner or later he found his way to her.

"Seems like I couldn't res' good at night if I hadn't seen her sometime during the day. I'd be thinking of how she must have looked for me, and how worried and hurted she must have been when I didn't come. Sometimes I'd get out of bed and get dressed again at night and go down there. Then I could res' myself, knowing she was all right."

If Emma's family had possessed just a little of Alice Zeno's understanding, if they had been more willing to accept their daughter's marriage, to adopt the live-and-let-live policy which had always ruled Alice's life, the marriage might have eventually rested on a more secure foundation than it did.

The first stunning impact of fatherhood did not quite floor the young man, although it came close. He was as happy and proud as his own father had been nineteen years before, walking on the same cloud. Still, he managed to pursue his normal activities during the time Emma was in Charity Hospital, working during the day, blowing his horn with a new triumph in its tones at night, eating his meals with his mother as vast numbers of new fathers do during times like these.

It was when Emma came home from the hospital, bringing their daughter Mildred with her, and he saw the actual proof, the living, squirming, crying, drooling, nose-wrinkling, miraculous

proof of his new status, that a sort of mental fog set in, obscuring reality. The day after the baby came home he started for work half a dozen times. Each time he returned for another look, another half-frightened, tentative touch, another reassurance that this incredible achievement was real. The last time he returned, he stayed. While the baby slept, he simply sat and stared at her; during the infrequent periods when she was awake he either held her and talked to her, or rushed about commanding everyone to come and look at what he was sure was a smile, until his wife pleaded with him to leave, go out, get a beer, do anything—just get out from underfoot. Babies were almost entirely new to him; there had been no younger brothers or sisters that he could remember for him to break in on, so to speak. And he was by gentle nature a born pushover for their wiles.

It never occurred to him (in fact nothing occurred to him that day) that his employer would fail to understand that a brand-new baby couldn't be left, even if it did have a mother and two grandmothers to handle any situation that might arise. He was, wasn't he, the baby's *father*?

He was mistaken about his employer. When he reported to work the next morning he found another boy on his job.

A father for the first time and jobless. It was not a good beginning. The money he made playing was small; it certainly was not enough to cover rent, food, clothes, and baby-type expenses. It was hard for either Emma or his mother to judge him harshly, but life had to go on and the added expenses must be met. The incident did not endear him to his in-laws to any degree.

The knack he always had of landing jobs brought him work within a few days at the big Whittemore shoe-shine stand. The money was not a great deal, but he made more than the other boys because of a New Orleans judge who, every day that court was in session, stopped for a shine and always wrapped the dime with which he paid for it in a dollar bill. It seldom meant less than four dollars a week additional, and sometimes more.

The job did not last long. Within a few months of their daughter's birth an undiagnosed illness brought him to such a state of physical debility it was necessary for Mrs Zeno and Emma to hire a carriage, wrap him in blankets, and practically carry him to his mother's rooms. There had been a long fever,

and, when that broke, the strength that should have returned did not.

There were two rooms in the place on St Claude Street where Alice was living and in one of these George, Emma, and the baby lived for nearly a year.

Alice was delighted with the arrangement. Her reaction to her first grandchild was not as extreme as her son's reaction had been to the young lady's arrival; after all, she knew quite a bit about new babies, but she gave each one that came along, in those middle years, the love that she had never been able to give her own babies, whose time with her had been so short. It was as though that love had never left, but had been in her heart all the time, in abeyance, waiting to be awakened again.

George put it more simply. "My mamma was crazy for them grandbabies of hers. There wasn't anything too much for her to do for them."

His clarinet was in his hands almost as soon as he was strong enough to sit up after that illness. His mother raged futilely that he would never get well as long as he used up his wind like that, but she was gone most of the day, and he "ran it over" hour after hour.

As soon as he could walk without stopping to support himself on the nearest solid object, he was back on the streets, looking up musician friends on bands, searching for a place to play. He did not ask, then or ever, for a job, but he listened to the talk and learned where the bands were playing, and managed to show up fortuitously when a band was seeking a clarinet player. He found several jobs, and then Willie Parker found him, after a few days' search, and took him to "join up" with the Eureka Band.

The crisis caused by the first funeral he was to play with the band almost approached that of his first communion. The Eureka Band costume for funerals was black shoes, black trousers with a strip of grosgrain ribbon down the side seams, a black shirt with white collar, and the conventional band hat. Over the black shirt was worn a blue blouse with tie waist. He had none of these things except the shoes and hat.

Alice had an ally now in Emma. Between them they managed. The only expenditures they made were for the grosgrain ribbon and the blouse material. A pair of dark blue trousers was dyed black, as was a white shirt. A white collar from another shirt was sewed on the black one. Alice made the blouse while Emma

sewed the grosgrain rilbbon on the trousers. By custom, funerals in New Orleans usually are held within a short time of death, and for twenty-four hours needles flew in the little St Claude Street apartment, dye pots bubbled, and George took care of the baby.

It was then he learned the slow, precise walk of the cemetery-bound band. The BOOM BOOM of the bass drum, then the left foot forward on the third beat, with the music coming in on the fourth, and the half-beat halt between steps. It was a walk he was to make more than 500 times before his legs refused to carry him on another. Less than a year ago he was asked to play in a funeral parade—"Jus' a short one, George"—and had to refuse. In his first few funeral parades he played a B-flat clarinet, later changing to E-flat, an instrument that always held a special appeal for him.

There was seldom a night, and never a weekend, that his horn was not heard somewhere in New Orleans or the nearby countryside. After he had played until the small hours on a scheduled date, he did not put his horn away and go home, but instead ranged the streets of the French Quarter and the "district," for although Storyville had been gone since 1917, the cabarets and dives where the music was played were still going strong. Many times the hot morning sun was beating down on the banquettes before the slender, quick-moving, soft-spoken, hard-blowing young man found his way home, there to change clothes and start for his day's work. If he was not playing at one of the night spots with a band on any particular night, he was always a welcome "sit in." Pete Lala's, the "25," the Humming Bird, the Black and Tan, the Tuxedo, in the "district" or blocks away, it did not matter; the music was in these places, and that was where he had to be.

The nights when he "sat in" there was no pay; on other jobs the pay was sometimes as little as 75 cents a night. Nor did the daytime jobs he worked at pay much more. He and Emma had moved back into a place of their own by 1920, and a second child was expected. Family interference was fast changing what should have been a normally happy marriage, with normal ups and downs, into periodic states of turmoil. And he was learning at first hand what he sensed when he was a child and saw his mother cry because she could not have a first communion party for him: the pain of wanting to give and having nothing to give

except the bare necessities of shelter and food.

He found in those days for the first time the ease with which the hurt of living could be lessened by a few drinks. Found, too, that on those frequent occasions when he "didn't feel too good" he could quickly feel better with their aid. And it was amazing how many hours of playing music, after a hard day's work, could be managed with the help of the contents of a jug.

He was not unique. The musicians of New Orleans were a hard drinking lot, with legendary capacities for alcohol. Whisky was the favourite drink, gin would do if there was nothing better, and wine was for those who didn't know good liquor when they had it, or else for those too broke to buy anything else. The country was squirming under the restrictions of Prohibition, but it made no notable difference, except for whatever unseen damage there might be to stomach linings.

A New Orleans musician who is still living in that city, and would probably prefer not to be quoted, had this to say, when I marvelled at the capacities for drinking, and the amount of it done, in that city.

"Y'see," he said. "I figure it like this. In New Orleans in them days—an' pretty much today—the Negro wasn't goin' nowhere. Not nowhere at all. Might as well get good and drunk on the way."

In George Lewis there was an emotional continuum of child and man. His nervous system was as unstable as a cat's, that animal whose movements his own resembled in quickness and grace. Because he had never known rest, even as a child, the habit of resting had never been acquired. He, literally, did not know how. But even if he had known how he probably would not have done so, for he would have felt, as he did for most of his life, a deep sense of guilt at doing nothing. He was between fifty-five and fifty-six years old before the psychological resistance to rest he had built up could be broken down. When this writer planned work for the band in those years it was necessary literally to trick him into the time off, the rest that meant the difference between survival as a musician, or a lifetime as an invalid. Had this been done before he might today be playing as many of his contemporaries are, steadily and profitably throughout the year, instead of on spaced-out, short tours, with true economic security still an unattained goal.

His physical stature remained slight; he walked erectly, and no amount of liquor ever made the arrow-straight back stoop. He

spoke softly, as his father and grandfather had done, and unless angry was an amazingly quiet and gentle young man. He had never lost the mischievous quality that had driven his frequently distracted mother into further frenzies. He had always been, and still is, a mimic of no mean talent. Because of his innate horror of anything that smacks of "showing off" he seldom displays this talent unless it comes into play almost unconsciously, as part of a story or anecdote. Then, with uncanny effect, this 98-pound man will suddenly assume the burden of an extra hundred and fifty pounds, if a fat man is involved in the story. The load of excess weight is before your eyes; the walk, legs wide-spaced, feet planted solidly to balance the bulging abdomen; the arms held slightly away from the body because of their size; the voice, fruity from good living. Or it might be a woman, fussy, over-solicitous, nagging, supercilious; somehow he creates them all, then as suddenly they vanish, and quiet, gentle, little George Lewis remains behind, with just a residue of mischievous twinkle in the eyes. But it is never done with malice.

He never learned the art of bragging; Alice Zeno had done her work well. And because bragging might conceivably hurt another, it is probable he would never have developed it, for his sensitivity increased reather than decreased with the years, and with each hurt that came to him he became more reluctant to inflict hurt upon another. If he felt undue pride in his own playing, he hid it well, although he never backed down before another musician, and never feared another musician's skills. After his experience in Muscle Shoals he avoided fist fights, keeping his temper a little better reined. He dreaded and loathed the violence and fighting that sometimes disrupted the festivities when he was playing. Attacked himself, he could fight like a demon, but he was a poor bystander.

"I was the quickest one in all New Orleans at finding a window to get through if a fight busted out on the floor," said George. "It wasn't so much that I was small and knew I'd be better off outside as it was that I hated to see blood and people fighting."

His revulsion to bloodshed became a permanent reaction of faintness and almost physical illness at the sight of it after his small body was used as a shield by Evan Thomas the night that great trumpeter was murdered. The murderer ignored the shield and with complete singleness of purpose reached over the frightened young musician's shoulder and cut Evan's throat,

severing the jugular vein. The physical results of this, as far as George was concerned, would be better left to the imagination.

On another occasion a fight broke out on the floor of a night spot called "Egg Head's Place." The participants were two women, one of them known as "Black Gold." All exits were blocked. George climbed up on a bench that ran along a wall on which there were hooks to hang coats and hats. Suddenly the bench was knocked from under him, yet he did not fall. He could not. His vest had become ensnared on one of the wall hooks and he hung there, his body too light in weight to tear the fabric of the vest, and far too light to dislodge the hook. When the fight was over and an uneasy peace came to the place, he unbuttoned his vest, slipped his arms out, and went back to his job of making music.

His dislike of bombast, bragging, and self-aggrandizement became almost an obsession in later years, after he himself became the unhappy and bewildered victim of the almost sadistic cruelties of a psychopathically jealous leader, who was also a master braggart and who, throughout his life in New Orleans, had antagonized everyone with whom he played by his constant criticism and "running down" of other musicians, to many of whom he was deeply indebted. Each recountal of impossible anecdotes drove George farther into himself, squirming with vicarious embarrassment; each belittling remark left a scar deep enough to affect all his relationships with the outer world, until it has become difficult even for this writer to learn some of the basic truths of his early career. Not until long after this particular chapter was written did I learn—and then only by picking up an unguarded remark—that Lorenzo Tio, Jr. sought George Lewis out after a parade to ask where he had learned to play, to flatly refuse to believe him when he said he had taught himself, and to offer his help whenever the young man needed it. "I never would have thought a kid like you could play like that, not without a lot of teaching," said Tio. And when I at last wormed the story from George, I was made to feel that by recounting it I would be breaking a confidence.

Only wounds deep enough to have left lasting psychological scars would have driven George Lewis from the apartment in which he was living into the snowy night cold of a pre-Christmas season in New York, to a bench in Washington Square, there to weep with hurt and loneliness and homesickness. In his hand his

return ticket to New Orleans was a warm comfort. His plans were made to leave the next day, his group clamouring to leave with him. He was found there by one of those to whom this book is dedicated, one of those whose name brings the quick, gentle smile, the sudden light in the eyes, and the quiet words: "He's my frien'." With infinite patience and understanding Bill Russell persuaded him to remain.

The year of his son's marriage Henry Zeno left New Orleans for the last time and moved back home to Mandeville and the countryside he loved. He was growing old now. The weakness following the surgery that a doctor in Mandeville told his sister had been badly bungled had made him for years the helpless victim of a taunting, greedy woman. His ability to earn money was lessened in ratio to his increase in age and loss of strength from illness. He felt that if he could only have Alice's strength to lean on, things would be as they had been, and when he at last accepted the fact that she would give it to him only as a friend, never as a companion and wife, he packed quietly, and moved without fuss or fanfare to the place in which he had grown up.

At first he stayed with his sister Hortense. The murder of her fourteen-year-old son had left her shocked and grief-stricken. It had also left her materially worse off, for the little money the boy had earned had gone a long way towards keeping the family in food. Henry helped her all he could, and with second hand lumber, working when he was able, he built himself a small cabin on the family property, next to his sister's house. It was snug and ship-shape, as anything Henry built would be, and behind it he planted a vegetable garden, and strawberries, and settled down, as he put it: "to live out my days." Each nail he hammered, each board he secured, was done with the warm knowledge that he was building a place where his son could come, and his son's children.

When George played, as he frequently did, in St Mary's Hall, he often was not able to get over the lake in time to see his father before the start of the engagement. On those nights Henry, eating with Hortense or spending the evening with her, would suddenly leave his chair and walk to the porch or window and stand, head on one side, listening until the last note had died away.

"That's the boy," he would say to his sister. "Listen y'ere, Hortense. You hear that? That's the boy. That's George. Keep the coffee on the stove, sis."

Now it was the father, not the boy, who stood outside a hall and listened to the music, head nodding, feet tapping, murmuring to himself: "Yeah, boy. I hear you." Saying afterwards to his son: "You fellas played mighty fine tonight, son. Sure sounded good."

"Yeah, pappa? You think so? Don't always sound just right to me yet. You're not just sayin' it? You think it really sounded good?"

"Sure, son, sure."

six

THE twenties roared just as loudly in New Orleans as they did elsewhere in the country. Many musicians had left, or were leaving, and were being heard in Chicago and New York, but the music stayed where it had been born. That the Negroes of the South played music uniquely their own wherever they might live cannot be denied, and the statement of many latter day writers that jazz, as it came to be called, was not necessarily indigenous to New Orleans alone has some truth in it. But the music of New Orleans had a quality not found in the music of any other area, for in no other city did the cultures of so many countries intrude. Here the ships put in from Spain, Italy, France, Germany, Scandinavia, and Latin America, and the songs of the sailors and the expatriates of those lands, sung in bar and bistro and played in parades and at dances, were taken up quickly and alchemized into the peculiar gold of the Negro interpretation. In England I was told by a student of folk music that "St James Infirmary," one of the most widely known of all Negro blues, came directly from the port of Bristol, England, and was based on a song sung there in the early part of the century. There was

great classical music in New Orleans too, and opera, and this music also found its way to the Negroes' instruments by various and devious routes.

Some of the men with whom George Lewis played in his teens were old enough to have picked up instruments left in the pawn shops by returning Confederate soldiers. To have handled them with delicate, understanding, gifted fingers; tried them tentatively at young lips, pushing first one valve, and then another, adding the sounds together, this one here, that one there; experimenting with the tones and what could be said with them; hearing spaces that needed filling in with tones from another instrument, playing a phrase, a run that needed an answer yet finding meaning in the tones; gaining courage, and then, suddenly: "Stand back and listen to my story, man!"

Theirs was not the technique of the conservatory. It was the technique of the pearl-divers in the South Pacific, of whom I once heard the member of an Olympic diving team say ruefully: "I watched them for weeks. And I knew that if I won every medal in every event I could never dive as they do. I had to learn it. They've *got* it." It was the technique of the Indian on his horse, who has never heard of a riding academy, or knows the definition of the word "dressage" but is completely adept in demonstrating it because it is second nature to him. It was the technique and skill of the man with a sail boat who has grown up with the feel of rudder ropes in his hands. It is a technique that others, with years of academic training, have been outspokenly frank in envying, and in admitting that they have striven for, yet have never achieved.

Each man brought to his music, besides his inherent gifts, the garnered experiences of his own life and the memories of his race. By the time he was seventeen the Negro youth of New Orleans had usually garnered more experience than comes to the sheltered in a lifetime. Yet it still came as a shock to some of the older men when George Lewis, a boy of nineteen who looked fifteen, would suddenly set a band on fire with a searing clarinet that had in it the cry in the night of Zaier when she sent her son from her, or the despairing rebellion against his own fear as he ran from a mob like a fox running from a pack of dogs. Yet whose clarinet could bring that fire to a soft glow in an instant with tones as tender as those of the Creole lullabies his mother had sung to him.

It is difficult to understand why it should have been assumed by the general public and the starry-eyed "discoverers" of this music that because a comparatively small handful of Negro musicians had left a city that was literally teeming with them, the music should have stopped or been in any way "lost." Even if the only men left had been Kid Rena, Buddy Petit, Chris Kelly, Evan Thomas, Roy Palmer, Lawrence Marrero, George Lewis, Alcide Pavageau, Jim Robinson, the Fritzes, Paul Barbarin, and a score of others, the music would have had a hard time dying. But there were several times several score left, and the music lived and grew strong, while in the north and east and west it lived, but did not grow strong. Instead, perhaps for the sake of survival, it succumbed, in instance after instance, to outside pressures and influences that left it impotent, eunuchoid, devitalized. But not until the hunger-filled years of the thirties came along was there a lessening of the sound of the music in the city.

And now it was becoming "jazz" instead of "jass' and dotters of i's and crossers of t's have covered many reams of paper in an effort to trace the origin of the word. George Lewis's comments on its origins are no more valid or necessarily nearer the truth than anyone else's, for no one seems to know. He says:

"When I was just a kid, befo' I'd even started playing music down around the district, I used to walk by the cheap sporting houses and cribs and the women would be standing in the doorway, faces all chalky with powder and make-up, half naked, and I'd hear them say to the men walking by: 'Don't you want to come in and jass it up? Come on—come on in and jass it up, boy.' That's the first time I ever heard the word. I don't know where it came from before that. It wasn't what we'd started calling the music then, and it was a long, long time before I ever used it for one of my bands. A little later on you started seeing the signs 'So-and-So's Ragtime Jass Band' then it was 'Jazz Band.'

"Maybe the word for it started down there in the district. But to say that the music started there—that's plain crazy. If I'd never even seen the district I'd be playing the music the way we all did. But everybody asks 'Where did the name come from?' I don't know, and I don't think anybody else does. An' you want to know something? To tell you the truth I can't see what difference it makes."

He heard the word frequently when he was a youngster, running like a hare down Eclipse Alley, most unsavoury of all the

Storyville by-ways. A boy always ran down Eclipse Alley, for the women in Eclipse Alley sat in the doorways of the tiny cribs, displaying and peddling their wares for dimes and two-bit pieces, and they'd grab a child as quick as a wink and take his money. The men who frequented Eclipse Alley were no higher in the human scale than the women, and if the police caught up with a child in Eclipse Alley they'd swat him none too gently on the rear with their billies and run him out.

And a coloured child always ran as fast as his legs could carry him when he went through that tough district known as the Irish Channel. Grown men didn't exactly linger, either, if they were coloured, and musicians tell of walking through the Irish Channel on their way to a job, carrying their instruments and being forced to stop and blow, then and there, while a crowd gathered. Guns would be brought out if they tried to quit, and sometimes the job would be missed entirely because the musicians didn't dare stop.

Because he had attended only the Catholic Church in childhood, the stirring congregational singing of the Negro Protestant churches did not come into his life as early as it had come into the lives of many of the musicians. He heard it through the open windows of the churches, at the picnics, and at the gravesides, and in the churches during the funeral services, and it moved him as no other type of music ever had. When he practised on his horn he would remember the transcendent lyricism of a woman's voice, breaking away from the others, riding the ensemble sound as a gull does the wind, soaring out and up and back, and then in a moment taking wings again, praising the Lord or seeking His hand. When he got home he would run over his clarinet, trying to bring out the sounds he had heard in the voice, trying to say the things he had heard the voice say, for he knew what they were and he understood them, and he could not rest until his horn could say them too.

And it did say them. Once in the twenties when he was playing cemetery-bound with the Eureka Band, his instrument an E-flat clarinet—that most piercingly emotional of all horns—a sobbing woman dashed from the sidewalk. She broke through the ranks of the band, and snatched the clarinet from his mouth, trying to wrest it from his hand. "Make that man stop!" she cried. "Make him stop, for the love of Jesus! He's breakin' my heart!" The band went the next few blocks with the E-flat clarinet silent.

Small wonder George Lewis does not even bother to read the

gymnastically literary critiques of the music, written with such self-conscious intellectualism by men—and women—sentenced by their own objectivity to forever stand on the side-lines, listening only with the inadequate and timorous ears of the mind.

Before their second child was born George, like most fathers, stated to anyone who would listen, that this one would be a boy, and he wouldn't settle for anything else. Still, he wasn't in the least disappointed when Mary put in an appearance, born at home with a midwife in attendance; a fine sturdy baby, who had only to wrinkle her nose to have him in the palm of one tiny hand. He did not make the mistake he had made when Mildred was born, and managed to stay away from home after her birth long enough at a time to earn a few dollars each day.

When the baby was ten days old, and he had just become used to being the father of two very absorbing new human beings, the midwife who had delivered the child called routinely to check on Emma's condition. Within an hour after she had seen her patient the ambulance she called was at the door. Emma had contracted smallpox. Her mother was in the hospital with it at the time, and her step-father had just recovered from it.

George pleaded with the authorities to let the baby remain at home but was told that it would be safer for the baby if she was taken with the mother.

For two weeks he worried, checking daily at the hospital, receiving encouraging reports about both his wife and the baby, learning at last that they could come home the next day. Emma would not even be scarred, they told him. It had been a light case and she had been most cooperative.

When he called to get his little family the next day they told him neither his wife nor his child could leave. The baby now had small pox. Forty-eight hours later she was dead.

Suddenly he was very young again, and hurt, and uncomprehending.

"Can I see her?" he asked. "Can I see my baby?"

Gently they told him that no one could see her. That she must be buried from the hospital. The health laws would not permit an open funeral for any one who had died of such a lethal, contagious disease, not even a small baby.

"You mean," said George. "I can't even see her before you buries her?"

The answer was a firm negative. They said, however, that he

must arrange for transportation to the cemetery, and for the burial.

George made arrangements for a service to be held over the tiny, sealed coffin, and stood outside the hospital and watched it being placed in the hearse. No one attended the service, but the baby's father stayed as close to the little church as they would permit him to while it was going on. After the service he followed the hearse in a streetcar which went past the cemetery, and the hearse remained in sight all the way. When it turned into the cemetery George jumped from the car and stood where he had been told he must stand—on the street corner. From there he watched them place the little pine coffin in its vault, then turned and walked blindly through the streets to his mother.

"I couldn't believe it," he said. "Not a little baby like that. Why would God want her, I kept asking myself. When my great-grandmother died, and my grandmother, it didn't seem wrong. Sad, but not wrong. They were old. My mother tried to help me and make me understand. She'd known what it was to bury a baby. Seems like I couldn't take it in for a long time."

seven

DURING the period between 1920 and 1930 what Kipling called "fate's weight cloths" proved almost too much for George Lewis. There was too much work, and too little money; too much responsibility too soon; and too much outside dissension and criticism brought into his home. He might have carried the weight and made the run without faltering had it not been for the latter factor, but these taxed a highly strung nervous system almost to the breaking point, and brought about bewilderment and rebellion in an acutely sensitive nature that, given opportunity,

warmed and developed with appreciation, shrank and became inarticulate and prickly under constant fire.

He was headstrong and mulish and had been so since childhood, firing up suddenly if crossed, yet completely reasonable when it became apparent that the course upon which he had determined spelled hurt or harm to someone else. His mother had learned, not without difficulties, that he could be led through his mind and heart but never driven. She tried to steady him as those difficult years went on, but was only partially successful. She was too fair-minded a woman not to see that there were two sides to the question of his domestic difficulties, but she had the wisdom to remain in the background, keeping her own counsel, offering her son and his wife only the love and understanding which she possessed in such abundance. He saw her daily, and this perhaps was the one thing responsible for keeping him on an even half-way even keel.

The reasons for his nervous instability lay buried in a conglomerate heap of early, unremembered pressures, fears, imagined dangers, illnesses, deprivations, and to these a body pushed to the uttermost limits of physical capacity throughout his life added its weight. There were physiological as well as psychological factors to blame for it, plus those intangibles that were within him at birth, vivid imagination, emotional intensity, the need he shared with every human for acceptance and appreciation.

The new burden of material responsibilities that he carried now was not made lighter by the need for adjustment—almost impossible for him—to the new emotional climate of censure, criticism, and rejection. He carried the burden of material responsibilities well, not always able to meet them but always willing to; the emotional adjustments he made at the cost of becoming cross and irascible, and of seeking the solution in drinking which, at least momentarily, brought relaxation and a feeling of well-being.

There had been no bridge between childhood and manhood. When he was a child he had, in many ways, perforce to live almost as an adult; when he was an adolescent, entirely as an adult.

Writers who have commented on George Lewis's playing on early records, although these records post-dated his first marriage by many years, on several occasions used the word "nervous." There is some truth in this, for despite the emotional impact, the highly imaginative, sensitive execution, and the clarity of tone,

there is discernible at times a nervous, quick, almost excited attack not wholly explainable by the strangeness and self-consciousness of first recordings. In later years that "nervousness" gave way to sureness, increased depth, with no loss of inventiveness.

If there were difficulties in his path at home there were, at least, no difficulties in his path as far as the music which he played was concerned, and this, perhaps, coupled with his mother's love and understanding, was his salvation. He could have been forgiven had he become over-confident and youthfully "cocky." Yet he never did. When he was little more than a boy he had marched beside and been accepted as an equal by such early-day masters of the music as Frankie Dusen, Willie Cornish, Henry Allen, Sr., Louis Keppard, George Bacquet, some of them men who had blown what many believe to have been the first trump of jazz with Buddy Bolden. He had never heard Buddy Bolden, and was always more than a little critical of many of those who claimed they had, for he knew the claimants must have been in diapers when Buddy was carried off to the mental institution in which he ended his days.

Such troubles as he did have with his music were economic. Pay was never high, and sometimes it was non-existent. No musician expected to be paid for "sitting in" but many times the pay for regular work was either less than promised, or the promoters of affairs would vanish before the night was over, never to be seen again. Vanish, that is to say, with the gate receipts. It would be safe to say that ninety per cent of the humbugs (New Orleans slang for an argument that just falls short of actual slugging) and violence, and that most of the near-fatal and sometimes fatal fights, had as their origin a money quarrel.

If employers of New Orleans musicians in later years, away from that city, have found them or their representatives hard and adamant in business dealings, wanting advance deposits, unwilling at any time to wait, even overnight, for a week's pay, reluctant and sometimes flatly refusing to accept cheques instead of cash, there is good reason for these attitudes. Memories of past injustices and cheatings have crystallized into a hard core of mistrust, even of those who have always treated them justly. Sidney Bechet, in his biography, admits going to his friend Milt Mezzrow and demanding money he believed he had coming to him from recordings, and of pulling a knife when he thought he

was going to be refused. The Negro had little hope of legal recourse in collecting money due him, yet money meant survival. Many persecuted minority groups have this preoccupation with money, this demand for exactitude in money dealings; money is their only bulwark against destruction.

The contrast between the two worlds of the South, the right and the left hand side of the two-lane "way of life," is shown by the fact that Kid Rena was sentenced to six months in jail when he defaulted on a contract with a utility company. The charge was "obtaining money under false pretences." There is no case on record of an employer being jailed or even fined for "obtaining music under false pretences."

The musicians had no great trust in each other, either. It was a life lived under the rule of "Root, hawg, or die." They knew the other man's children were as hungry as theirs, the other man's need as great, and the fight was a basic one—for survival.

George Lewis tells of a picnic he played in the twenties, and how, at its conclusion, the pay-off man laid the money on a table preparatory to counting it out. The musicians were to have been paid six dollars. The man started a long explanation, a drawn-out tale of woe, leading up to the announcement that instead of six dollars they could only receive two dollars and a half. When he finished he drew a gun from his pocket and laid it on the table beside the money, keeping his hand on the butt. George, before any of the others there had a chance to react to this news, reached across the table, across the man's hand where it lay on the gun butt, and picked up a five-dollar bill and a one-dollar bill. He placed the six dollars in his wallet, and then got up and walked out of the room. "That six dolla's," said George, "was *my* money." The rest of the band settled for three dollars each.

In 1922, after the birth of his first two sons, William and Joseph, born in 1921 and 1922 respectively, George joined Buddy Petit's band when Edmond Hall quit. Buddy, who had taken the name of his foster father, discarding his own name of Joseph Crawford, was one of the most sought-after and popular leaders of the era. Like most of them he drank heavily, and would die of it eventually, and George was to play his last date with him. Before Jimmy Noone left for Chicago Buddy and Jimmy had shared leadership honours in a band known as the Noone-Petit orchestra. Buddy stuttered badly, but there was no faltering or hesitation in the clear, commanding tones that made him one of

the most famous and among the greatest of New Orleans cornetists.

A leader in those days did not have exclusive rights to a sideman's talents. Whenever his regular leader did not have a gig, the musician could usually find one elsewhere, and leaders themselves would take on sideman jobs on off nights. Turnover was rapid, and there were no hard feelings when a musician left a leader for another band if he thought he could better himself, or if the new leader seemed to have more work. He was always welcome back on the stand with the old group if they needed him.

The system for booking dates in New Orleans was simplicity itself. Across from the famous bar known as Tom Anderson's was a barber shop run by a barber-cum-drummer named Red Dugas, and it was there the musicians hung out. Each musician kept a book at the shop and as the calls came in they were jotted down in the book, and each day the musicians would check. A $1.00 deposit was paid, and if the musician accepted the dollar he was considered to be under contract for the date. Bunk Johnson was in and out of New Orleans then. "He was the wanderin' kind," Lawrence Marrero, a musician who remembered him well, told me. "Most times he'd get a call for a job, take his dollar— an' wander off. Got so he didn't get too many jobs. They couldn't be worried with him. He'd just wander away with his dollar."

In 1923 George Lewis brought a group of his own together for the first time. On one date he wanted as his trumpeter a young teen-age lad named Henry Allen, Jr., son of a much beloved and admired musician who watched over his boy with the all-seeing eye of a mother cat. Henry, better known as Red, had been playing with one of the Sam Morgan groups but on the night George wanted him he was free.

Red's father would not let him come alone, and brought him to the door of George's home astride a horse, and turned him over to George with gentle, implicit instructions as to what his son was and was not to do, and what time he was to be brought home. George did his best to comply, but his best was not good enough to overcome the forces at work that night which were destined to bring poor Red what seemed to him, at that age, utter disgrace and disaster. Again it was a yard party and in the group, besides Red, were Albert Mitchell, bass fiddle, a man named Barnes on trombone, a man known as "Dad" or "Clarence" on banjo, Albert Martin on drums, and George. As the night

wore on the party followed the usual pattern of yard parties. At midnight some exuberant reveller shot out the overhead lights. A timid neighbour called the police. Before the musicians could pack and vanish, a feat they had grown adept at performing in a matter of almost seconds, the wagon arrived. The entire crowd of guests and musicians who were still on the property when the police drove up spent the remainder of the night in jail. Red, faced with the grim realities of life after dark in New Orleans, was panic-stricken. Most of the night he spent in tears, not only because of the disgrace he thought had been visited on him by being thrown in jail, but also for fear of what his father would say. George's words of comfort did little good, inasmuch as all they could possibly consist of was the none too relaxing advice that Red might as well realize that these things happened, and if he was going to keep on playing music out in the big and wicked world, he was, sure as he was born, going to see the inside of a jail now and then.

Red, who is playing in New York today, never fails to stop the proceedings at the club his horn keeps popular whenever George Lewis walks in the door.

In 1921 when George's first son was just beginning to put one fat and husky leg in front of the other and maintain a precarious upright balance, Mildred's health began to fail. The child lost weight and appetite, and each cold or illness seemed to follow the last within a few days. The doctor advised Emma that it would be best for the child to leave New Orleans for a drier, healthier climate, and he suggested the pine-woods country on the other side of Lake Pontchartrain, not far from Mandeville.

Henry Zeno sent George to apply for a caretaking job at a hunting lodge where he had himself been employed several times. It was about forty miles from Mandeville and was run on a co-operative basis by a group of wealthy Orleanians who used its facilities mainly on weekends. It had a closed membership, and members served alternately in handling the administrative details.

He found there was more than caretaking involved. He and Emma were required to do all the cleaning, cooking, and serving. During the week there might be only occasional guests, but on weekends every room and bed was taken. His father and mother had taught him to cook superbly, but only in small quantities. When he faced his first job of cooking a dinner for an unknown

number of hungry gourmands, appetites whetted by a day's hunting, he almost gave up.

"After I cooked that meal, and it came out all right, and they liked it, nothing ever seemed too much for me to do again," he said.

Mildred's health improved almost from the first day. Her appetite returned, and her eyes became clear and shining and mischievous again. They had been there only a short time when the man in charge of the lodge's affairs during that period found out that the new "boy" had applied for the job because of his little girl's poor health.

He waited until after dinner had been served before giving George his orders.

"Sorry, boy," he said, using that form of address, 'boy', so loathed by the Negro, so universally used by the white, "you'll have to send the children away. Their mother can go with them if you want, and we'll get somone else here to help you weekends. Morning will be all right."

"We'll leave tonight," said George. He was shaking with anger, his eyes suddenly flat black, without expression or lustre, all Indian.

"You don't understand," said the man. "You're not going. Just the children, and your wife if you want. We can't have sick children here. Some of our members might carry something home to their families. But you'll stay. You've done a fine job."

George was past thinking or counting the cost.

"There's nobody sends George Lewis's family away from him. They go, I go. We leaves tonight."

George said the man's eyes narrowed and his face grew red and then dead-white.

"You know what you're saying, boy? You realize what you're doing?"

George knew, and George realized. He was defying white authority. And what was worse he was showing anger, rage even, at an edict of that authority. He knew the anger within him, the bottled up resentment and rage, would eventually make him ill, as it always had since childhood. Whether he lost his temper, or managed to control it, the result was always a muscle-shaking sickness that started at the pit of his stomach and spread throughout his body.

"I know what I'm doing," he said. "I know what I'm saying.

I'm saying I'm leaving here tonight. With my family. Get yourselves another 'boy.'" Then he walked from the room, legs trembling, but not with fear.

They washed the dishes that night in silence, he and Emma. Then they bundled up William, and with Emma carrying the baby and George carrying Mildred they left in time to catch a train that would take them near Mandeville. From the station they walked to Henry's cabin, and were welcomed warmly and given a hot drink, and bedded down somehow.

Research for one of the new wonder drugs which acts as a blood-pressure depressant was carried out in a clinic in the deep South. The reason that particular clinic was selected was because doctors had found such a "surprising" number of cases of hypertension among the Negroes. With modern medicine discovering more and more of the links between the mind and emotions and the physical body, the "surprise" at finding high blood pressure prevalent among Southern Negroes is hard to understand. George Lewis himself was warned repeatedly, even in his thirties, that his blood pressure was dangerously high. Yet not one of the many physicians who cared for him in his later years outside of New Orleans was ever able to report a blood pressure reading that was not within normal limits.

The next day, at his father's suggestion, George found a small house for rent, at four dollars a month, and lined up some odd jobs. These, and resumption of regular playing, would keep them going. Henry was as happy as he had ever been. At last his son and his beloved grandchildren, whom he spoiled shamelessly, would be near him. He felt that it was recompense for the suffering he had been through since he had left Alice, although he was fair enough to admit that the suffering had come to him through his own action.

George was also happier than he had ever been. He had his own place, and he had his family to himself. There was no time to rest, but that didn't matter. They planted vegetables and berries in the back, and set out flowers and plants in the front. They kept chickens and ducks, and in spite of the all-work-no-rest régime that had become second nature to him, he felt better than at any time he could remember.

He saw his mother every time he was in New Orleans, which was usually several times a week. Ironically, things were easier for Alice now. She was working almost exclusively for the Ren-

shaw family, and a deep and lasting bond of affection and loyalty was being forged between her and the family she would stay with for the next twenty-five years. Hours were shorter, days off more frequent, and she was at last getting the opportunity for the occasional rest her sick and exhausted body had been crying out for all through the years her son had been in her care. If there was money left over at the end of the month she gladly shared it with her son and daughter-in-law if they needed it. And a little went now and then for some of the neighbourhood children.

"So many children lived near my mamma," said George. "Some of them was real poor. Even poorer than what we had been. Many's the time I've seen my mother bring home some little shoes, or maybe a toy, or something to eat for them. Nothing hurted my mother as bad as seeing a hungry child."

One morning in 1922 Henry Zeno did not feel well enough to get up. His head "worried him," he said, and there was a look in his eyes that frightened his son. The doctor who was called by his sister diagnosed his trouble as a "brain tumour." He left instructions for Henry's care, and told George and Hortense he did not believe the old man would pull through.

As he always did in grief, George became numb and quiet. He continued working, and spent all the time that he could with his father, sitting with him at night before he left to play in New Orleans, holding his hand, talking to him. Sometimes Henry recognized him, sometimes he did not.

The night that Henry died he seemed much the same as he had on previous nights since the onset of his illness. George left for a playing job in New Orleans, but immediately afterwards his father's condition became markedly worse. Hortense went to the village and telephoned the place where her nephew had said he was playing. George received the message before he had played even one set. He found a substitute and caught the first boat for Mandeville.

Henry had gone into the delirium which sometimes precedes death, and which is occasionally broken by brief spells of lucidity. Towards midnight he struggled to a sitting position. "Hortense!" he called. "Hortense!" His sister came to his side.

"George is coming," said Henry. "My boy's coming, over the lake. He's hurrying but the boat's broke down. You hear, Hortense? The boat's broke down." He fell back on the pillow,

called: "George!" and lost consciousness. He never regained it.
George arrived at the little cabin in the early hours of the morning to find his father within moments of death.

"Couldn't you have come earlier?" scolded his aunt. "I called in plenty of time. He come to himself earlier and he was a callin' for you."

"I tried," said George. "God knows I tried. I caught the first ferry I could get. I'd have been here long since if something hadn't happened to the rudder. The boat broke down."

eight

AFTER his father's death George closed and locked the little cabin Henry had built. He left Henry's tools inside, the paint brushes he cleaned so carefully the last time he used them, the carpentry tools, and the odds and ends the Henry would somehow have put to use if he had lived. His fishing equipment and gun George left there also, for he could not bear to touch them. Henry was a man whose house was always in order; his life left no debris to be cleaned up by those who were left behind. Then, numb with a grief whose memory still has the power to sting, George walked away.

The cabin remained untenanted and untouched. It was many years before George Lewis returned to it. Whenever he played in Mandeville he stayed away from its reminders. When he did return to it, thinking that at last he could face its memories, could bear now to use some of the things his father had left, he opened the door with the key he still carried on his key ring and stood on the threshold. Nothing had been changed by human hands. Only the cruel and destructive hands of time and disuse had been at work. Cobwebs wreathed the paint brushes, the fishing equipment and the gun; rats and other marauders had found their way in and shredded the pillow and mattress of the cot on which Henry had slept, and stuffing lay scattered over bed and floor.

"I just stood there," said George. "I couldn't go in any further. Everything came back to me, all the things we'd done together. My daddy loved me and I did him, maybe more than most fathers and sons. Everything came back to me at once, walking together on Sunday mornings to get our shoes shined, him teaching me how to swim and fish and hunt, and listening to me play standing there at the window half the night, and holding my babies on his lap. Everything. I just backed out of the door and locked it and went away. I never even went inside. I never went back, not to this day."

Within a few weeks after his father's death George, Emma, and the children returned to New Orleans, renting rooms in her family's home. Emma's family had been urging her to come back, and Mandeville never again meant anything to George except another place to play.

It was only natural that in a temperament like George Lewis's the inter-relationship between his mind and emotions and his body should be close. Already, even in his early twenties, his digestive system was beginning to respond with unerring—and unpleasant—accuracy to emotional pressures as a finely adjusted barometer responds to atmospheric pressures. He, of course, ignored completely all physical symptoms unless totally disabling.

"How did I feel in those days?" George tried to recall. "I don't remember too well exactly. There were lots of times I didn't feel too good, I know that for sure. Lots of times I had things wrong I didn't know what they were. But I never laid off or anything. Not unless I fell down when I got out of bed or something like that."

One of the times when "something like that" slowed him down came in the mid-twenties. A sore throat "worried" him one morning. When he looked at it he saw a small white spot on one side. Not too painful at first, gradually it became worse. When fever made him light-headed Emma insisted that he go to the hospital clinic. Fretting and protesting that it would be all right, and there was no need for such nonsense, he finally went. He waited from eight in the morning until six that night in the out-patient waiting-room before he was seen. Then a hurried doctor told him to come back the next day when, he said, he would give him a shot.

If he had ever had a hypodermic injection before it was when he was a child and too sick to know or realize. Like many others,

he was terrified of needles. Nor was he exactly happy about the long, sick, feverish ten hour wait in the crowded, odorous clinic waiting room, and he shared the feeling of most of his people that it made little difference to the powers that were whether he got well or not. He did not return and each day the pain grew worse.

"I never suffered such pain in all my life," he said. "Not even when I broke my leg and walked on it and they had to pull the bones back in place and put weights on me. Never."

A few days later a call came to play a club dance. Even George realized he could not play as long as he was in that much pain, but he accepted the job. *En route* he stopped at a druggists and asked for something to relieve him, even if it was only for a few hours. The druggist swabbed the throat and for three and a half hours he was completely free of pain. Then it returned, doubled and redoubled. Now one entire side of his face and neck was involved, and his jaws had begun to lock.

For days he lay in bed, getting up only when the heat drove him outside. sitting under a tree in the yard, whittling aimlessly to distract his mind from the pain. Now his jaws had locked so that he could not even drink water, and he had become stone deaf.

At last he was no longer able to sit beneath the tree, and early one morning Emma called the parish priest to give him the last rites of the Catholic Church. The priest, used to death and recognizing its face, gave little encouragement, but he suggested that as a last resort Emma call the hospital and ask that a doctor be sent. He administered the last rites to a young man who accepted their need, and after he had left Emma called the hospital to ask that a doctor be sent. The doctor to whom she spoke refused to come, and refused to send another. He looked up the record of George's previous visit and noted that the patient had been told to return. "This man had an appointment to come back and he didn't come. Tell him to come in now."

Sobbing, Emma repeated what she had already told him.

"He's dying," she told the doctor. "He can't come."

Still the doctor at the hospital refused to send anyone, nor would they send an ambulance to bring George in. His family, said the doctor, would have to get him there if he was unable to come himself. One cannot help wondering what his remarks were to his colleagues after he hung up the telephone; if, perhaps, they

resembled those of Alice's employers many years before who had warned their daughter against too much sympathy for the "darkies" who really enjoyed their ailments.

Alice, who had not left her son's side all night, was stunned. She had not dreamed a call for aid in so serious a case would be refused. Had not her mother and her grandmother, voluntarily and without thought for the possible results, gone into the streets and the homes of the people, white and black alike, to do what they could for the plague-stricken dying? They had been bound by no oath of service, but had gone because they believed that if it lay within their power to help, it was their duty—and God's will—that they do so.

Somehow Alice and Emma scraped together enough money to hire an ambulance from a funeral home, actually the conveyance used to transport corpses from house to mortuary. They carried George from the ambulance to the emergency room at the clinic. Apparently the attendants on duty at the hospital believed him already dead, or at least moribund.

"When they threw me on that hard table," George relates. "I swear to God I bounced, they threw me that hard. I wasn't unconscious, but I was dead weak and I couldn't see, and I couldn't speak. I was just one big pain."

They prised his mouth open, for his jaws were now fimly locked, and treated his throat. Then one of the doctors gave him an injection. "I don't know whether he can take this injection or not," the doctor told Alice. "It's a powerful one, but it's the only chance he has. If he can take it, it will probably fix him up. If he can't, he'll be gone in 24 hours." And they sent him home to die or get better.

Twelve hours later the throat started to drain, and the relief and improvement were almost instantaneous. He was almost completely dehydrated, for he had taken no fluids in days. He drank water greedily, began to eat soft foods in another day, but recovery was a lengthy process.

It was not the first time he had felt the brush of black wings, nor would it be the last.

When he was scarcely into his twenties he was already treading the vicious circle of frayed nerves and exhausted body seeking relaxation and stimulus in alcohol—which in turn created the very conditions it was consumed to allay.

He never lost sight of his faith, but that faith did not always

bring him the surcease from strain, the inner peace that it brought to Alice, who had been granted more time in her youth to secure her faith firmly. Life had presented monumental obstacles to George's faith before he was even out of adolescence. That it lived with him throughout his life, as it did with most of his people, is one of the authentic miracles.

George left Buddy Petit's band to join Chris Kelly's group, though he and Buddy remained good friends and he gigged often with him through the years. He also played frequently in those days with Lee Collins. It is almost cruel to those readers who are avid record-collectors to mention here that in 1926 he recorded with Lee in the back room of a music store. It was the first time he had ever recorded and he recalls taking two days off from his regular job to make the records. The only other members of that group whom he recalls were a piano player known as "Tink" and the drummer, Irving Joseph. The discs were never issued and the most diligent searching (and there is no more diligent searcher than a record-collector) has failed to unearth the masters. George states that he was told a few years later that they had either been destroyed or "thrown away." There will be sarabands danced in the streets if they are ever discovered.

Old timers say that the Chris Kelly Band in which George played was probably the best all-round group Chris ever brought together. It comprised Roy Evans, drums; Arthur "Yank" Johnson, trombone; Manuel Manetta, alto horn; George Lewis, clarinet; and Ricard Alexis, second trumpet.

The trumpet of Ricard Alexis was already bringing him considerable renown in the city, but his career on that instrument was short-lived. A few moments after he left his house one night, *en route* to a playing job with Kelly, while he was standing on a corner waiting for a streetcar, an auto, top down, containing two roistering white youths, careered around the corner on three wheels. According to eye-witnesses who described it later to the men in the band, one of the youths, laughing uproariously at Ricard's fear and involuntary jump to avoid the car, swung at him with a tyre iron, striking him on the side of the face, shattering his jaw. Ricard spent weeks in hospital while the wired-together fragments of the jaw knit. After he was released he never regained proper control of lip and cheek muscles, and laid down his trumpet, changing then to bass fiddle.

"After that Ricard drank real heavy," says George.

George played on Ricard's last date in 1960, at a wedding reception in New Orleans. For years Ricard had suffered with high blood pressure, and a form of heart failure that caused his legs and ankles to swell to such an extent that walking was difficult, and he could not walk half a block without becoming short-winded. Yet he continued to play. George saw him, on this last date, struggling vainly to carry his bass to the back entrance of the hotel. The others had gone in. George picked up the bass, which was twice as big as he was, and carried it in.

"God knows how he got through the night," says George. "All the time I could hear him puffing and gasping back there. He was dead in just a few weeks."

George Lewis was by no means the only New Orleans musician who played compulsively, literally wedded to his music "for richer for poorer . . . till death do them part."

George quit Chris Kelly's band the first time after an argument over non-payment for a job. The next night when he did not report for work Chris sent a friend for him. George told the messenger that he was not working for Chris any more, but the messenger told him Chris had said: "Don't come back without him." To ease the mind of the man who had come for him, George went to talk with Chris.

"Shucks, George," said that man of great good nature. "You was kiddin' wasn't you?"

Never a man to keep an argument alive, and a complete stranger to malice, George said he had definitely not been kidding, but that he'd be happy to forget about it.

Many dates were played in the rural back country of Louisiana and Mississippi. These were approached warily, for it was on these the bands were most often cheated of their money, the promoters of dances and parties frequently disappearing just before the end of the affair, taking the gate receipts with them. Dates in the Cajun country were dreaded more than any others, for they could—and often did— wind up in nightmare. The Cajuns were intolerably insulting to Negro musicians, and often physically abusive. The trips were made in rattle-trap, make-shift conveyances, ranging from open trucks with canvas stowed aboard in case of rain, to broken down Model T's, and occasionally slow, filthy, unheated trains.

On one trip to Jackson, Mississippi, the car they were riding in was hit head-on by a truck, and George was thrown to the

ground and knocked unconscious. When he recovered consciousness, with pounding head and badly sprained neck, the driver of their car had patched it up somehow, and they continued to the date, George more than half-sick from shock and pain.

Not only did the promoter, avowedly in search of a "jug" for the musicians, disappear that night with the gate receipts, but their plans to play on the streets for eating and rent money the next day were washed away by a torrential rain that drove every living creature in the town to cover.

Although most of the band members protested that it would do no good to seek redress for their wrongs from the law— "Hell, George, you know no one ain't going to do nothin' for us"—George insisted on trying. When they approached the local law enforcement officer and stated their case they were met with profane abuse as "out of town niggers" and ordered to be on their way within an hour. If they were not, this guardian of law and order told them, hand on gun, they would spend the next six months in the town's jail.

They were on their way in half an hour. They had not eaten since they left New Orleans the morning before.

"I was so hungry," said George, "I remember I picked up half an apple lying on the ground under a tree and I ate it. That and some pecans I got off the ground was all I had for two days."

A few miles from town a tyre blew out on their car, and they had no spare. There was nothing to do but abandon it, and walk and hitch-hike the remainder of the way. When they finally arrived in Lafayette, Louisiana, where a number of them had friends and relatives, they separated, and George went to the home of his godmother.

She gave him one look and started plying him with coffee and food. After she had fed him she told him the bad news. His mother, knowing that Lafayette was on the route they would take going home and thinking he might stop at his godmother's, had sent a message for him. He was to hurry home at once. His son Joseph was very ill and they were taking him to hospital. His godmother gave George carfare to use when he reached New Orleans and he continued the trip without rest.

In New Orleans he proffered his nickel, the only money he had, to the streetcar conductor, who refused it.

"Seven cents," said the conductor.

"*Seven cents*?" said George. "Since when?"

"Since this morning," said the conductor. "Fares went up."

Although he pleaded the urgency of his case with considerable feeling, the conductor was adamant. No seven cents, no ride. George walked the more than thirty blocks home.

His son Joseph recovered. So did George, in time.

At home domestic crises were becoming more frequent. During that decade he and Emma separated several times, he seeking self-respect and independence in temporary bachelorhood, she remaining with her family. But after each reunion, brought about by genuine affection, and his emotional ties to his children, the rift between them was wider, the gulf harder to bridge.

Shortly after the disastrous trip to the country which was climaxed by a thirty-block walk to reach a sick baby, George joined Kid Rena's band. Kid had signalled to George when the Rena and Kelly bands were slashing each other to musical ribbons from the backs of two trucks, wheels locked, at a New Orleans intersection. The information that Rena had taken George from the Kelly band in this fashion was hard to come by, as it had been hard to extract the information about Lorenzo Tio, Jr.'s interest in him. To volunteer information when this could possibly be constructed as bragging or a show of self-pride is almost impossible for George. Such information must be caught on the fly, as it accidentally emerges in conversation, or is overheard in a talk between George and someone already familiar with the facts. Then detailed amplification must be obtained by means not always fair. How many incidents like these lie buried in the memory of this frustratingly modest man the writer knoweth not.

Chris did not object strenuously to George's leaving, because he was, as they all were, a realist and he knew that at that time Rena's band had more work than his, and George was bettering himself.

"Just so long as you don't leave mad, George," said Chris. George himself sought and engaged his successor for Chris.

George had great respect and affection for Kid Rena, perhaps more than he had for any leader for whom he played during that period. The reason for it was typical of George Lewis.

"Kid was mighty kind to young musicians," said George. "You didn't find many like that in those days." And he said something then he was to say again, when he was approaching sixty

years of age and a brash and untalented young clarinettist had bothered him throughout an evening by sitting in. "Me, I hates to hurt a young 'un." Then he went on. "Rena always used to let the young 'uns sit in when he was playing anywhere, except a parade. He never used to give them a bad time, or try to 'cut' them, or louse up their playing just for fun, or show off how good he was. I felt real bad when he had a breakdown. He got over it but he never played as good again. He was a terrible drinker, too. It killed him, like it did Buddy and Chris. Like it did a lot of them."

George frequently points out a fact about the musicians of those days, and going back beyond those days for many years, that does not seem to be generally known: that a great many of them came to New Orleans from the back country. As young men have, since cities began, they came in an effort to better themselves, seeking fortune and excitement, finding the latter but not the former. Chris Kelly, Jim Robinson, Edward "Kid" Ory, Evan Thomas, Joe Darensbourg, Bunk Johnson, Papa Celestin, Guy Kelly, were but a few. Guy Kelly, said George, "gave 'em all fits, even Evan, when he blew."

These country boys brought to the music of the New Orleans bands the plaintive, poignant expressiveness of the rural Negro, and this expressiveness wove itself into, and became a part of, the more intricate, sophisticated musical patterns the native Orleanians were playing. No finer example of this can be heard than the haunting sadness of the Guy Kelly recording of "The Blues Jumped the Rabbit" in which trumpet and voice combine in starkly simple phrasing to tell the story of how, when the blues jumped the rabbit, he "cried like a natural chile."

As the roaring twenties were approaching the wailing thirties George Lewis was advancing to the point he had been striving for when, often sore-lipped and sometimes tearful, he had practised, day after day and night after night, in the tiny French Quarter rooms he and his mother lived in. His horn was speaking for him now, speaking truth. The words he had never been able to find when he tried to express himself in speech were there, in the clarinet, and so were the laughter and the tears. But he was no more content then with his musical achievements than he was as a child or is today, and his practising was as faithful, his judgment of himself as unrelenting. There has been no time in his life when he could not have said to his father in all sincerity,

as he used to when he was a boy: "You aren't just sayin' it? You think it really sounded good?"

George became well acquainted during and following his period in Chris Kelly's band with a young bass drummer, powerful and skilled. He was a quiet young man, short, heavy, dark-skinned, and placid-appearing. His name was Lawrence Marrero, and his father, uncle, and brother were also musicians. Eventually their acquaintance was to develop into a friendship so close that both men seemed to forget they did not belong to the same family. There was no basis in fact for the nickname each used for the other: "Brudder-in-law," pronounced as it is spelled here. They were "Lawrence" and "George" before the public, but in private I seldom heard them use any other name than "Brudder-in-law."

Lawrence's appearance was deceiving. The band uniform he wore concealed a frame of tremendous power and muscularity, and in his early youth he had been a prize-fighter. The uniform also concealed an ugly scar on his chest under which a bullet still lodged, result of a gun fight in his youth. But there was a calm and peaceful benignity about Lawrence's manner and bearing that was bound to appeal to the quiet and basically gentle George Lewis.

Lawrence had been a member of Chris Kelly's band before George joined it, and the two men played many gigs together throughout the twenties.

Another man whom George saw frequently in those days, but did not play with until much later, was a dashing French-quarter Creole who had been a neighbour of the Zenos on St Phillip Street. When there were no wagons or parades to follow, or bands playing at Hopes Hall to listen to, the young George Lewis could frequently be seen listening, entranced, to the street-corner playing and singing of this young guitarist and his wife. The guitarist embodied to the child the essence of dash, gallantry, romance, and glamour. His name was Alcide Pavageau, and his Creole accent was so involved that not even the Creoles could always understand him. As the years went on he earned the nickname of "Slow Drag" because at every ball he attended he won the contest as the best performer of the dance by that name, one of slow, rhythmic, measured grace. His black moustache, jauntily held cigar, courtly manners, all added up to near-perfection as far as George Lewis was concerned. His acceptance of the nickels

and dimes tossed his way for his street playing was as gracious as might be the acceptance of tribute by a reigning monarch.

George also heard frequently in the twenties the rousing trombone of a tall, gangling, big-framed country boy from Rayne, Louisiana, named Jim Robinson. His round, brown face had the high cheek-bones of the Indian. He was like a huge St Bernard puppy and was unlettered and unschooled. His big, long-fingered, expressive hands were used constantly to make his points when talking. He stuttered slightly, especially when excited. He had learned to play the trombone in the United States Army during World War I, serving both at home and overseas, and the effects that he achieved with his horn must at times have rocked his instructors back on their heels. He always retained a certain amount of staccato, parade-ground style, but once out of the army and on his own musically he joyously tore into the music his people were playing with an ebullient, shouting, "tailgate" style that—in those days—knew no rival for inventiveness and force.

In a few years George was to play with trumpeter Avery "Kid" Howard, and these four—Howard, Marrero, Pavageau, and Robinson—formed the nucleus of the George Lewis Band which rode the crest of the wave of popularity of traditional jazz in the late forties and early fifties. It would become the most widely imitated and copied of any American jazz group in the countries of Scandinavia, Germany and Great Britain, and its leader a living legend.

In Denmark they tell of a group of young musicians in Odense, known as the "Cardinal Blusicians" who, in 1951, literally wore out the grooves on both sides of a George Lewis record in their efforts to emulate its driving rhythm and distinctive sound. The record, an early American Music Company release, featured George Lewis with Kid Shots Madison. It was a special import, and expensive. They wore it out in six months time.

"Iss a funny thing in Scandinavia," said a young Dane I met a few months before going to his country with the Lewis band. "Wherever you go you see little groups of blonde Norvegians and Svedes and Danes with their cheeks bulging—so-o-o-ooo, and their eyes popping—so-o-o-o-o, all trying so werry hard to sound like the George Lewis Band. Iss werry strange to see. Iss good, too."

But thirty years ago George Lewis could not know, nor would

he have believed it if anyone had told him, that the time would come when he would consider Denmark his "second home" or that the people throughout that tiny, lovely country would ever proudly and with love refer to him as "our sunburned Dane."

nine

BY the end of the twenties George Lewis had realized many times over the consuming ambition of the small, estatic child who had stood beneath the balcony of Hopes Hall and listened to the musicians "calling the chil'ren in" with their horns. His childhood always remained close and vivid, and when he played there now and watched the boys and girls of a younger generation dance and tap and clap their hands he blew a little harder, and smiled a bit more broadly, for he knew what they were feeling.

He was learning the art of leadership in these days, and learning it as much by adverse as by good example. From his start as a leader in 1923 with the group that accompanied young Red Allen on his first trip to jail, down through the years, the men he led found that while he had every phase of their playing under quiet control, no one but the bandsmen seemed to know it. There was none of what he calls "brutalizing" of the men, a thing he had seen far too often; no hogging of the limelight, no reluctance to share with his men all honours due. Yet the men who played for him are unanimous in saying that he was the hardest-driving leader, in a musical sense, for whom they had ever worked.

I sat at a table in a Chicago night club with Baby Dodds, two years before his death, and listened to him for more than an hour as he talked about George and the times he had played with him as a sideman, and under him as a leader, and of their

days together in New York in the forties. There was no player out of New Orleans better qualified to discuss drive and rhythm than Baby, long acknowledged the greatest drummer that city of rhythm has ever produced.

"I'd rather play for George than anyone I ever knew," said Baby. He knew I would not doubt the sincerity of his statement, for he had proved his words many times. "But man, does he drive! He never lets up. And yet you know—" and he pointed to a man sitting at a table across the room— "that man over there, he asked me which one was George Lewis. His eyes bugged out when I told him. It's not always the leader that shouts the most and makes the most show that drives the hardest. It's something you feel inside you, when a leader's got that kind of drive."

George's eyes glowed when I told him what Baby had said. Ever since the day in 1910 when he counted out his hoard of nickels and dimes in Uncle Dave's pawnshop, the opinions and judgments of other musicians have always mattered far more to him than those of any layman, however exalted. And from fellow musicians and artists these judgments have been unstinting in praise and appreciation. The warm spontaneity of tributes from such widely divergent personalities as Louis Armstrong, Benny Goodman, Omer Simeon, Burl Ives, Odetta, Leadbelly, Ornette Coleman—to name but a few—have brought him his greatest satisfactions.

It is sometimes difficult to reconcile these tributes and the aloof disparagements of a small coteries of *avant garde* writers who have seemed bent upon making George Lewis the symbol of an art form they apparently dare not stoop to praise for fear of betraying some semblance of emotional response; or, possibly, admitting to a common humanity with the vast public which has shown how little it cares for their opinions by turning out to hear him by the thousands.

George Lewis calls this avant garde coterie, with a grin, "the belittlers," and pleads their case with deadly effect.

"They just don't know," he says gently. "And what a man don't know he can't write about, really. Not and make sense."

One of these writers has referred to the hand-clapping of the members of a New Orleans band, (and these musicians have been doing this since childhood's muscles began to coordinate) as "hokum," and a bop dance step on stage by Dizzy Gillespie as a

"delightful caper." Which is not to say that Dizzy is not a delightful gentleman, because he is indeed.

Another will display a breath taking ability to perform mental gymnastics by referring to the Lewis clarinet as "certainly the most lyrical clarinet ever heard," and in the same article describe it as "primitive." One has a mental picture of the writer finishing the article without using the word "primitive" then, perhaps on his way out to lunch, clapping a hand to his forehead as the thought flashes into his mind: "My God, what will the public think. I must tell them or they will not realize how truly learned I am, that this man, being without academic training, is a primitive. Heavens!" One then sees him rushing back to the copy desk, snatching his article from the man in the slot, and revising it. A "lyrical primitive" calls to mind a chuckle-provoking picture of a musically gifted caveman sitting before his fire, mate and children (clad in the skins of wild beasts) gathered round him, bringing forth from a hollow reed the poignant, precise, and deceptively simple beauty of Lewis's "Burgundy Street Blues."

On the continent of Europe this attitude was seldom—if ever—encountered. It was occasionally found in England, although almost entirely confined to London. In Germany, critics whose attention previously had been devoted to classical music but who came to hear Lewis because of his historicity—and their own curiosity—found themselves using words and phrases like "miracle clarinet" and "genius" in their reviews. Quite probably to their own astonishment.

It was not in the cards for George Lewis, either in his youth or later, to become the type of leader whose name would resound as loudly as did some of the others. There are a number of reasons for this, not the least of them his total lack of aggressiveness, and his lack of any desire for power. Also, he was never able to attain any eminence, however slight, by using the bodies of others as stepping-stones. Nor did he ever have any over-weaning ambition to become a leader.

When he was fifty-six years old he called his good friend, trumpeter John Lucas, in Los Angeles, and said he was anxious to return to the West Coast. He asked John if he could help him line up a job as sideman. Lucas was so astounded he called me long distance to inquire if, by any chance, George Lewis had lost his mind. I assured him he had not, and that the request was

definitely in character. After 1957, during the brief periods he played in New Orleans with his own band, his drummer, Joseph Watkins—who was also his strong right arm through many years—assumed leadership responsibilities and prerogatives, including the additional pay. Physically exhausted nine-tenths of the time, even in youth, shoulders weary from the burden of cares and responsibilities, nerves racked with worry, Lewis was quite content to play his music with kindred souls and let the glory go.

The road of the future had been just ahead when he was a boy of fourteen, quivering with nerves on his first job as a full-fledged musician. He saw with youthful eyes only the enticing promises of what might lie along its route. But as his eyes grew older and he travelled farther he found, as his people had been finding for centuries, that he travelled not a road but a dark labyrinth, without destination. Beyond each curve there lay in wait the Furies and the Harpies. Their names were many: rejection, sorrow, illness, humiliation, man-caused grief, wantonness, hatred, bigotry, and—most formidable of them all—the smiling Harpy of the closed heart, with the dread name of Objective Compassion.

Each man holds at bay with his own weapons the Furies and the Harpies that lie in wait along his road. The cave-dweller built a fire, and its crackling flames held them back; modern man uses wealth, or power, or the skill of his hands, or the strength of his intellect, or his pen, or the love of his fellow man, or offers the beauty that lies within him as a sacrifice of appeasement.

George Lewis and his people held the Harpies and the Furies at bay with their music. It was their nepenthe; it was light and warmth; it was the hand that led them through the darkness of the labyrinth, the link that held them together in their common journey, the channel to the source of the deep strength that lay within them. It was in its own way power, and it was their faith made manifest.

It has been called, in some of its expressions, a "happy music," and this is so, for they had the gift of great laughter, and the sight of a Fury at bay is a joy to behold. It is perhaps the only music in which there is true humour, the slyness of barbed wit—and the barbs are stiletto-sharp. But in all the world there is no sadder music than the bitter beauty of a blues played by a man when a Harpy has its talons in his soul.

It would be logical to expect that in such music there would be

a lack of discipline, a frenetic display of pure emotion. Yet in no other music, except the classical forms, is there more rigid discipline than in classic jazz. It is a discipline seldom found—and herein lies the difference—in the so-called "Dixieland" of the white groups, excellent though many of them are.

The most notable exceptions to this were the fine groups that sprang up in Chicago and San Francisco, the "Austin High" group in Chicago, and the Lu Watters group in San Francisco. Realizing their limitations, they imposed upon themselves the needed musical checks and balances.

The Negro of the South did not have to learn this discipline. It was inherent and it gave to his music the added beauty of cohesiveness. It is a discipline that seemed for many years to be in the process of complete destruction by later schools of "jazz." The swing of the pendulum of experimentation has brought it back now to the opposite pole, until at times this newer form seems more a mathematical formula than it does the music whose name it claims, and which originated many years ago in the heart of a people. There is an almost Euclidean beauty in the efforts of today's groups far removed from such unscientific motivations as emotion.

In the classic jazz of the early New Orleans groups one listens in vain for a squealing clarinet; a trumpeter searching for a high note, not because it belongs to the music he is playing, but because of the personal satisfaction it will give him to blow it. The tuba player does not become automatically a musical clown, but a man with a rhythmic job to do. In this music there is no "going to hell in a hand basket" frenzy. However strong the drive, however intricate and subtle the counterpoint and polyphony, it remains completely under the control of the musicians. Nor is the individual musician ever the captive of his instrument, hypnotized by its possibilities. And always there is something withheld, something promised, as there is in the narration of a story by a master story-teller who knows just when to bring in his climax with the most stunning impact.

The patronizing comments by a certain type of critic on the much-belaboured subject of technique are in themselves revealing. It is usually granted to any artist that he be permitted to perfect a technique which will give him results satisfying to his own inner compulsions for expression. And in any art, whether

it is music, painting, writing, or sculpture, one man's technique is all too frequently another man's downfall.

In this music there are the necessary, physical techniques which must be practised by each individual; breathing, fingering, drum-tuning, and handling of drum-sticks. Few good musicians are identical in their techniques.

But besides the practice of the physical techniques, there is in this music things that are not learned, but known; the rules of an untaught grammar instinctively spoken correctly; the niceties of a deliberate and ordered beauty of musical diction that have never found their way into the musical speech of others.

Small wonder those who bring to bear upon it the utterly inadequate light of their own erudition find themselves baffled, and turn from it to forms more readily understood, and which they can discuss more facilely.

"Listen to my story!" sings the traditional Negro musician. "Understand my song!"

"Clap hands, here comes Charlie!" shouts the Dixielander.

"Look how far I've come!" cries the modern.

For many years the younger generation of Negro musicians turned their backs and stopped their ears to the music of their forefathers. They had new weapons with which to keep the Furies and the Harpies at bay, the weapons of education and solidarity, and a weapon put into their hands by others: world opinion. They did not want to think upon or listen to reminders of the shameful state of servitude in which their ancestors had been forced to live, and they overlooked completely the magnificence of the spirit of these ancestors. The lack of logic in this attitude is evident, yet it is comprehensible to an understanding mind and heart.

Today there is clear evidence that these young musicians are outgrowing that adolescent phase of their musical development, the feeling of contept for a music born in the darkness in which their forefathers lived. The Negro has too keen an appreciation of beauty to close his ears forever to the poignant loveliness of the only true folk art our country has given to the world: the music of his ancestors before they began their slow journey into the light.

These younger men, whose wounds are slighter, no longer laugh quite so rudely at the scars of deeper wounds.

When the few who are playing today, whose music still has its

roots in the soil of a great heritage, lay down their instruments, this music will not be heard again. It will be imitated down through the years, but its imitators will never be able to bring to life its emotional and technical complexities, for theirs will be a different message.

To regret that this is so is to regret that there have been different and stronger weapons forged to subdue the Furies and the Harpies, that there is a lessening of the need to hold them at bay.

To mourn its loss is to mourn that no longer is it true that there are "no footsteps backward" from the cave where the lion dwells.

ten

In 1929 George Lewis walked for the last time out of the house that he and his wife shared with her family. He never looked back, nor returned, and no quarrel preceded his action.

Today he and Emma are friends, but there was never a reconciliation as there had been following previous separations. He remained in touch with his children and helped them when he could. It was simply that he had, in today's slang, "had it."

But before the final break-up, grief and tragedy were to remind him that they had not yet finished with him. The last child born to him and Emma had been a girl, and they had named her Hilda. It was good to have a little girl again, after a succession of boys. She was the first girl to be born since the death of their second child, Mary.

When the baby was a little more than two weeks old the midwife, who was still checking routinely on her patient, was taken ill and sent her niece, a young girl, to inquire if Emma was well, and to help her with the baby. The girl placed a belly-band, still damp from washing, around the baby's abdomen. The baby developed a cold but did not seem to be acutely ill.

On the nineteenth day after her birth, George, home from work in the late afternoon, went in to see her.

"The baby was lying on the bed," he said. "We was watching her mighty close. We couldn't afford cribs and baby beds and all like that. The youngest always slept on the bed with us. I went in and laid across the bed and took hold of her hand. She had real strong little hands and used to grab hold of my fingers real tight. This day she didn't. She didn't grab at all. When I looked closer I saw she was dead."

It was a long time before George recovered from the shock of the baby's death, and Emma came close to a complete breakdown. He has never forgotten this child, with them so short a time, and throughout his life his memory of her has been clear and vivid.

Many years later, when life was more difficult and hopeless for him than it had ever been, he dreamed of her. George Lewis has always dreamed in technicolour and full stereophonic sound. He has kept his entire band enthralled through many breakfasts on the road with a recountal of the plot-filled, complicated adventures of his subconscious mind during the night. Although other people's dreams are usually boring, George's have always been the kind one listens to with a certain awe that so much can happen to anyone while he is asleep.

The dream of Hilda was different. It was a simple one, and its very simplicity made its uncanny element of prophecy all the more startling.

"She had grown up, in this dream," George told me. "She was maybe fo' or five years old. But I knew it was Hilda. We were walking together and she was holding my hand. What we were walking in was nasty, thick mud, up to our ankles. It was a long, long walk, seemed like, and I was carrying a bucket, a real heavy one, full of some kind of stuff, I don't know what. I know it was mighty heavy and I was real tired. After a long time we come to a pretty little house, with a fence around it, and there was a man sitting out in front, and Hilda, she led me over there. The man had a kind look about him, and Hilda was talking to him. I don't know what she said but he came to the gate and he said to me: "Keep on going, son. Straight ahead. When you get a little bit farther you'll see a fork in the road, and there'll be a big dog there. But don't pay him any mind. He won't hurt you. Just keep on going."

George stopped there in his story of the dream and said, as if convincing himself: "Shucks, it wasn't anything but a dream." Urged to continue he went on.

"Me and Hilda did like he told us. We walked on, and I still had the heavy bucket and the mud was still bad, and I could hardly get my feet out of it to walk. I was so tired I wanted to quit but seems like I couldn't because Hilda was still holding my hand. Then I saw the fork the man had told us about. We kept going, and sure enough, there was the dog. He was a mean-looking one. I mean, he looked fierce. When we came along he stood up and growled, with his fur up straight on his back, and then he stopped, and he laid down, and I knew he wasn't going to hurt us none. Then, all of a sudden, Hilda was gone. And there wasn't any mud any more and I put down the heavy bucket. I walked past the dog and ahead of me there was this long road, and it was as smooth and nice and pretty as anything you'd want to see. And I started walking towards it and I got to it and then I woke up. I used to tell myself it wasn't anything but a dream, but still sometimes I used to wonder what it meant."

Book Three

There be many shapes of mystery
And many things God makes to be
Past hope or fear.
And the end men looked for cometh not,
And a path is there where no man sought.
So hath it happened here.

Euripides

one

THE music to which George Lewis had devoted his life, that had sung in his heart long before young fingers could bring it to life on his horn, was not greeted with unanimous enthusiasm in the rest of the United States. Some of the outrage and some of the amazement is shown in the following comments: *

"Unspeakable Jazz Must Go!"

Title of an article in the Ladies Home Journal, 1921.

"What's the Matter with Jazz?"

Title of an article in "Etude" in March, 1924.

"Jazz Has Come to Stay." *Leopold Stokowski.*

"When America regains its soul, jazz will go."

Dr Stephen Wise.

". . . . . . mongrel music . . . . malarious . . ."

Robert M. Stults.

"Vulgar . . . . debasing." *Mrs H. A. Beach.*

"Jazz is not spiritual." *Charles Wakefield Cadman.*

"This music will point the way for tomorrow."

Edwin Ansermet.

"Jazz . . . . . is caricature." *Dr Frank Damrosch.*

"His (Louis Armstrong) style of music would seem to have combined the highest reaches of instrumental virtuosity with the most intensely disciplined melodic structure, and the most spontaneous emotional expression." Virgil Thompson, writing of

---

* Taken from "Shining Trumpets" by Rudi Blesh, published 1949 by Cassell. London

Armstrong in 1936. Of the music itself Thompson wrote: "It stills . . . . the nerves and allows the mind free play in that purely auditory perception of feeling that is the alpha and omega of music."

In an interview with Frederic Ramsey, Jr., the Brazilian composer, Hector Villa-Lobos, said: "You see, when the jazz musicians play it is an expression of themselves as musicians. It takes great originality and spirit to improvise. When a composer writes down he is working with the intellect consciously . . . the composer is the individual in the romantic tradition of European concert music. That is why, also, the classical musician cannot approach the jazz musician—he simply cannot do the things a jazz musician can do with his instrument . . . But as for transposing the great jazz improvisations into concert music . . . that is ridiculous, it is silly. But you know the business of writing down jazz and using it in composed music . . . *c'est du pur chichi, du chichi du musiciens*!"

And so the battle ranged across the country. From malarious to magnificent, the adjectives were used as cudgels with which the critics beat each over the head, and the long, involved, and tortuous analyses of the music that appeared in those days were the forerunners of today's intellectual donnybrooks. Today's battlefield is wider, its front more extended, for in the comparative simplicity of the early days only traditional jazz was at issue.

Now the self-righteousness of yesterday has become the intellectual snobbery of today.

And after the battle of the critics came the battle of the writers, extending over three decades, still being waged. One writer would say of George Lewis's playing: "primitive . . . of limited technique." Others were to share with Rudi Blesh the opinion implicit in his citation of the Original Zenith Brass Band record "If I Ever Cease to Love." Earlier he had referred to George as the "finest living exponent of the New Orleans clarinet solo." In his citation of the record Blesh says: "The whole creative spirit of Negro jazz seems revealed the moment when Lewis's masterful clarinet leaps out in solo stop-time. Stop-timing consists in a series of breaks, like improvised cadenzas, invented at the moment, over a broken, pulsating rhythmic figure supplied by the band. Lewis's electrifying breaks run like chain lightning over the basic rhythm barriers."

Blesh received for his pains, for his years of research and

study, some of the most unnecessarily cruel blasts levelled at any of the upholders of traditional jazz. This writer disagrees on many points with Blesh, feels that he was frequently enticed into mistaking myth for reality by some of the musicians who "told the man what he wanted to hear." Yet this in no way lessens the importance of his findings, and of his meticulous searching into the past for the roots of the music. It is significant that almost every book on jazz, which deals even remotely with its origins, shows evidences of the author's "brain-picking" with Blesh's brain as the picked.

One of the loudest cries, from those who would carry the myth of white supremacy to its ultimate in ridiculousness, was that he was a "racist." Yet those who accused him of this would not have raised an eyebrow at the statement that the difference between the operas of Guiseppe Verdi and of Richard Wagner could be traced to their widely differing Latin and Teutonic temperaments.

In England I was amused to hear a critic speak slightingly of Blesh because, he told us, he and a group of others had played back a Bunk Johnson record and found that a note stated by Blesh to be B-flat (I believe this was the note) was in actuality one either half a tone higher or half a tone lower. That the early Johnson records were made under appallingly difficult engineering conditions; that even a split second's difference in playback speed in any part of a tape or from a disc can alter the tone of a note considerably (as witness the distortion of the human voice as a recording tape is varied in its speed) had not apparently occurred to these experts. For a half-tone—or even a whole tone—the years of research and work, the months and years spent in the South and in New Orleans, were to be sold down the critical river.

Yet—"They all loved Art with a capital A."

Writers from the North thronged into the South and in particular into New Orleans. Then the writers of the South awakened to what was going on in their midst, and joined the not-always-merry throng. And in the midst of the feuding and the fussing, the praising and the damning, the musicians themselves were completely forgotten. They had no more status as individual artists than an innocent bystander at a streetcorner brawl.

To many of the Southern writers the musicians were principally the descendants of the "dear old darkies" the authors'

ancestors had kept as slaves on their plantations, this latter circumstance apparently constituting a form of status symbol and guarantee of understanding and expertness on the part of the writer. They were "our people," and it is fortunate few Negroes bothered to read these, for this is a phrase calculated to bring their blood to a rapid, though smilingly concealed and invisible, boil. From this extreme these writers went to some of the less fortunate descendants of the plantation slaves, and the "snores in the barrel house," the drunken brawls, the knife fights, the whorehouses of Storyville, and the songs of the prison chain gangs, took centre stage.

The Northern writers were little better. To them the Negroes of the South, whose music either entranced or infuriated them, were Symbols; they were a Race; they were Characters, and they were always set apart by invisible quotation marks. They were never, to either the writers of the North or the South, just plain people. A Henry Zeno, an Alice Zeno, would have baffled these scribes completely. There were no individuals, men with wives and children, mothers and fathers, family pride and family traditions; heartaches and sorrows and ambitions. One looks vainly through American non-fiction writings on jazz for something identifying the subjects of these writings with the rest of humanity; for the common touch, for any sense of kinship.

Nor did the artists offer many worth-while contributions to the cause of truth. For every understanding drawing or painting of the Negro, there are hundreds of semi-caricatures, dragged out at the slightest excuse with great pride, labelled as art, and showing all too clearly the astigmatic artistic vision of their creators. They seldom missed, and often exceeded, caricature, and they appear even today on many modern record covers, exclaimed and titillated over by those who most assuredly "all love Art in a seemly way."

But George Lewis, playing his music the "best he knew how" in New Orleans, was oblivious to the battles raging around that music. No one had heard of George Lewis in the twenties and thirties, outside of New Orleans. In fact, as late as 1957 a book by an American college professor purporting to trace the history of jazz to modern times does not even mention his name, although the name of George Lewis has meant as much as any other—and more than a great many—in the perpetuation of this

music since its early exponents travelled North in the migrations of the twenties and thirties.

The book, presented to George in Basle, Switzerland, in May of 1960, is inscribed with unwitting irony: "To Mr. George Lewis, the finest clarinet ever played jazz . . . in true love and admiration from his sincere friend, Werne Ruoff. May God always be with you for we can never return the things you gave to my folks."

Only one adverse comment on the music causes George Lewis to react noticeably, and that is reference to it as "whorehouse music." This will bring a visible wince of real pain. But even if he had known of the furore over the music in the twenties and thirties he would have paid as little attention to it as he does to the furores of today. There were too many important things to worry about: food, rent, shoes, clothes, the whole miserable fight for a bare economic survival in a depression-ridden era.

If, in the twenties, the going had been hard sometimes, the thirties were to serve up hell-with-trimmings three times a day.

In the decade just passed, pay might not always have been sure, and was usually low, but there had always been the certainty of opportunity. If last night's gig had ended in a humbug over money, tonight's was sure and reliable. No week ever passed without some income. If there had been times when he and Emma had been forced to use all their ingenuity to make certain their rapidly growing family had enough to eat, if George Lewis himself had frequently been forced to tighten his belt another notch and substitute for food the liquor that always flowed freely on every gig, yet there had been no element of panic in the circumstances.

It was unthinkable that there would not always be the music. It was as much a part of life as the broad expanse of the river that flowed around their city, as the spring rains, and the summer's torpid heat, unchangeable. There might be times when its financial rewards were slight, perhaps only the money that found its way to the kitty, but there would always be the sounds of the horns and the drums. This was as certain as death or birth.

Yet, now, unbelievably, the sound of the music was growing fainter.

Economic conditions were not wholly to blame, for the slow process of attrition from age and illness was being felt. Men who were middle-aged or elderly when George Lewis had first started

to play had either died or become too feeble to continue. The sounds of the horns of Keppard, Kelly, Petit, were gone. Rena was to blow his for the last time in the middle of the decade.

In nineteen-twenty-nine George played his first gigs with Bunk Johnson, one of the few remaining veterans of Buddy Bolden's historic band. Bunk was a man who played a trumpet with a devastatingly sure attack and compelling purity of tone. He was not playing in New Orleans then, in fact had not played in that city for almost ten years, but instead was gigging in surrounding parishes and towns. George played frequently with the Louis Fritz Band, taking the younger Fritz's place when he had other jobs, and it was on a job for which Louis Fritz had sent for him that he first met Bunk.

Johnson was then about fifty years old, but he was not quite the "legendary" figure he has been credited with being. He was a trumpeter of outstanding talent, although he freely admitted to a limited range, and because of this limited range had usually been found playing second trumpet with various groups, a band position he is said to have created. He did not lead a band of his own, and he was a musician of whom leaders were wary. He was also, as has been noted, a wanderer.

Although he was esteemed as a musician he did not rank as high in the opinions of other native New Orleanians as did Kelly, Keppard, Rena, Petit, Thomas and others of an older generation than these. Early in his career he alienated most of his fellow players by a constant habit of "low-rating" other musicians. Leaders and sidemen quarrelled frequently, sometimes lethally, in those days; leaders often gave their sidemen more than a little grief in money matters; there were bitter enmities and long-lived feuds, but there was an unwritten code that forbade a man to low-rate a fellow-musician's playing. It was quite acceptable to call him a thief, if you thought he was one; but let his playing alone. This was hitting below the belt; it was taking money from his pockets, for by so doing you might be cutting him out of work. Survival was involved. Yet whenever Bunk was heard—and he could usually be heard wherever he was—he was usually profanely commenting on the lack of playing ability of some absent musician or group of musicians.

Certainly Bunk Johnson had no need to resort to this as an over-compensatory device, for Bunk need never have lacked work. And lack work he definitely did before he left New Orleans

about 1922. His playing made him a definite adjunct to any band, and could have resulted in his being one of the most sought-after trumpeters in New Orleans. His phrasing was impeccable, his quality of tone individual and uniquely his own. More than any of them he was a master at "pushing" the beat, and he had to an extraordinary degree the instinct for discipline in ensemble work. His trumpet was never heard to even skirt the edges of freneticism. No one will ever know what dark bitterness lay within this man, beneath his engaging personality, that accounted for his perverse pleasure in the hurt and discomfiture of others. A raconteur of surpassing talent, he managed—with everyone except his own people—to force acceptance of himself at his own valuation by sheer force of verbal power and personality.

George Baquet, backstage at a Johnson concert in Philadelphia in the forties, called one of the musicians over to him, and, pointing to Bunk, said: "Who's that man doing all the talking?" Told that it was Bunk Johnson, Bacquet shook his head. "Can't seem to place him," he said. "Seems like I ought to be able to. I've been around a long time. But the way he's talking he was the one who started it all."

There is far more that is pitiable than censorable in the manner in which Bunk Johnson destroyed himself in his latter years, when, as did Armstrong, Noone, Ory, Hall and others, he might have become great and honoured in the eyes of his own people. Only a man driven by deep and painful inner conflicts so wantonly inflicts pain on those with whom he lives and works.

The blight of the economic distress of the thirties at first hit the city harder than it did the rural areas, and during that period George played, leading his own group, on many country dates, and on some of them playing as sideman with Kid Howard's band, or others. Then he abruptly refused any more of them.

"Look, George," said the young white man who made the bookings for him, "you need the work. I've been down there and talked to those people and they won't treat you or any of the other bands like they have before. They've promised to be decent."

"I'm sorry," said George. And he was. He genuinely liked the young man. "It's no use you're wasting your time. I'm not playing in those parts again. I do thank you very much for your help, but I'm not going."

The young man ran his fingers through his hair in exasperation. He was fond of George Lewis, and he knew how badly Lewis

and his men needed the work. He knew, too, of the insults and abuses that had been their lot in the "Cajun" country, a country whose residents were largely of mixed blood themselves.

"If the other men—"

George stopped him quietly. "What the other mens do is their business. If they want to go there's nothing to stop them. George Lewis isn't going."

"They won't go without you." It was a plaint to be heard often in the years to come, when the men who played with George Lewis developed an almost fanatical loyalty to him and dependence on him.

George shrugged the statement off. "They don't like it no better than I do. But I know they needs the money. Maybe you can get Howard."

"How much money you and Jeannette got in the house now, George?"

George grinned. "Maybe four bits. Maybe two. That don't make any difference. If it was nothing at all it would be enough to keep me from being insulted and treated like that. Honest, I'm sorry. And now I got to go. I got to see about a job. Thanks for stopping by."

With an innate desire to please, to help others, to avoid making trouble, George was sincerely sorry to "let the boy down." But he had had his fill of the rural South. Four bits, or "maybe two," could still buy beans and rice. And even if there had not been that much it would have made no difference; his father had taught him years before that pockets that contained self-respect were never empty.

He managed somehow, in those days of nightmare worry and poverty to find some place where he could play his music. His very weariness seemed to drive him to it. The halls in which he had played for years—St Theresa's, St Catherine's, Hopes, Globe, Perseverance, St Elizabeth's—were dark most of the time now, but occasionally the windows were thrown open, light flooded out, and the sounds of a band sent the phantoms of want and despair fleeing before them down the banquettes and through the alleys of the city by the intensity of their golden drive. There were still bars and taverns where a band willing to play for tips, or fifty or seventy-five cents a night, could blow. Two-dollars-and-a-half a night was, during the depression, a downright princely sum.

It was during the late twenties and early thirties that George first played with trumpeter Evan Thomas, the only musician of whom he has ever been heard to say: "He was the greatest I ever heard." Many of Evan's engagements were in the rural areas, and he invariably sent for George.

"I'd never heard anyone before Evan and I've never heard anybody since blow a trumpet like he could. He could hit a note a whole octave higher than most trumpeters, as easy as I can whistle Yankee Doodle. But he never did it just for the sake of doing it. It had to be there naturally, in the music, in his mind. Sometimes I'd take down playing, just to watch him and hear him. Playing with him was something I wouldn't have missed for anything."

Evan was one of the first of the New Orleans trumpeters to play what is called the "non-pressure" system, taught exclusively today.

Evan is dead. Today, because there are many living who might be hurt by comparison, George Lewis will not be drawn into a flat statement of opinion of any musician. It is my distinct impression, however, that, in George's judgement, Evan's only competitor—had they played there during the same period—would have been Louis Armstrong.

By the time he was thirty George was a veteran of such bands as the Olympia, Tuxedo, Eureka; he had played with most of the great trumpeters who were active during his lifetime. He had followed in the footsteps—literally—of men like Picou, Noone, McCurtis, Baquet. Through those years he must also have played with a number of mediocre and inferior instrumentalists, but he has never been heard to refer to them.

It would be a long time—twenty years—before the long road that was as "smooth and nice and pretty as anything you'd want to see" would open before George Lewis. Now more than ever he sought the comfort and strength of Alice Zeno's love and faith. She had been upset over the separation between her son and his wife, yet she made no criticism, for she had sensed for a long time before it happened that her son was nearing the breaking point. Sometimes when his work on the docks or on some labouring job kept him away from her during the day he would come to her apartment late at night, rousing her from sleep, keeping the promise made to her years before when he had left her to found his own home. There was always coffee waiting,

needing only to be heated, and if on these nights she smelled liquor, or noted that he had been drinking, her remonstrance was brief, though her worry was great. When he was able to come to her at the end of the day, before he went to his night's playing job, she would always lay her fingers on his forehead as he left her, and say, as she had when he played his first job in Mandeville: "Offer it to God, son. Ask him to help you."

"And I know He did," said George. "I *know* it. Many's the time I'd be so tired getting on a job to play it seemed like I couldn't make it. And I wouldn't be drinking either. I'd remember what my mother said, and somehow I'd make out. Seems like the tireder I was, the sicker I felt, the more real I prayed, and the better I played."

Many years later he said to me, with a sort of exasperated patience, after I had remonstrated frantically over his playing when he was ill:

"You don't understand. George Lewis has played most of his life—most all of his life—sick, or half-sick. It don't matter. Not one bit. I'll do all right." And of course he did, not "all right" but magnificently.

He had come a long way from the nights when he would dart, hysterical with relief, into heavy traffic as his mother stepped wearily from a street car, crying: "Ma! Here I am, ma!" Yet basically he was still that small boy who, smiling with happiness, gave his mother the nickels and dimes he had earned cracking pecans in a factory, yet who would rush to her arms in a frenzy of relief at the security he found there. Two things were essential to his happiness: the feeling that he was needed, and emotional security and fulfilment.

Life had denied him many things, but it did not deny him these. If through the years to come he did not have the hand of his dead child Hilda in his own, as he had had when he was walking ankle-deep in the mud on the road of his dream, he did have the hand of a woman whose basic strength and understanding, whose unquestioning love, would lighten the load of the "heavy bucket" until at last he could put his feet on the smooth and pretty road that lay beyond the fork, past the dog who growled so fiercely.

Her name was Jeannette Williams, and it was their marriage in the early thirties that became the rock upon which his life was founded.

There was no discord in their life. The quarrels which they had, in common with all couples, were based on matters that concerned only themselves. If George drank too much, Jeannette did not by any means suffer in silence, but she never tried to destroy his respect for himself, and her resentment was directed against the drink and not the man. She seemed to know instinctively the meaning of the teaching: "Love the sinner; hate the sin." Whatever their differences she knew unquestioningly that his need of her was all-encompassing, and that no other woman could fill that need.

George frequently speaks with the formal phraseology of his mother's generation, in the phrases we call "clichés" today. Just as we have succeeded with our own particular brand of intellectual self-righteousness in virtually eliminating emotion from the music, so we have eliminated it from speech, shunning it in both forms of communication as a minister would shun certain Anglo-Saxon four-letter words. But George had learned his early lessons from McGuffy's reader, from the nineteenth century poetry and books which his mother read aloud to him, from hymns, and from the Bible. On those rare occasions when he speaks of something or someone close to his heart he falls back on their phraseology. Of Jeannette he says:

"She held my head above the waters."

two

GEORGE Lewis and Evan Thomas sat basking contentedly in the sun by the side of the railroad track near the station in Crowley, Louisiana. There were several hours in which they could relax before getting ready to play that night. It was early November, 1932. In the distance they heard the sound of an approaching freight train. It came in sight, rumbled near, and slowed down to enter the station. It was loaded with sugar cane, and on a flat car in its centre rode the workers in the sugar cane, men, women, and children. As the flat car drew opposite them a tall, spare, familiar figure stood up, waved and jumped from the still-moving train. It was Bunk Johnson, carrying a trumpet case and

nothing else. He was not sure where he was going. Anywhere, he said, where there was work.

The three men sat and talked and reminisced, and discussed the hard times. "Things," said Bunk, "are mighty bad." Evan had picked up George in New Orleans the day before to travel with him on a round of dates he had managed to secure in the country. The work was a godsend to both men, and Evan told Bunk that if he wanted to travel with them he would give him a job. Later George and the others agreed to take a little less money to make this possible. The band included Abby Foster, Walter Preston, Louis Robertson, and a man named Goff, whose first name George does not recall. Bunk joined the group as second trumpeter, they travelled for about two weeks, returned to Crowley for a play date, then to New Iberia, and then to Rayne. When they arrived in Rayne it was less than a week before Thanksgiving.

The men scattered, finding lodgings wherever they could. Evan rented a room in a boarding house near the club where they were playing, run by a woman named Mrs Gilbey, whose husband, John, was away, and from whom she stated she was separated. John Gilbey was one of the thousands of Negroes of mixed blood in that area, whose skin is so light in colour it is possible for them to pass back and forth across the colour line at will.

The band had been in town only a day or two when Gilbey returned. He did not make his presence there known to his wife, but instead remained out of sight, hanging around in the bars and taverns, picking up what gossip he could. Some of this gossip (wrongly, George says) linked his wife with Evan.

Two nights before Thanksgiving, their evening's work almost completed, the men were playing easily, contentedly, the crowd with them, happy, relaxed. Suddenly the floor cleared. The men on the stand were puzzled for a moment. It had happened so quickly. Then they saw John Gilbey walking toward the stand, the crowd melting away before him and in his hand a razor-sharp hunting knife. Evan knew instantly for whom the knife was intended. He had been warned that afternoon and had laughed the warning off. There was no time to run. He ducked behind George, grabbing the smaller, shorter man by the shoulders, pleading with Gilbey to listen to him. George says: "I got twenty years older in less'n ten seconds." It was over so quickly the other men scarcely had time to jump from the stand. Gilbey

reached over George's shoulder, and with one swift slash cut Evan's throat, severing the jugular vein. George was drenched with blood, and every instrument on the stand was splattered with it.

Doctors have said that what followed is impossible, yet more than a score of people saw it happen. Mortally wounded, Evan staggered from the stand, and with a strange, lurching run, blood spurting from his throat, ran across the hall, through the door, and for several feet beyond, finally collapsing, face down, hands digging and scrabbling at the dirt, then suddenly lying quiet.

The murderer had vanished. The police came and removed the body, questioned the witnesses and left, admonishing the musicians to be ready to appear in court the next day. George, shaking with horror, almost in shock, stripped off his blood-soaked shirt and returned to the stand to pack his horn. He put it in its case and placed the case at the back of the stand, while he looked for his coat. At that point the murderer returned. The other men, still talking about their experience, had not yet put their instruments away. This time Gilbey did not carry a knife but a gun. There was a window at one side of the hall and George was the first one through it, head foremost, followed in rapid succession by the others. Crouched beneath the sill on the outside, they listened to the murderer shouting obscenely inside the hall, and heard the sounds of crashing and banging.

"There they goes," groaned one of the men, in the tone of one who sees his whole family massacred before his eyes. "All of 'em. All our instruments."

It was true, with one exception. George's horn was overlooked, tucked safely away in its case at the back of the stand. Every other instrument on the stage was kicked, bent, battered, almost completely destroyed. The drum heads had been slashed to ribbons, and Bunk's trumpet was smashed beyond hope of repair.

The murderer was apprehended that night, tried and sentenced to the penitentiary, but managed to escape after a few months. Months went by before he was re-captured, and then it was by accident, in a white restaurant in New Orleans. All restaurants in New Orleans, whether working men's or posh society, were Jim Crow as they are today, and Gilbey had thought to evade the police by crossing the colour line and passing as white. Only the quick memory of a policeman dropping in for a cup of coffee and recognizing him from the "wanted" posters was responsible

for his capture. But during that capture he killed a policeman, and was himself shot to death.

The Rayne engagement ended the night of the murder. Bunk returned to New Iberia, and for ten years never left that town, working in its rice fields and on various labouring jobs, and during those ten years he never blew a trumpet.

George returned to New Orleans and the unending search for work. Not long after he returned he played a parade, for the guaranteed price of two dollars and a half. There was little food in the house; coffee, rice, some beans. He and Jeannette had seven cents between them. At the end of the parade there was no pay.

"I was so tired," said George. "I was tired most to death, and I didn't even have the stren'th to get angry. I went home and I'm not ashamed to admit it—that night I cried. Jeannette, she told me not to mind. Something would happen."

It did, and within a very short time. "I've always been lucky," says George, with something less than accuracy.

He was playing a little later in a club frequented mostly by gangsters and gamblers.

"We didn' have no coal in the house, and not much food. I was working for 75 cents for the night's work and whatever we could get in the kitty. It was a pretty good kitty that night, because the place was full of gamblers. After we finished working I went in to wash up, and I saw on the floor of the men's room, off in a corner, a little pile of what looked like dollar bills. Everyone was gone but me. I went over and picked it up. The money was all wadded up like gamblers carry it. There weren't many bills, but most of them was big ones. There was a hundred dolla's in that little pile."

After he got home he and Jeannette sat, speechless, looking at the money lying on the table. Enough coal to see them through the winter; enough staples to have a supply of food on hand for the days when things were really bad, money for the rent, and a pair of shoes for each of them.

George was willing to take any form of work that came along, and did. He continually accepted jobs from sheer hungry necessity that were far beyond his physical capacities to perform safely, and by sheer force of will performed them ably. He reported to the docks almost daily, seeking any kind of work, knowing only one kind would be offered to him. He was

fortunate enough, now and then,—"I was always lucky"—to be given occasional jobs unloading coffee, or loading cotton. The Brazilian coffee came in bags weighing 135 to 140 pounds each, the Guatemalan coffee in bags weighing 160 pounds. Four was the usual number of bags to be loaded on a hand truck, but George quickly learned a trick of loading that had two beneficial results: it made the foreman happy, and it made it easier on his arms and shoulders. With only four bags on the truck, two bags on top of two others, the weight of the fourth would jerk the truck down with the full weight of the nearly six hundred pounds on his arms and shoulders. A fifth bag thrown on the back of the load acted as a brake.

"They was wooden wharves then, and a man's legs caught hell trying to push those trucks."

He developed muscles like rawhide, and he also developed a heart that would eventually give out just when his feet were starting on the "smooth and pretty" road, and legs that would give him trouble the rest of his life.

He was a first-class passenger on the Cunard Liner "Mauretania" *en route* home from England when the first of many blood clots in those legs became a matter of critical concern, frightening the ship's doctor and nursing sister half to death, and his manager almost into a decline. A doctor in New Orleans told him reproachfully, as though he should have known better than to accept the only work open to a Negro—thus insuring survival—that it was the work on the docks and its strain on his legs that eventually brought about the recurring attacks of blood clots.

His digestive troubles now were beginning to assert themselves more painfully and frequently than they ever had before. They had started when he was a young man, but now the recurring pain was sharper, the attacks more frequent. Periodic nosebleeds were also bothering him, some of them of haemorrhage proportions. One of these nasal haemorrhages continued, off and on, for three days and two nights, and he played on each night almost choking from the blood that flowed into his throat, finally being forced by his employer to quit on the second night. Again he was bullied by his mother and Jeannette into reporting to the hospital for treatment. There he was told that he had been extremely fortunate that his nose had bled because if it had not he might have had a stroke. His blood pressure, they said, was

abnormally high. The nose was packed, he was sent home and ordered to remain quiet and did so. The reason he did is easy to understand. There was no work to be found. These attacks never really subsided until well into the fifties, when he was playing almost exclusively in cities outside of New Orleans. And they never occurred when he was playing in any of these cities.

In 1934 George started work at a night club at Ursuline and Decatur Streets, at one dollar a night. He remained there, with one interruption, for two years, never missing a night, seven nights a week. His hours were from eight-thirty until two-thirty in the morning, and sometimes when there were more than the usual number of gangsters and gamblers in the place he played later. These men tipped well, and they were never offensive to coloured musicians, as were many of the other patrons. In fact they showed such open hostility to Negro-baiting or patronizing whites that the latter found themselves leaving earlier than they had intended. And it was by no means unusual for them to find, when they reached their cars, that all four tyres had been neatly slit.

After he had finished at the club in the early morning hours he would go home, catch what sleep he could, and start out early the next morning for a labouring job on a WPA project, or wherever he could find one. During the two years he played at the club he never averaged more than four hours sleep a night. When he returned at the end of the day from labouring he would wash up first and then drop exhausted into a chair and sleep for an hour or so, until it was time to get ready for the night's work.

"Me and Jeannette had a real fuss one night," George relates. "I came home tired, and cleaned up and took off my shoes and sat down and fell asleep. When it came time to wake me for supper she didn't do it. She thought I was too tired. I woke up 'way late. I burned up. It's about the only time I ever in all my life been late on a job. Any job. That's something I don't like—being late."

Just before the end of the two years the club, unable to keep up during the height of the depression, closed. But before it closed George was to learn the true mettle of the woman he had married.

One night while he was playing he was picked up by two policemen and, without a word of explanation, hauled off to the city jail and lodged there as a "suspect." What he was "suspected"

of he had no idea, nor was he told. Later, when the facts in the case were finally uncovered, it was shown to be a case of mistaken identity. The man who had committed the crime, in the neighbourhood of the club, had been glimpsed briefly as he fled, and was said to be a "small, dark, thin man, wearing white shoes with brown saddles." George answered the description to perfection.

One of the musicians went, the night of his arrest, to the little apartment at 1117 Burgundy Street and told Jeannette what had happened. The fear the Negro knows when word comes that a husband, or son, or lover has been jailed is a different fear than the white knows under the same circumstances. They know white justice will accuse him, white justice hear the evidence, and white justice pass judgement. It is not always a comfortable feeling.

By morning Jeannette was ready for action. She had stayed up all night, cleaning out table and bureau drawers, working feverishly. They had their own furniture, bought, it was true, second hand, laboriously acquired a piece at a time over a period of years, and with a chair here, a table there, representing a slim meal now and then. But it was good furniture, solid and substantial.

The whole lot brought forty dollars. By noon the last piece was gone. Only a mattress, some bedding, the old stove that had been in the house when they rented it and some pots and pans and dishes remained.

By two o'clock she had found a lawyer who would take the case for forty dollars. They would not let her see her husband; not even his lawyer was permitted to see him. In fact, to this day, George has never met the lawyer.

Late the following day he was released. No charges were ever filed against him; the real criminal had been identified, and there was not even a hearing. The lawyer returned to Jeannette the forty dollars she had given him, knowing what she had sacrificed to obtain it. She tried to buy back the furniture, as Alice had tried to retrieve her chairs many years before, but the purchasers asked exactly double the amount they had paid her.

The night he was released George and Jeannette made up the mattress on the floor—there had been no time to get replacements— and were getting ready to go to bed when someone knocked on the door, it was a messenger from the club.

"Boss wants to know why you aren't at work, George," he said. "Sent me to find out were you sick or something, after all that trouble."

"You all think I'm crazy or something?" said George. "I'm not going back there. How do I know everybody'll believe I didn't do it? How do I know there won't be a bunch of peoples there wantin' a little trouble just for fun? Tell the boss I'm sorry, and I should have gotten a substitute only I was so upsetted I forgot. I'll send him one tomorrow night."

The next night the boss refused to accept the substitute and sent again for George. One of the reasons for George's repeated refusals to return was Jeanette's obvious fear. At last, the boss himself appeared at the door, late one afternoon.

"Look, George," he said patiently. "You don't think I'd ask you to come back if everything wasn't all right? All the boys down there want you back. In fact they want you back so bad I wouldn't be surprised if they didn't come out here and bring you back bodily if you don't show up tonight."

It was a convincing argument and George agreed to return, ignoring Jeannette's protests. Once he had given his word he would not back out. She finally subsided and cooked supper in grim silence. After supper George dressed for the club, and then noticed, as he walked toward the door, that Jeannette was walking with him, dressed for the street, and, although it was a warm night, wearing her winter coat.

"Where you going, girl?" he asked.

"With you."

"What you saying?"

In reply she unbuttoned the top buttons of her coat and George saw the handle of the hatchet it had covered.

"My God!" gasped George in horror. "Put that thing up, Jeannette. What you trying to do? Get us both in jail?"

"I'm going with you, and I'm staying outside the window, and I'm coming back with you," she said with finality. "Anybody tries to come at you, they got to kill us both."

For almost a week Jeannette kept quiet, grim vigil outside the window at the back of the club. George fretted and fumed but it did no good. Sometimes the gaiety inside was loud and rough and, horn at his lips, he would roll an apprehensive eye towards the window. He knew that Jeannette, a God-fearing, strictly-reared Baptist, was not used to this sort of rowdyism and he was

afraid she might misunderstand. It is probable that his playing was not at its best. Lullabies were what he wanted to play, slow and soothing; when the rough-housing crowd demanded fast numbers or low-down "funky" blues, he broke out in goose-pimples of fear. As the hair-suspended sword had worried Damocles, so Jeannette's hatchet worried George.

Just before the end of 1935, shortly after the club closed down, his abdominal pain became almost unbearable. At its worst excruciating, it was always bad. Whisky acted as a local anaesthetic, soothing it temporarily, only to have it return with doubled intensity when the effects of the drink wore off. He returned from one gig in a rural community, doubled up in agony on the floor of the band truck. Eventually he found himself at the hospital. After the usual wait the doctor who examined him asked quizzically:

"Are you planning to play that horn tonight, boy?"

"Yes, sir," replied George between clenched teeth. "If you'll just give me a little something for this pain, I'll be okay. Seems like something I eat all the time gives me trouble."

It scarcely needed X-rays to tell the doctor that a perforated duodenal ulcer was only a matter of hours away. Could come, in fact, at any moment. Somehow he convinced George that surgery meant, quite literally, the difference between life and death.

It was a long and critical procedure. The duodenum and a goodly portion of the stomach were removed under spinal anaesthesia, while George listened with doped and hazy pride to the surgeon as he said to the medical students grouped around: "Never saw such abdominal muscular development in a man this small before. Look here—and here—"

The surgeon left a drain *in situ,* and George remained in the hospital for two weeks. The wound was still open, the drain still in place, when he returned home. It was a matter now of healing, and the doctors felt that he would be happier and recover more quickly at home. He was told to remain quiet, refrain from exercise, and return for dressings.

At home there was little in the way of money. Jeannette had worked as often as she could find jobs, but pay had been farcically small. She used it to stock the cupboard with staples, with Alice Zeno adding what she could to the supplies, so that there would be enough basic nourishment for George during his convalescence. There was a pitifully small amount of it.

Three weeks from the date of the operation, a week after he returned home and before the drain had been removed from the operative wound, George received a call asking him to play a funeral parade. He would be paid, he was told, three dollars and a half.

"You *sure*?" asked George, mindful of other parades, other promises.

"Positive. Got the money in advance."

"Okay. What time?"

Jeannette raged again, and again it did no good. Before he left to report for the job he and Jeannette took strips of towelling and bound them tightly around his body, fastening them with large, strong safety pins.

"Leave me, for God's sake," gasped George at one point, "enough room to breathe."

"Man crazy enough to parade in the shape you're in don't deserve to breathe," she observed tartly.

And then history repeated itself. As he started to leave for the funeral parlour he found Jeannette beside him at the door, dressed for the street, wearing an old, comfortable pair of shoes.

"Where you going, girl?" he asked as he had asked before.

"With you," she replied, as she had replied before.

George grinned. "Got your hatchet?"

Throughout the long parade, from funeral parlour to church, church to cemetery, and cemetery back to town, Jeannette walked beside the band, only a few feet from her husband.

"In case he fell out," she said.

After the operation, George stopped drinking, not gradually, but all at once. He lost all taste or desire for alcohol, and did not touch it in any form, however mild, until nine years later, when he was a thousand miles from home. No one could blame him for it at that time in the circumstances in which he found himself.

It was some time during those days of illness and poverty, overwork and underpay, with the weeks following each other in a grim parade of want and worry; when Alice Zeno's prayers, and his own, and Jeannette's, all combined, seemed scarcely strong enough to hold life at bay; that he experienced the clear, vivid dream of Hilda, and the man with the "kind look about him" who directed his feet out of the mud and mire.

As 1940 drew near, work became more plentiful, and he was able each week to bring home enough to keep things going and

once in a while to "put up" a little for the future. On March 28, 1941, Shirley Lewis put in her appearance, a chubby, happy infant, with her mother's solidity of bone and muscle, her father's features. Perhaps the unexpectedness of her tardy arrival, perhaps the feeling both he and Jeannette had that this might be their only child, put her in the forefront of their lives, so that every move and every thought revolved around her. The children of his first marriage were grown now, two of his sons worked with him on the docks, it would not be long before grandchildren would be burbling and burping their way into his affections. He remained, at 41, the same gentle push-over for a baby's wiles as he had been the day in 1919 when he had lost his job because he could not tear himself away from the delectable charms of his first daughter.

Alice was nearing eighty now. The vacation she had day-dreamed of so guiltily had never come to pass, but she was content. She still went to work every day, far better physically, even at that age, than she had been so many years before when it had been necessary for her to push a sick and pain-racked body almost beyond its endurance in order to take care of her son. Her life still centred, and always would, about that son, and her saints heard his name daily as they had since the day her mother laid him in her arms. When he was ill, she sensed it, and would stop in at his home on her way from work.

"How did you know he was sick, Gram?" Jeannette asked once.

Alice shrugged. "I always know. Sometimes I wish I didn't. When he was just a little thing, not much bigger than a pint of milk, and I had to leave him all day I'd know long before the day was out those times I'd find him sick when I got home. I guess he could be a thousand miles away and I'd know."

Then she would say resignedly: "I suppose he went to work?"

"Yes, Gram. He went to work. There's nothing anyone can do about that, I guess. Not you or me or anyone."

three

It is seldom that the course of a legend can be charted accurately from its beginning. The legend that is George Lewis can be pin-pointed almost to the day of its birth, during the month of November, 1942, when George answered a knock at his door and found the future on its threshold.

"Me and Jeannette and the baby were living at 827 St Phillip Street when I heard the knock. I went to the door and Bunk Johnson was standing there with three white men. I hadn't seen him for ten years, not since Evan Thomas was murdered. I asked them to come in, and they did, and then they asked questions and we talked a long time. There was something about them that was different, and I had a good feeling about them. There was Bill Russell and David Stuart and Hal McIntire. There was something different about the way they talked to me and Jeannette and the way they acted. They shook hands with me, and later on David asked me did I have a horn, and I got it out and played some for them."

On January 7, 1961, David Stuart wrote to me, at my request, giving his version of that meeting and the resultant recording session.

"The Jazz Man records were the first Bunk Johnson records . . ." he wrote. "The first trip to New Orleans was made by Bill Colburn, Hal McIntire and me—from Los Angeles. We met Bill Russell and Gene Williams down south, m'am. Bill, Hal and I brought Bunk in from New Iberia and it was while driving to New Orleans that Bunk brought up George's name. I had asked for a clarinet man other than ——— or ———, who were playing less than great by then. Bunk said he knew a George Lewis who played fine, remembered his address—or found it somehow—and when we made it to New Orleans we went to the house and found George. Bunk hadn't been to New Orleans for twenty years.

"A shy, handsome man, he eventually brought out a beat-up, wired-together clarinet and played for us. So damned beautifully I waltzed out to a hock shop and bought two horns and gave him his choice. I still have the one he didn't take. With the new and complete horn he truly wailed! Marvellously!! And the recording session was without a doubt the most exciting day of

music I've ever attended. Just sitting here writing of it, my spine tingles."

David's verbal account of the meeting, given to the writer a number of years ago, was even more explicit.

"When I asked George if he had his horn there he smiled shyly and said yes, *sir,* he certainly did have a horn. And then he went and got it out of a chest and showed it to us. He said it 'wasn't in very good shape' and it sure wasn't. I never saw such a clarinet in all my life, literally held together by elastic bands and bits of wire. I didn't see how anyone could play on it, and then he stood there and played like an angel. I'm not ashamed to admit that when I heard that damned beautiful tone coming out of that beat-up, battered horn I took a walk to the window and looked out till the mist cleared away."

Bunk by his own admission had not been in New Orleans for twenty years, and a band must be brought together that would give David what he had come thousands of miles to find, the sound of New Orleans music before it had become adulterated and commercialized, the music that had been heard when Bunk was a young man, and George was a boy playing his first job on a mule-drawn wagon in Mandeville. George had little trouble in selecting the men, for he already had a group of his own, playing the music the white musicians in the north had long ago dubbed "the righteous stuff." He selected his close friend, Lawrence Marrero, business manager of his band; another good friend with whom he played often, Jim Robinson; and for bass he chose a player named Austin Young. He had not started playing yet with Alcide "Slow Drag" Pavageau; he was to hire him the following year. Ernest Rogers was selected as drummer. The whole group then went to the home of pianist Walter Decou and with Decou they journeyed to Grunewald's music store for the session. Negro musicians were not permitted to use professional recording studio facilities, and David had to "make do" with the acoustical horrors of a piano showroom on the second floor of the store. It was there he experienced his "most exciting day of music," and listening to the records it is easy to understand why, almost twenty years later, his spine tingled writing of it. During those twenty years David had recorded some of the greatest of the traditionalists, and many of the most outstanding of the modern or "progressive" jazz artists.

The records, imperfect as they are from an engineering stand-

point—they could be nothing else—have in them all the fire, the drive, the hope, of the men who made them that memorable day. The occasional clang of a streetcar as it rumbled past the building can be heard if one wants to listen for it, but so can the message of the music, a message so clearly stated that every note on the discs is a tribute to the director who, just by being himself, was able to bring it forth. The clang of the streetcar does not matter to the listener who knows what he is hearing. And this, of course, marks the difference between the human approach to jazz and the intellectual.

There was to be another man to whom George would feel as drawn as he was to David Stuart and Bill Russell—Alfred Lion. But it would be more than a year before Alfred's gay, understanding laughter, and warm, pixie personality would fill the little St Phillip Street apartment with a kind of friendship and companionship George had never experienced before with anyone not of his own race until he met this triumvirate.

That these three men were initially responsible for bringing him the fame he knows today through the distribution of those early recordings has nothing to do with his love for them.

Of Bill Russell he says: "He's a livin' saint. Now I don't mean that like folks say it today, kidding. I mean it really. He's a saint walking around on earth. He's my friend."

Of David Stuart: "He's real. I'd play for David if I had to do it standing on my head in a bucket of hot coals. He's my friend."

Of Alfred Lion: "I'd go to hell for Alfred and keep on playing on the way. He's a real person. He's my friend."

There are a few others whom George Lewis also calls "my friend." One does not need the fingers of both hands to count them. Each is distinguished by the fact that at some time he dared the conventions under which George had lived his life, flouted the prejudices and black codes that had controlled his destiny, and stood beside him as an equal and a companion, never as a "patron."

That George Lewis was able to recognize and grasp this hand of friendship extended by the members of a race from which he had previously known only—at best—patronage and "kindness" was unusual in the people of his generation. It was Alice Zeno, teaching him as a child that all men were alike in the eyes of God, whatever they might think themselves, requiring him to show to his own people the same courtesies he was to show to

white people; it was the inborn dignity and knowledge of his own worth, and pride in his own race, that had come to him from Zaier, and Urania, and Henry Zeno. There were musicians in New Orleans sought by writers and curious traditional jazz enthusiasts who would not open their door to a white man. In the days of the great migration north some never lost their bitterness, so deeply had its acids been etched into their minds and hearts in childhood and adolescence and this bitterness can be heard in the biting tone of their horns. "Give me the child until he is seven—"

Lewis had felt hurt, and resentment, but he had also learned tolerance and sad acceptance. He viewed the attitude of the white man and woman in the south as the inevitable result of the way they had been reared, of the influences of their childhood, and is far more tolerant of the bigotry and prejudice displayed than are many white persons who find it intolerable and beyond understanding.

"They can't help it," he said to me once when I was fuming with anger at a patronizing snub the band had received from a touring Orleanian, when they were playing in Los Angeles. "It's the way they're raised. Mostly it's ignorance. We know it's not Christian, but they don't. And there's nothing anyone can do about it. It'll be a couple of more generations of both white and coloured before things really change."

For the most part, except for the very few who earned his accolade of "he's my friend" George remained withdrawn with others, keeping within himself a quiet place of objective watchfulness; giving graciousness, charm, and loyalty, but witholding affection and complete acceptance.

A few months after David Stuart left, Gene Williams returned to record Bunk for his own record label, "Jazz Information," named for the publication which he edited. He accepted Bunk at Bunk's own valuation, and his devotion to Bunk, his patience with that erratic and arrogant gentleman through the coming years were matched only by those same qualities in Bill Russell. That Bunk proved somewhat less than grateful, that he repaid these men who sacrificed so much for him in coin that rang less than true, was of no concern to them. He could do no wrong. The world today is indebted to them, and there will be generations of jazz historians to come who will also be indebted to them, for

their tolerance and selflessness, their singleness of purpose, and their understanding.

Although Bunk had never led a band in New Orleans, those early records prove that his admittedly limited range did not stand in his way of being, musically, a good leader. It is true that he was leading a group already coordinated, men who had played together often, either under the Lewis leadership or under other leaders, yet these men subordinated their own talents to his horn, embellishing it with their own skilled musicianship, and the over-all sound, the push, the drive, the impeccable phrasing and rhythmic discipline of these discs make them among the finest of early traditional jazz recordings. Had Bunk not been engaged, apparently, in a constant battle with some dark force within himself, these records give evidence that he might have become a truly great leader in a city of great leaders; might have been a reality rather than a myth, for no one ever "low-rated" Bunk's talents on a trumpet.

When Gene returned to New Orleans to make these records he had with him a young white clarinet player, Ellis Horne, who is today as thrilled as he was then that on portions of these recordings George played his clarinet. As David Stuart had been forced to do, Gene had to battle the acoustical problems of recording in a mid-town building, unable to control the street noises, with the band's sound hard to manage and balance from an engineering standpoint. If the past sheds light on the future, the reverse is also true. Something of today's smug contempt for yesterday's greatness, for the musicians of that era and their music whose very name—"jazz"—has been appropriated by almost every combination of popular musical groups known, from swing to near-symphony, is shown in a "review" of a re-issue of these records that appeared in a West Coast paper. The reviewer, once an ardent follower of jazz in its classic, freely improvised, unstudied, unarranged form, but more recently finding greener pastures in the modern purlieu, announced briefly that such a record had been re-issued—"if any one was interested"— listed the numbers on the disc, and ended his "review" with the name of one of the numbers, thus: ". . . and Sometimes My Burden Is Too Hard to Bear."

No one believed it inadvertent. There were many, reading it, who thought of the burdens the musicians bore, the humiliation of being forced to record under inferior conditions because of

their colour, still nervous under the comparatively new experience of recording, Bunk "blowing like five hundred," to quote George, his chance come at last after years of oblivion and hard labour in the rice fields. They thought, too, of the dedication of the young man, Gene Williams, struggling so hard to bring about the realization of a dream of years, fighting against handicaps that would have floored one less earnest, less dedicated.

Yet despite these handicaps Williams produced records that were vital and alive.

The burden carried by Gene and the musicians who gave him the best they could under those defeating circumstances, both psychological and physical, must conceivably have been at least as heavy as the burden of the Bright Young Man who sat at his typewriter years later and dismissed those recordings with such dull-edged sarcasm and intellectual snobbery.

Work on the docks was plentiful now. The country was at war and they hummed with activity; night and day the clang of the cranes, the screech of the winches, the shouts of the stevedores could be heard, George Lewis knew few idle days. This was unfortunate. An idle day—or even week—now and then might have saved him from grief later on. Already the lines of inner fatigue were deeply etched in his face, the cheeks beginning to hollow, the facial bones stand out with startling prominence, the eyes become more deeply set. At night his legs ached almost unbearably, and exhaustion would mercifully bring him an hour or so of sleep after he reached home. Then, later, driven as he had been when he was a child and, sick with fever would jump from bed to follow the sounds of a band, he would take his horn and range through the French Quarter, seeking the music. On weekends there were gigs in the clubs on Bourbon Street (where it is difficult to find a Negro musician today) and on Sundays there were picnics and parades. Often he would call his friends together, Jim Robinson, Lawrence Marrero, and others, and they would play in the yard or in the old green-shuttered house on St Phillip Street while the baby, Shirley, watched in plump, round-eyed ecstasy, and Jeannette would not let them stop until George had played "Over the Waves" for her. She called it the "Singing Clarinet" and little dreamed that her title would travel across the continent and over the Atlantic, so that in far-off Sweden almost twenty years later a fan in an audience in the Konsert-

huset in Stockholm would call out to her husband in halting English: "Singing Clarinet, Jorge—Singing Clarinet!"

In the late thirties a young man, Alfred Lion, came to this country from Germany—a jazz enthusiast since he had first heard the music in 1925 in a record store in Germany—and founded the Blue Note Record Company. He was joined soon by a friend of many years, Frank Wolff, who became his partner. They recorded nothing but jazz, and they recorded only the jazz that they liked, and gave no thought to the profits. This is unique in the history of commercial recordings; nothing like it had ever been done before; nothing like it will probably be done again. And, either because of, or in spite of, their dedication, they have prospered materially, and been enriched spiritually by the affection and loyalty of each musician they have recorded.

In 1943 Lion was in the United States Army, stationed in Texas. Wolff was taking care of the business in New York. In New Orleans Bill Russell had set up a recording date for Bunk Johnson, only to find that he was in California with Rudi Blesh, playing with the Lu Watters Yerba Buena Band. Bill made the recording—which was more in the nature of a rehearsal session—substituting Kid Howard for Bunk, under the leadership of George Lewis. He sent the masters to Wolff in New York, who in turn sent them to the Army post where his partner, Lion, was stationed. Lion took them into town and played them at a record store. Without having been there, it is still easy to imagine Alfred's delightful, delighted laugh, the laugh that one hears before one sees him bounding from the control room during a recording session, eyes dancing, accent suddenly stronger with excitement, the fine-featured face twinkling like a Christmas tree ornament, crying: "That is it, no! Yes, that is it!" Gracefully leaping the linguistic hurdles of the "th" and the "w" without even slowing down, setting the band laughing without the vaguest idea of why they were laughing.

"Buy it!" he wired Wolff, and the George Lewis legend, already stirring, became a vital, living reality.

A few days after Christmas, 1960, I wrote to James Asman in London, a jazz enthusiast and historian as well as writer, and asked him if he would write and tell me just when the first George Lewis records were heard in England. In my letter I said: "I know that while George Lewis was working as a stevedore on the docks of New Orleans, pushing hand trucks loaded

with coffee, wrastling bales of cotton, playing wherever and whenever he could for as little as fifty and seventy-five cents a night, jazz enthusiasts in Great Britain and Europe were fighting to get hold of his records; and that clarinettists on both sides of the channel were driving themselves into nervous breakdowns trying to play like George Lewis. It would help if you could give me any information about the introduction of his records to Great Britain."

His reply was the answer to any biographer's prayer. Condensed only slightly, and paraphrased not at all, it follows:

> " *As to the first impact that George Lewis and Bunk made over here . . . As far as we are concerned the emergence of George Avakian's reviews of the first Bunks with George on clarinet excited us in Britain. When the records finally arrived—some smashed in the journey—the recording technique was very rough and the balance questionable after the clarity and expert handling of the 1929 Mortons and Olivers.* Particularly were we thrilled by the purity of the clarinet playing, and the smearing foundation of the New Orleans trombone of Jim Robinson . . . and we learned perhaps for the first time that true native Crescent City jazz had laws all its own. We began to see that the Armstrongs, the Olivers, the Mortons, and the Dodds which had been put out until the end of the 'twenties were not absolutely faithful to these original New Orleans laws.*
>
> " *It soon occurred to some of us, myself to the forefront, that native New Orleans jazz band music was much more severe, much more concerned with pure ensemble improvisations built on clean, simple patterns. These simple, clear patterns formed merely the basis used by the New Orleans Negro musicians who had left the South so many years before and had "moderated" their own music in a new environment. We realized that audiences in New York and Chicago must have found the continual ensemble playing too difficult to understand and appreciate, and these jazz migrators had slowly changed to cope with their surroundings. Playing to crowds who quickly applauded*

* The Mortons and Olivers were not made in New Orleans.

solo work, they were soon forced to start solo improvisations and use the typical New Orleans ensemble style for first and last choruses only. It was, it seems now, the beginning of the jam session pattern which eventually gave rise to swing music and to modern idioms. The neat, strict tradition of Bunk's and George's playing, which paid full respect to their own native musical laws, was nothing short of a revelation.

" *Together the first Bunk Johnson-George Lewis sides and the parallel output of San Francisco's Lu Watters Yerba Buena Band gave British amateur musicians the impetus to begin playing more closely to the native New Orleans pattern . . . This impetus did more than anything to bring to the forefront the first "purist" British revival jazz bands, the Yorkshire, Crane River (Ken Colyer), Albemarle, Zenith Six, and Mick Gill's group. From these groups, all playing determinedly during the 'fifties, came the present influx of popular "Trad" jazz figures: Ken Colyer, Chris Barber, Monty Sunshine (who began his career with Ken Colyer), Acker Bilk, Ian Wheeler, Terry Lightfoot, and so on—all modelling their playing on George Lewis.*

" *Nevertheless the greatest impact of all took place when the Climax records came to this country. Kid Howard was on trumpet, playing much more earthily than Bunk was accustomed to do—and the George Lewis Climax records made jazz history in Great Britain.*

" *My first meeting with these wonderful records in the early to mid-forties is perhaps worth recording. I lived in a small Midland town, Newark-on-Trent—working in a ball-bearing plant during the war years, and jazz record collecting was my greatest relief from the long hours . . . Dot (Mrs Asman) and I invited a British collector, Bill Rankin, to stay with us and he brought with him a case of precious imported American 78's.*

" *I shall never forget the first full force of that immense sound, the sound of pure jazz unadulterated by any kind of commercial considerations whatsoever, unchanged by alien audiences. This was jazz at its finest and we all knew it. I remember rolling over on the carpet in a wild delirium of sheer happiness and excitement—and I have a vague*

impression that the rest of the company were equally affected. We had around us a goodly group of very intelligent and ardent enthusiasts, among them Tony Short, Graham Boatfield, Bill Kinnell, Graeme Bell and several others.

" *Of course, I managed to import copies. It cost me more than I could afford and poor Dot gladly sacrificed what small savings she had put by for a cheap fur coat she had set her heart on. We did without food. We did without beer —but we got those wonderful discs. And then, after we had mortgaged ourselves to the hilt to buy a three speed gramophone, we got the whole treasury of Bill Russell's unforgettable American Music L.P.'s with Bunk, Robinson, Marrero, Slow Drag, Baby Dodds . . . and the sweet, delicious, Elizabethan styled clarinet of George Lewis—the pivot of the whole British jazz revival. He was, to us, an unbelievable legend.*

" *We suspected then, from listening to him play, what we learned later. That he was not only a great musician, but a great man.*

" *That is why I say that hearing and seeing the George Lewis Band some decade and a half afterwards was the greatest musical experience of my life. For despite the heavy hand of time, these unique veterans still made music which brought the hair erect on the back of my neck, and prickled my skin like a hedgehog's.*

" *Good luck to your biography of this wonderful person whom we are so proud to call our friend. If these verbose and excitable notes help in any way, I am glad. But nothing I can say or do will ever repay those electric moments back in the 'forties when I rolled like a madman over the floor and glued my eager ear to the loudspeaker for hour after hour to catch every magnificent note that George Lewis played.*

Our love to you all—

Jim and Dot Asman."

"And a path is there which no man sought—"

four

For three days during the summer of 1944 George Lewis lay in bed in the hospital in New Orleans to which Negro industrial accident cases were taken. Since he had been brought there with a badly injured chest, he had received three trays a day containing food of sorts, an electric light bulb under a blanket tent had been placed over his injured chest, and he had received no further treatment. He had not been bathed since he was admitted, gasping with pain and in shock, after being struck in the chest by a wildly swinging cargo hook while unloading cotton. This was, to the fastidious Lewis, the most revolting feature of the whole experience. No X-rays had been taken, at least that he ever recalled, and nothing had been said to him about the extent of his injuries. He does not recall receiving any medication whatsoever.

By the third day the pain, the neglect, and the completely abhorrent conditions of dirt were more than he could stand. He had seen his clothes in a locker at the end of the ward, and in the afternoon, when the ward was deserted by attendants, he made his way to it painfully, and managed somehow to dress. His wallet and change had been placed in the hospital safe until his discharge. No one stopped him or paid any attention to him as he walked out of the door of the hospital and into the street. He had no money for carfare or taxicabs, but he would rather face the long walk to Charity Hospital than run the risk of asking for his money at the desk and being forced to remain. Every breath was a knife stab through his chest and he remembers the walk only as a nightmare. For once George Lewis was ready to admit that he was a fit candidate for hospital care, and he did not go home but directly to Charity Hospital.

The doctors there were in full agreement. His chest presented an appearance of extensive and deep bruising, and other symptoms indicated possible internal injury. X-rays were taken, and though he was not told what the findings were, they must have been positive for definite injury, or his hospital stay would have been shorter, the numerous conferences between internes and doctors less frequent.

When at last he was discharged the pain was still an agonizing stab with every breath. The heavy supportive strapping that had

been put around his chest was all that kept him upright.

"Can I play my clarinet all right again?" he asked when he was discharged.

"We'll see, George, we'll see," said the doctor. "Come back next week and we'll take another look at this. We can tell better then."

"We'll see——we'll see——" Scant comfort to a man whose whole life was centred on blowing a clarinet.

"You're damned right, 'we'll see'," muttered George on his way home.

The next day, confined to bed, the strapping tight round his chest, each breath bringing fiery pain, George called Lawrence Marrero, and Slow Drag Pavageau, whom he had, the year before, taken on as a sideman.

"Come on over," said George. "Let's make us some music." Bill Russell came by, found out what was planned, and set up a portable tape recorder close to the bed.

"We'll see," said the sick man to himself. "We'll see can George Lewis still play his horn."

Not only did George Lewis find out that day that he could still blow his horn, but the results of that informal session, issued on Bill Russell's American Music label, became one of the most famous of recorded blues in traditional jazz history.

He had never played it before. He had heard it, in his head, in his heart, when he was a patient in the hospital, despairingly anxious about the one thing that mattered to him—his ability to "make music." It came out almost without a falter on the first attempt, and the second run-through was a perfect "take." Composed by Lewis, without a note on paper, it is the life history of a man, and the life history of a race since it was transplanted to a strange and hostile land. He has recorded it several times since, under perfect conditions, but there has never been a recording that matched that first one in feeling or in tone. As all blues are, it is deceptively simple. It has been said: "the blues are a little song; the blues are song itself—." In "Burgundy Street Blues," named on the spur of the moment that day, and always pronounced by the Orleanian with the accent on the second syllable, the song is one of ineffable sadness, despair, all-conquering faith; there is in it the weeping of a million Rachels, the crying of a child, and the strength of spirit of a man and his people. It is responsible for more tears, on both sides of the Atlantic, than

any other piece of music this writer knows of. These tears I have seen, at home and in the great cities of half a dozen countries; they have come unbidden, without benefit of a sad or heart-rending vocal, for "Burgundy Street" has only once been recorded with a vocal accompaniment. It is a story told only in music.

Later that same year Bill Russell and Alfred Lion moved in—literally—with George, Jeannette, and Shirley. The house on St Phillip Street was small, but it managed to accommodate them, and Jeannette took the situation calmly.

Of his stay with George and Jeannette, Alfred said to me: "There was a warm friendship between us. We were good companions and we would talk for hours. With me George talked, and I am very proud, as he would have with one of his own people. But I do not like it there, in the South. I was given a bad time by many people because I was living at the home of a coloured person. How stupid can these people be! And we could not go places together as friends should. One night I invited him to go with me to the movies, before I knew all their crazy laws, and he was a little embarrassed. He told me he could not; that even if we went as far as the theatre together we must separate at the door. I could sit downstairs but he must sit upstairs because he is coloured. Then I said 'We do not go!' I have been sorry all my life, ever since, that there has not been more time to be with George, only once in a while when he comes to New York. Some day perhaps we can all take a vacation and be as we were then again. I have always hoped so. He is my good friend."

It was during this period that the majority of the American Music Bunk Johnson records were made, the ones mentioned in the Asman letter which, although made after the Climax records, apparently arrived overseas before them.

George had taken Alcide Pavageau, who appears on all these American Music sessions, under his wing the preceding year when that lively, cricket-like, greying, but gallant Creole was playing with Herb Morgan at the Silver Star. George had dropped in at the club and had watched and listened from the rear for several sets. He was appalled at what he described as "the shameful way some of the other mens in that band was treating that old man. It made me sick. When the set was over I called Slow Drag outside and I said 'You don't have to take that kind of talk from no one. You come see me and I'll see you get work.' "

From then on not only did Slow Drag follow George like a particularly adhesive shadow, but he never played regularly with another band; only on occasional recordings or on private gigs did he accept another's leadership.

During that period, the National Jazz Foundation was formed in New Orleans, an organization which was eventually to be supplanted by the New Orleans Jazz Club. The Foundation did much to further the cause of the Negro musician in that city. It was at their instigation the men joined the coloured local branch of the American Federation of Musicians in New Orleans. George expressed it: "They made professionals out of us. They did a lot for us."

By the spring of 1945 Bill Russell and Gene Williams had already taken the preliminary steps to bring Bunk Johnson and George Lewis and his group to New York under Bunk's leadership. An engagement had been arranged for September at the Stuyvesant Casino.

Shortly before they were scheduled to leave New Orleans George received a wire from Bunk stating that another bass player had been engaged and it would not be necessary to bring Slow Drag.

"If Drag don't go we all stay home," George wired in return. Drag went.

The Lewis group arrived in New York the last week in September. They are frank to admit that their first reaction was one of sheer fright. In the first place, they said, they couldn't seem to see any coloured people. There seemed to be nobody but whites. Except for Jim Robinson, none of them had ever set foot in a non-Jim Crow city in their lives, and they did not know where to turn, or what doors would be closed against them. There is, after all, a certain security in knowing that you'll be arrested if you sit in the front of a bus, or downstairs in a motion picture theatre. You sit in the back of the bus, or upstairs, and are safe. But they did not know the rules here, and for several days adjustment was difficult. A day or two after they arrived, Jim, Drag, and George stood looking through a restaurant window searching vainly for the sight of a coloured person inside that would indicate it was safe to enter. They were hungry after a long sightseeing walk. They finally decided it would be better to walk back to Gene Williams's apartment in Greenwich Village,

where they were staying, than take a chance. As they turned away, the cashier came to the door.

"Did you men want something?" she asked.

"We was thinking about lunch," said George.

"Then why," she asked reasonably, "didn't you come in? You scared me, standing out there, just looking."

The importance of the first trip to New York from the standpoint of George Lewis's career has been over-estimated. Another five years would pass before the event transpired that would bring him and his band to the attention of the American people from coast to coast, from the boundaries of Canada to those of Mexico.

The crowds that came to see and hear the Bunk Johnson Band were much the same as the crowds that later were to fill the concert halls and night clubs when the Lewis band made its tours through the country: young college students, scores of awed and happy young white musicians, and an older age group of the discriminating and scholarly. Many of them were hearing for the first time, during that 1945-46 period, true collective improvisation, and were completely enthralled by what they heard.

In 1956 a San Francisco night club owner said to me: "Trouble with the Lewis band is this: when George is here I get in one night more Phi Beta Kappa keys sitting at the bar, more crew-cut and horn-rimmed characters at my tables, than I get the whole rest of the year. Big crowds, and very intelligent crowds. Only thing is they're too intelligent to drink a lot of whisky."

The engagement lasted into January, the men returned home, and were then brought back again to New York by a commercial promoter, and after a few months, with the city still buzzing with excitement over their music, they returned to their native city and to what has always seemed an unnecessary five years of almost complete obscurity, as far as the world outside of New Orleans was concerned.

The entire band, Bunk included, were staying at Gene Williams's apartment. It was not an easy time for George Lewis. He had known strain, and little else but strain, throughout his life, but it had been the honest, uncomplicated strain of wondering where the rent, the coal, food, and clothes for his family, were coming from. True, he was surrounded by old friends. Lawrence Marrero, almost a member of the family, "Uncle

Lawrence" to Shirley; Jim Robinson, a neighbour and friend of many years with whom he had played on countless gigs; Drag was his friend and had been an idol of his childhood; he had known Baby Dodds for years and played with him many times. Alton Purnell, who came with them as pianist on the first trip, had been playing in New Orleans for years as a 'single' in various clubs, and was an integral part of their lives together in that city. There had been little friction among them; only shared hardships, shared pleasures, and common goals and destinies.

Suddenly they found themselves at the mercy of an arrogant, domineering, almost psychopathically jealous leader. They turned, as one man, to George, small, quiet, peace-loving, and he became the bewildered and unhappy comforter and peace-maker for a group of volatile, proud, and individualistic musicians who were finding that the greater their public acceptance, the more difficult their lives became, both at home with Bunk and on the platform.

Bunk had always been a heavy drinker. On the first trip to New York Gene Williams and Bill Russell were able to keep him under control to a certain extent. On the second trip the pattern appeared to be a clearly established one of alcoholism. He was obscenely profane, a habit that "upsetted" Lewis to the point of illness, and this profanity, used nightly on the stand towards the members of the band, was frequently far too audible for the comfort of those who sat nearby. That a leader might become upset at crowds who gathered around other instrumentalists in his band would be understandable, if this adulation were accompanied by any lessening of their acclaim for him. But he continued to be to the public the great and legendary figure of an early New Orleans musician, an alumnus of the Buddy Bolden Band, and the outstanding discovery of the century in the jazz world.

It always infuriated Bunk particularly when the crowd requested—as it did several times a night—George's "Burgundy Street Blues." "Now," he would say, "they wants to hear the ——— composer." And he would embellish his remark with certain verbal adjectival phrases that cast considerable doubt on the "composer's" antecedents, personal habits, and relationships with his family.

A young fan, Sam Rudovich, an almost nightly visitor to the Casino, whose patience had been wearing thin for some time,

overheard the remarks once too often. Only quick and timely interference of other nearby guests who dragged him from the stand kept him from knocking Bunk down. It was the first attempt made to slow down Johnson in his unreasoning tirades and, had it been carried out to its conclusion, might have been the best thing that ever happened.

Bunk's talents as a raconteur were not viewed by the members of his band with quite the tolerant amusement they were viewed by others. Many of the anecdotes he told they knew to be ridiculous and far-fetched. George squirmed with vicarious embarrassment at his bragging, and they all had inner shudders as they heard his needling of absent musicians, and statements that he had left other bands because "they didn't play so good." Many of the bands he sneered at had been among New Orleans's greatest.

As a result George drew into himself more and more, grateful to the public for its appreciation of his playing, warming to the friendship and the acceptance, but growing daily more homesick.

In 1960 Sidney Bechet's autobiography, a tape-recorded story, was published posthumously. It told a strange tale of Gene Williams and Bill Russell during this period, and the former's alleged attempts to "keep Bunk drinking" in order to control him and secure his services for recording. And, strangest of all, it recounted an attempt by Gene to have Bunk "seduced" through the co-operation of a woman friend. The entire story, as related by Sidney, came to him through Bunk, and in justice to Sidney, he may have believed the yarns to be true.

It seems unworthy of mention, yet it is brought out to clear the memory of a fine and dedicated young man. Told of Sidney's accusations, George Lewis almost stuttered in amazement.

"That's not true," said George. "It just isn't true. I know. I was there. Gene was a fine, good boy, and he loved Bunk. And Bill gave up his whole life to Bunk while we was there. There wasn't anything wrong Bunk could do, ever, no matter what, as far as Gene and Bill was concerned. Gene wouldn't ever do anything to hurt Bunk. And as for getting Bunk to drink, no one ever had to do that for Bunk. He could do that for his own self."

If there was difficulty on stage and back stage, and on the home front, the manœuvrings and intrigues going on in the ranks of the fans and those who wanted to "move in" and control the band were of such complexity that they became impossible to unravel before the men had played two weeks.

Alfred Lion, who wisely remained an amused onlooker at these antics, said: "There were cliques. Then there were cliques inside the cliques. And then inside those cliques there were more cliques. And sometimes it happened that people came to the Casino because they must see what their rivals were doing, and because they were afraid they would get ahead of them. The week before those rivals would have been in their clique. It was fan*tas*tic!"

It was shortly before Christmas that the sensitivity that had been George's outstanding characteristic throughout his life gave way under the bludgeonings of the leader for whom he was playing. He told his men, quietly, without apparent emotion: "I'm going home. I can't take no more."

He left the Williams flat in the blustery cold and found his way to Washington Square, where he sat for hours on a bench, unmindful of the weather. Every once in a while he would take the return half of his New Orleans ticket from his pocket, look at it, and feel better. He wept as he sat there, not only tears of deep hurt, but of reaction and relief that he was leaving at last what had become an intolerable mess. Before he left the apartment the men had joyously announced that they were going with him, but he urged them to stay in New York. Leaving would hurt them professionally, he knew. As for himself, he was past caring.

It was there that Bill Russell, with Baby Dodds, found him, and sat beside him and talked with him, and at last George put away the warm and comforting thoughts of home and agreed to stay.

"When I realized I'd be hurting Bill I come to myself and knew I couldn't go through with it," he said. "God knows I never wanted to do anything so bad in all my life as I wanted to go home. But if I had ever done anything—or ever do anything—to hurt Bill Russell, I couldn't live with myself for the rest of my life."

During that period the men went back to the apartment one night after work and found it locked against them. Bunk had hurried home earlier, in an uglier mood than usual, and secured the door. It was, of course, well past midnight and they had nowhere else to go. They returned to the Stuyvesant Casino and spent the remainder of the night on its chairs. Jim Robinson, the tallest, unearthed an old settee, on which he could stretch out partially, for a cramped, uncomfortable sleep. The next morning

they found lodgings elsewhere, and not until the return engagement in New York did they take up a communal and precarious life again with Bunk at Gene's. On this second trip a white player from Baltimore, Don Ewell, took Alton Purnell's place. Don is one of the most accomplished of all traditional jazz piano players, whose style, while definitely individual, is founded on the rhythmic figurations of earlier Negro players, Jelly Roll Morton, Tony Jackson, and the scores he must have listened to, and learned from, during the five years he spent in New Orleans after leaving the Baltimore Conservatory, turning his back on classical piano, dedicating himself to the freer forms of jazz.

At Christmas, George's loneliness for home reached its climax. Christmas carols rang across the unfamiliar snow; the hurrying New York crowds, in once-a-year good nature, streamed through the streets with harassed, smiling faces, arms piled with packages; traffic jammed routinely; there seemed no place, despite the scores of friends who sought to entertain the men and share the season with them, for a man whose heart was so far away.

In December the band recorded for Victor, and the first session fell on the afternoon of a day in which he had fourteen teeth extracted. For years his teeth had been "giving him fits"; in New York the pain and discomfort became almost unbearable. The small salaries which the men were making on that first trip did not allow for money to be sent home, plus civilization's most expensive necessity, dentistry. In New Orleans he had merely waited until a aching tooth became too much to stand, and then had it pulled. The money for the dentistry appeared suddenly and magically, through the efforts of New York admirers and friends. All the teeth, the dentist told him, must come out except two, to which a lower bridge could be anchored. Fourteen were taken out on what George describes as "the first pull" and he reported within a few hours at the recording studio. When the session began he found that all the tunes selected by Bunk had heavy clarinet solos. He says he was never so worried, not even after his chest injury, about his ability to play as he was that afternoon. That he overcame the handicap and the pain more than creditably is evidenced by the almost hysterical acceptance of his playing on these discs by traditional jazz enthusiasts, both in this country and abroad.

Just as Alice Zeno had never failed to give him her blessing before he played, ever since that first exciting engagement in

Mandeville in 1914, so she never failed in the years after 1946 to repeat a routine she started when he returned to New Orleans in January of that year. After the flurry of greetings was over, the questions asked and answered about the health and welfare of assorted relatives and friends, she would unbutton his shirt and with long, still graceful fingers, feel over his ribs and chest, searching for a gained pound, seldom finding it; judging for herself the pounds lost, talking to him as she had when he was a child.

"You're too thin," she would say. "You should not be blowing that horn. It's not good for you."

Then she would make another search, through his heart and his mind, for any hint of those things she had always fought so valiantly: pride and self-aggrandizement. When, as was only human, he would tell her of the things that had happened, of the acclaim and enthusiasm of the crowds for which he played, she would refrain from praise or comment.

"You are still George Lewis," she would say. "Remember that, son. George Lewis does nothing. It is God does it."

Her own pride, though, showed through in the comments she made of his father, and what she knew would have been that quiet man's deep joy in his son's achievements. In this way her conscience was satisfied.

five

THE crowd in front of the El Morocco Club at Iberville and Bourbon Streets in the New Orleans French quarter stretched half-way up the block. Those who comprised it were waiting for some of the more fortunate ones, already inside, to leave and make room for them. It was early 1950, and the club's proprietor was living on that particularly comfortable cloud all night club owners inhabit when they discover they have a hit attraction. Over the doorway and along the sides of the building huge signs proclaimed "The George Lewis Band."

A year before the scene would not have been possible. It had come about almost overnight, with the publication in LOOK

magazine of a picture article devoted to the Lewis band. The editors of that national magazine had sent a team to New Orleans with the happy assignment of finding the most authentic New Orleans musical group still playing. They returned with a full picture story of the Lewis group. Be it forever to the credit of the editors of the magazine that they did not seek help from any of the big-time agents, or from musicians, but instead gave instructions to their team to work independently. For many years fame for a musician or entertainer had lain in the hands of a small group of people: the big booking agents and talent bureaus, with their highly-paid, high-pressure staff of press agents, their interlocking relationships with radio and television producers. It was then, and it remains today—even more powerful— a smoothly running, well-oiled machine for the brainwashing of a hapless public that listens to what it is supposed to listen, sees the entertainers it is supposed to see, and which is expected to accept the views of the latter-day "critics" who go along joyously in the profitable company of the successful, and those responsible for their success.

When one considers the deliberate efforts made, as the years went on, to discredit the music that had surged up from the South, the contemptuous belittling of its forms and the build-ups of the more arranged, composed and stereotyped band offerings, the taking over of the name "jazz"—originally, certainly, far from the commercial product to which its name was being given —one cannot help but be reminded of the young lady who, having been forcibly robbed of her virtue, remarked: "The least he could have done was kiss me."

The public, however, showed that given an opportunity to listen to the music at its source, it would not only accept the pure and the unadulterated with enthusiasm, but would cry for more.

Many individuals have claimed credit for bringing the George Lewis Band out of New Orleans and to the attention of the rest of the country, beyond the boundaries of New York. None of these claims is valid. It was the picture article in LOOK Magazine, with its splendid photographs by Joseph Roddy, that worked the miracle. There were many who could have accomplished what this article brought about, but they did not bother. Among them were several who had come to New Orleans in the early days of the excitement over Bunk Johnson, and spent long hours with George Lewis, hours when he was tired

and exhausted from work but too polite to deny them, asking questions, "picking his brains," learning from him many facts they had never known about the music, and by which they would profit. These, of course, did not include his good friends, Stuart, Lion and Russell, or Rudi Blesh, who were primarily interested in recording, and who did all that was in their power to help him.

Within a short time after the article appeared the band was engaged for a run of several weeks at the El Morocco. A once-a-week radio programme was arranged, and ran for a year. By then the Lewis legend was well launched in Great Britain and Europe; Lewis records were at a premium overseas; the "Cardinal Blusicians" in Odense, Denmark, were about to perform the extraordinary feat of literally wearing through a Lewis record in an attempt to pattern their playing on its sound, but the American public had heard little or nothing of him since he had returned to New Orleans in the Spring of 1946, to his work as a labourer, and to the gigs and parades. Rudi Blesh had returned to New Orleans and recorded him for his Circle label; David Stuart was to record him again for his Good Time Jazz label, in 1950, but no efforts were made to bring the band out of New Orleans again, although New York would have welcomed them with open arms.

George had remained throughout the years the same quiet, soft-spoken, meticulously neat and conservatively dressed little man he had always been, leading his band with the surge and drive of a high-powered dynamo without apparently lifting a finger. Baby Dodds was in the north, and Joseph Watkins had joined the band as its permanent drummer, Alton Purnell as its pianist. Two things George Lewis insisted on, besides musical accomplishments: punctuality, and neatness and uniformity in dress. Unreliability, sloppiness—these were the cardinal sins he could not forgive. By these things, almost as much as by their music, did he feel his men would be judged by the public that now thronged to hear them and that waited on the street in long, patient lines. They were qualities that had been of paramount importance to him even in the early days of the yard parties and picnics played for his own people, when he had spoken with all the sharpness of which he was capable to musicians who reported for work unkempt or late.

George would no more wear the same suit for day-time activities that he wears when he is playing than he would, con-

ventional soul that he is, go out with no clothes on at all. No one has ever seen George Lewis throw a coat casually over a chair. Each night, before going to work, clothes are carefully inspected for spots or microscopic fragments of lint, shoes carefully polished. The same care is exercised with all his possessions. When a friend in Los Angeles complimented George on a brown suit he was wearing, which looked brand new, George said he had worn the suit for five years, and told how it had been purchased.

He had come home from a day's work on the docks late one afternoon, and, after washing up, sat down to rest and relax. Jeannette disrupted this programme. "We're going shopping," she said.

"No, we aren't," said George. "I'm too tired. What's so important you can't buy it without me?"

Jeannette did not answer, but instead pulled back a corner of the rug. Under it were green bills. She pulled it back farther and revealed more green bills, and much silver. George's eyes almost started from his head.

"Where'd you get all that money, Jeannette? What—what's it *for*?"

"I been saving it," said Jeannette. "For a long time. I knew you'd never find it there; it was the safest place I could think of. I've been saving it up so's you could get a new suit. You been needing one a long time. Let's go, George."

And once again George and Jeannette set forth together, this time without benefit of hatchet or towel-bound middle, this time to buy him the suit she had saved up for so carefully.

After their engagement at the El Morocco the band played for a while at the Mardi Gras, in the French Quarter. It was there that Ken Colyer, a slight, bearded, blue-eyed young Englishman found them, and—to quote him—sat down and "went into a trance."

Ken was Norfolk-born, with the Norfolk burr in his speech. He had been, at various times, construction worker, milkman, toolmaker, seaman,—and, primarily musician. His musical career had started when he was in his teens, playing cornet with the Crane River Jazz Band, leaving it to join the Christie Brothers, then leaving that group to go to sea again with the hope that some day he would be fortunate enough to sign on with a ship that would eventually reach New Orleans. Before he

reached New Orleans he sailed on ships that took him to Europe, Africa, and New Zealand, but at last the chance came for a berth on a tramp steamer taking cargo from Mobile, Alabama, to Venezuela. Ken was sent to join the ship in Mobile. He made two trips on her, but when she set out on her third trip Ken was on a Greyhound bus, bound for New Orleans without visa or clearance. He had waited as long as he could.

All of the English jazz public, and a good portion of the American, know the story of Ken's trip to New Orleans. How the young musician, the first white man ever to do so, played in a Negro funeral parade; how he defied the taboos and prejudices of that supposedly cosmopolitan city and sought out the music in the gathering places of its originators, and how, eventually, he spent six weeks in the city jail for jumping ship and remaining in the country without a visa, his release affected only after weeks of wire-pulling and effort. But before this happened he had realized an ambition that made him the most envied young man in all England's jazz circles: he had "sat in" with the George Lewis Band, playing beside that great trumpeter, Percy Humphrey. It was a ticklish situation. Then, as now, white musicians may not play with Negro groups in public. Nor could Negro musicians—nor can they today—mingle with the public or the guests. At all clubs in which they play they must retire between sets to a back room, usually unventilated, never maintained. The reaction to this time-honoured custom among Europeans who have come to New Orleans, and who later, in their own country, commented on it to us, was often one of horror and dismay. Most of them say: "We bow to the customs of the country in which we are travelling. But we do not return to the South."

Somehow Ken Colyer managed the near-impossible. Whether his unduly long incarceration in the city's bastille was a result of the defiance of New Orleans' ever-active "Black Code" can never be known definitely. Although there are many among the white people of New Orleans who deplore these things, its police are strictly loyal to the majority element which elects its officials.

As James Asman's letter showed so clearly the impact of Alfred Lion's Climax discs on the listening public, so Ken's letters, written to his brother Bill, without restrain or knowledge that they would ever see print, show the impact on a dedicated musician of listening to, and sitting in with, the George Lewis

Band. From photostatic copies graciously made available to me by Ken and his brother, I have selected a few paragraphs which show, only in part, his happiness and joy in that experiences, Alvin Alcorn had told him where the George Lewis Band was playing.

" *I said good-night to the boys and floated down to the Mardi Gras. The Lewis Band was playing as I walked in. I sat down and ordered a beer and went into a trance. Marrero was about five feet from me with Drag just behind him. Alton Purnell on piano just to the right, Joe Watkins in front, George, Percy Humphrey in a line just behind and to the left of Joe Watkins . . . At the end of the set I met them in the back room. They all shook hands but were very quiet and didn't seem to want to talk much . . . A fellow came in with a lady and started talking ten to the dozen. He was an ex-Whiteman drummer and started yarning about Bix and Gillette and so on. 'Do you use any of so-and-so's arrangements?' he asked. 'We don't use no arrangements,' says Joe Watkins tersely. 'We just play.' I spoke up quietly, 'Tha's the way it ought to be, man,' I said. The fellow laughed and carried on talking but I don't think he liked it.*

" *Lizzie Miles came in as the band went back on. She is a wonderful person and is helping me considerably.*

" *I sipped my beer and got sent with every number, the beautiful changing tone colours are a wonder to hear, and their effortless, seemingly casual teamwork works uncanny wonders at times.*"

Of the first time he sat in with the band, then at Manny's Tavern, Ken wrote:

" *Glory be! Mine ears have heard the glory of the Lewis band again, and I'm going to sit in with them Saturday night at Manny's Tavern! Can you wonder that, though I was dead beat last night, I only slept three hours and am now up and writing this at 8 A.M.?*"

"*. . . George gave me the wave and I got my horn out and tootled a little bit near the piano till they had finished the number. I felt absolutely calm and played like I was in a dream from the first kick-off. . . . Percy would just flip*

his finger at me when to take the lead and, man, it's a dream to play with these men, no fighting, no carrying, just sit back, relaxed, blowing easy and play the greatest horn of your life . . . Man, that was something, sitting there with George Lewis standing right alongside me and blowing all those beautiful things right in my ear. Percy on the other side, and I'm matching his tone and we're weaving all around one another . . . 'You're all right, man, you're all right,' said George, leaning over and patting my knee. Lawrence Marrero was chuckling away and I nearly floated off the stand."

" I would willingly go through all that frustration and yearning all over again to experience playing with these men."

There was no possibility now that the George Lewis Band would slip back into obscurity, at least in the foreseeable future. The eyes of the country had been focused on it through the magazine article; record-collectors had begun to spread the story, and tourists had carried stories of the band back to their own cities. A few years before Ken's visit to New Orleans George had been fortunate in receiving the help, in a managerial capacity, of a young Italian-American, Nicholas Gagliano, who had asked George to play at a dance being given by his church. Following the dance Nick found other engagements for the band, worked with George closely, and took over the responsibilities and what George calls the "worriments" of its affairs. After the LOOK Magazine article Nick followed through on the requests that flooded in for the band to play in other cities, setting up tours and night club appearances, and arranging his playing dates in New Orleans.

In 1950 Alice Zeno was eighty-seven years old. She had at last retired permanently. There had been previous retirements, the first when she was eighty years old. She and her son differed on how long that retirement had lasted, one saying two weeks, the other saying three weeks. A habit of work that had lasted almost eighty years was hard to break. But at eighty-four she finally conceded that possibly she was too old to continue to go out to work every day. She lived, as she had throughout her life, in the French Quarter, in a little upstairs one-room apartment at 910 St Phillip Street, surrounded by mementos of her son's

childhood, and of the Renshaw family, for whom she had worked for more than thirty years.

Packed carefully in a trunk in her room was a silk faille dress of soft salmon pink, yellowing now with age, bosom and sleeves carefully stuffed with tissue paper. Frequently, over her son's shocked protests, she referred to it, extracting from him the promise that when she died he would see that she was "laid out" in it. It was the wedding dress she had worn, more than fifty years before, when she had married a tall, handsome, reddish-skinned man with a deformed jaw, a quiet gentle man with whom she lived for ten years and never forgot, Henry Zeno. "I never took another man," she told the writer. "I never brought a second father under my son's roof." Had Henry Zeno known, in the last years of his life, that this dress, so carefully tended, lay waiting for his wife's last appearance on earth he might have been more reconciled to her refusal to return to him; might have realized that, although she may have been resentful and bitter at times, these emotions had not supplanted her love.

Alice Zeno had cause to remember many times in those days the words of Urania the morning George was born: "Call him George; this one will live!" He had fulfilled that prophecy, and had lived now for half a century, but he was very tired. Ahead of him there stretched the road "as smooth and pretty as anything you'd want to see." The dog had growled and then lain down again to let them pass. He had set down his heavy bucket, but his step was faltering as it approached the road that lay ahead.

Now at the end of a night's playing his breath was short, and his ankles were so swollen that when he took off his shoes at home there were cruel, ugly ridges in the flesh. He had had his first agonizing major attack of angina pectoris and it had left him weak and gasping and very frightened. There had been minor attacks of pain before that to which he had paid no attention. They were old acquaintances, George Lewis and pain, George Lewis and illness. And just when the load of worry should have been lifted from him, just when every hour's anxiety could harm him physically, Jeannette was stricken with the same trouble. Her heart, the doctor told him, was very bad. So now, with his feet on the approach to the smooth and pretty road, his heart was heavy with dread and worry, his step halting with physical weakness.

six

On October 10, 1952, the George Lewis Band played its first engagement outside of the South, and seven thousand people surged to their feet in the Shrine Auditorium in Los Angeles and shouted themselves hoarse at the conclusion of the performance. The occasion was Frank Bull and Gene Norman's fifth Jazz Jubilee in that immense building, and Frank had sent all the way to New Orleans for the Lewis band, and had assisted Nick in securing a stand of several weeks to follow in a Los Angeles night club, the Beverly Cavern.

"I thought I'd seen crowds," said George of the Shrine Auditorium engagement. "And I thought I'd heard applause. But I never saw or heard anything like that. I couldn't believe it. I tried to say 'thank you' to the people and nobody could hear me. I couldn't even hear myself."

The weeks at the Beverly Cavern saw the club jammed to the walls, and on week-end nights the line outside extended, as lines had done in New Orleans, for half a block.

And in Los Angeles, as in New York, the intrigues began all over again. Cliques within cliques, and the cliques within the cliques spying on all the other cliques. Jockeyings for position and for power and for control. Fans went to strange and unbelievable lengths to have an "in" with the band. One record company representative told me: "These people fight about which one's going to get to carry the band's laundry."

Through it all George remained the same quiet, quizzical, gentle person he had always been, not bewildered in the least, but detached, puzzled in many instances, frequently admonishing his men that the day would come when they would have to return to New Orleans and "adjust" to a different social climate; having no trouble whatever in adjusting himself to this new atmosphere, for he was little changed from the small boy who had been spanked because he didn't tip his cap and ask Miz Todd did she res' well last night, and who received chastisement or at least scoldings if he forgot his manners with anyone, white or coloured. He could remain aloof from the intrigues and the manœuvrings of the band followers, for he had in Nick Gagliano a bulwark and defence, and he always managed to avoid any decisions, apparently agreeing to everything, then

passing the problem back to New Orleans, for Nick to iron out. It required all the reserves that he had to merely keep going, although conditions were far different from those in New Orleans, with shorter hours, complete freedom of movement, more opportunities for rest.

He worried constantly, as he always had; worried about Jeannette, and Shirley, and his mother, never relaxing completely except for a little while after his weekly telephone conversation with Jeannette. He worried, too, about the success of the trip, not the financial success, for he blandly laid that on Nick's shoulders, but the over-all success from the standpoint of the public's acceptance, the profit for the people who were hiring him. As long as he had been treated fairly, and an employer had kept his word to him, George had always been delighted when those for whom he worked made money.

His conscience nagged him constantly, and without reason. One of the few times one of his sidemen was late in reporting on a date—a one-night engagement in Chicago—he said he almost "fell out" and I believed him, for I was there and saw his consternation. The consternation was not due to any worry over his musician, a man he knew to be well able to take care of himself, but because he had a signed contract calling for seven men to be on the stand at a certain hour, and here he was with six and there could conceivably be all kinds of a humbug. His efforts to please were composed not only of a natural wish to give pleasure, a genuine enjoyment of the happiness of others, but of a stern sense of duty with a capital "D," imparted by Alice Zeno when he was a child, and she taught him that to give less than one was being paid for was stealing, just as much as taking money from a man's pocket. No matter if the pay was small; if one had agreed to do a job for it, nothing less than one's best would do.

The band, a tightly knit unit always, became even more closely knit during these early trips on the road. They gave each other strength and reassurance in this strange new climate of tolerance and acceptance which they did not, could not, trust entirely, for there had been nothing in their lives prior to this to inspire trust in any but themselves. Their loyalty to George was almost fanatical. Each man leaned on this slight, quiet, frail leader as though he were a towering oak.

The year following the first Los Angeles trip the band played

in San Francisco and the representative of a large record company came to the club with an offer for a recording. There was an "if" however. "If," said the recording company representative, "you will hire somebody else in place of ———."

"I'm sorry," said George. "And I thanks you for your interest. But I'm not changing my mens." He did not even consult or notify Gagliano. This was his decision and no one else's, and at no time throughout his life has he tolerated from managers or employers any interference with the personnel of his band.

The band played four consecutive engagements at the Shrine Auditorium for Frank Bull's annual jubilee, each time to the same thunderous welcome and applause. They travelled extensively throughout the midwest and west, playing at a score or more universities, in night-clubs, and for civic concerts. Their first concert after their initial trip to the west coast was at Miami University, in Oxford, Ohio. They were brought there by the rector of the Holy Trinity Episcopal Church of that town, and by the head of the university's English department, Dr John Ball.

How deeply the Reverend Mr Kershaw entrenched himself in their hearts, how great and outgoing were his understanding and genuine love for these men, is best illustrated by the fact that after their second engagement in Oxford he was "the Rev." to every man in the band. George, Joe Watkins and Slow Drag Pavageau were the house guests of the Kershaws during their stays in Oxford, and there, more than anywhere else, did George relax, warmed by their friendship, feeling "at home" as he did nowhere else.

I accompanied the band on the third trip to Oxford, handling the details of a long and arduous tour. The trip started in Los Angeles, and before it had even got under way Lawrence Marrero had been taken ill, and flown home. His blood pressure had assumed such proportions that the doctor to whom I rushed him told me that it was imperative that he be sent home—by plane—immediately; that he was in grave danger any moment of a massive stroke.

To replace him for a portion of the trip, making the seventh man called for in the contracts, George asked for John Lucas, the wheel-chair-bound white trumpeter from Pasadena, severely crippled with arthritis. He would play second trumpet until they left for New York, when, if he responded to medical treatment,

it might be possible for Lawrence to rejoin the band. Lucas was George's especial care, and George scarcely let him out of his sight. They roomed together wherever we stayed. George remained awake and pacing the floor until three in the morning once in Chicago, until Johnny came rollicking home after a night on the tiles with friends.

"Johnny," said George mildly, "you shouldn't have done that." And when he told me of it he said: "And that Johnny, he just gave me that sweet smile of his, like an angel, like he'd just been out playing tiddley-winks. He's something, that Johnny. I really loves him."

It was during one of their trips to Oxford that the band made ecclesiastical history, when they played for a vesper service at the Holy Trinity Church. There has been much publicity about "jazz" activities in churches of late, but this was the first time that a jazz group had ever played at a church service. The performance was recorded and later issued on a record greatly sought by collectors, although it did not enjoy any outstanding commercial success. On this occasion the men were genuinely nervous. Some of the tenseness shows in the recording, but so does all of the faith.

Perhaps one can overdo the emphasis on faith. I do not know. I do know that for eight years I was more closely connected with the band than any other person; that I travelled with them throughout the country, not once but many times; that we travelled the length and breadth of Great Britain and over much of Northern Europe, and that I lived with that faith, saw it, felt it, and heard it, every day. Time and again I have been caught blushing, with Joe Watkins's stern eye on me, because I have been chattering away at the start of the meal before he had "asked the blessing." When George was critically ill in New York, Slow Drag told me— as simply as he would tell of going to the corner for a handful of cigars—that he had "talked to the Man" about it, pointing almost casually to the skies; Kid Howard's worn Bible was the first thing to be unpacked in every city. Lawrence Marrero, after an afternoon at Mahalia Jackson's apartment in Chicago, with Bill Russell and the members of the band, stated flatly that he was going back to church music and not play jazz any more. She had sung to them all afternoon, as only Mahalia can, of the God and the Jesus who belong so uniquely to them.

A few years ago the writer was scheduled for surgery. It was not serious, but it is not a prospect any of us enjoy. The night before I went into the hospital I called George long distance on a business matter. Before the conversation ended he said to me: "My mother says I should give you a message. She says for you not to worry about the operation. She says her Dr Jesus will take care of you and that she's praying for you."

My faith had been, let's admit it, in the skilled, trained hands of my surgeon. Yet I do not hesitate to say that I definitely felt better when I learned that the redoubtable Alice Zeno was also on the job!

This, then, was the George Lewis Band as it travelled in the first half of the 1950's around the country, playing to crowds that seemed to increase in every city; and which, in between tours, played seven hours and more a night in New Orleans clubs, under conditions that killed the music, and left the players disheartened, exhausted, and without spirit.

George Lewis was tired now, with a weariness that had nothing to do with work or physical exertion. He was tired with the exhaustion only those with a failing heart can understand, the tiredness of just staying alive.

"I'd have to lie in bed all day when I was home," said George. "Me, lying in bed all day! But I couldn't help it. I was downright ashamed. Then, even though I'd rested all day like that, when I'd get up it would seem like I was too tired almost to even get dressed; too tired to make the trip over the river."

So had his mother felt, decades before, when she had wakened in the morning and known that she must, somehow, marshal her strength for a ten or fourteen hour day in order to provide for her son.

And, after he had pulled himself together and managed to dress, he would work from 8:30 at night until 3:30 in the morning, never able to get home until nearly five; playing sets of 50 minutes duration, sometimes longer, with only a ten-minute break between. And playing them all, at the demand of the proprietor, at top speed because that was what the tourists wanted to hear. And then he would somehow make his way home and to bed until the next night. On the road he was better, for concerts last at the most three hours, night clubs in most cities have band hours of from nine until two, and he could finish work, eat his first real meal of the twenty-four hours, and be at his hotel and

in bed at an hour when he would still be waiting for a cab in New Orleans.

On March 2, 1952, he and Jeannette moved over the river to the suburb of Algiers. For the first time in his life he was in his own home. In the early forties he had applied for admission to one of the housing projects, and found a waiting list of hundreds ahead of him. The investigator from the project had come to the little French Quarter apartment and had seen Jeannette bathing the baby in a hand-basin, with water brought from the cistern in the yard, heated on the battered stove. The investigator had noted these things, and the outdoor toilets which had, George said, "special accommodations for children." She agreed that the little family was definitely eligible for housing. Periodically George checked at the project office, but no units were available.

They had saved money during the fatter years, and George had bought a lot in Algiers. Now he saw in the paper that a group of war housing units were being torn down, and the lumber and fixtures were for sale. It was good lumber, and they were good fixtures, for the houses had not had a great deal of use. He bought the lumber and engaged the workmen, and the house on De Armas Street in which he still lives began to grow.

If he was glad for himself, he was glowing with happiness for Jeannette and Shirley. There was a big back yard; the house had a wide porch in front; a living-room, dining-room, two bedrooms, an unusually large kitchen, and a back porch. He had always been a home-loving man, even when that home was a rat-ridden, roach-infested apartment in the French Quarter. Now he was a home-owner, and it was a home of which his wife, who had been through so much for him, could be proud; a place where his child could "feel the grass under her feet" and grow up in the sun and not the shadows of the city. It was the nearest he had ever come to the peace and happiness of the childhood days in Mandeville with his father. During the next two years he bought for Jeannette the things she needed now to make work easier for her, for she was increasingly troubled with angina and shortness of breath. There were, in time, a new washing machine, vacuum cleaner, electric refrigerator with freezer, a new stove. George kept chickens again, and one of his greatest pleasures was caring for them and watching them as they clucked busily around the yard. He could never kill them. This chore was left to Jeannette, who was more pragmatic in her approach to these

matters. Perhaps in gratitude the Lewis hens were always phenomenal layers, and Jeannette had an "egg money" fund of sizeable proportions.

It is true that he was a sick man, but he was also a happy man, able at last in the middle years of his life to do for those he loved. "To have someone you love need something and not have the money to give it to them, that's a mighty hurtin' thing," he had said.

Now at last he knew the happiness of giving.

seven

In September of 1954 George and his men were preparing for their fourth trip to the West Coast. They had already broken records for "standing room only" crowds in San Francisco as they had in Los Angeles, appearing at the Hangover Club on Bush Street to packed houses. George added, in that city, two people to the ranks of those whom he called "my friend," Charles "Doc" Daugherty, owner of the club, and Norman Pierce, record store owner, and a serious and enthusiastic student of traditional jazz. In San Francisco the band had at first puzzled the crowds who came to hear them and to meet them, as they had in Los Angeles. They quietly retired to the background after each set, and still unsure of themselves in a strange climate, they waited warily for others to make the first move. They did not have long to wait. Both Norman and Doc, with bluff, no-nonsense heartiness, dragged them out from their self-imposed seclusion. The San Francisco public is a more sophisticated, urbane, and worldly public than that of Los Angeles, and there was no political jockeying and behind-the-scenes manœuvring as there had been in southern California. The band was flooded with invitations, entertained and lionized, and George began then, as often as he could, to deputize the men in his band to accept the bulk of the invitations on his behalf, while he fought to keep his strength up with the rest he could not do without.

He was no longer a man who moved with cat-quick motions; he walked slowly now, still arrow-straight, but as though it was

an effort. Although he had gone back to a no-drinking régime after he returned from New York in 1946, he drank now because the warmth of the alcohol drove the cold of the outer world from his bones, cold that knifed cruelly through a body that had only a modicum of red blood cells in its veins. He drank, too, because stimulant was almost a necessity through the night, to keep him going, to give him the impetus not only to blow but to meet the never-ending questions, the long, and often tiring, importunities of well-intentioned fans. They recorded their second West Coast discs on that trip, for Antone records, a company founded for that purpose by Hilaire Brown, an official of the Standard Oil Company, for his young son and daughter. The name of the company is a composite of their names. Later Delmar bought the masters, a new company started by a young man, Robert Koester, of Chicago, starry-eyed with delight at having the George Lewis Band on his label.

With the exception of Alfred Lion's Blue Note and Bill Russell's American Music records almost every Lewis recording has changed labels a number of times. The tragedy of it is that in all these changes and sales of masters, not one penny has gone to George Lewis, for in the United States a musician sells property rights in his music when he signs a record contract, and despite repeated efforts on the part of the American Federation of Musicians, no legislation has yet been passed to put a stop to this, nor will a record company even discuss a contract that does not give it these property rights.

In September of 1954, a few days before the band was scheduled to leave for their trip to Los Angeles, I called George to discuss last-minute arrangements. I talked with Jeannette also, and tried to reassure her about her husband's welfare. She knew better than anyone how ill he was, but she also knew that the work on the West Coast would be far easier for him than similar work in New Orleans, and that the trip was necessary from an economic standpoint. She spoke with warmth and cordiality and a gentle humour. Then, as the conversation drew to a close, I said: "Don't worry, Mrs. Lewis. George will be in good hands. Everybody here loves him." Suddenly her voice changed. In it there were strain, worry, and love. Each word was sharply defined, and each word etched itself in my memory until I can hear them today as clearly as I did then.

"You all take care of that man," said Jeannette. "You hear?"

I had my orders.

They played on that trip in a club on Hollywood Boulevard, and again the long line of customers waited for tables. It was on this engagement that I looked about the room for a vacant seat for myself one night and saw one—just one—at a table occupied by a man I had noticed in the club almost every night. His absorption in the music was absolute, and I knew he would not even know it if I slipped into the empty chair. The band played "Just a Closer Walk With Thee" and he kept his eyes closed throughout, hands shading them. When it was over he looked at me, but I did not feel that he really saw me, and I noticed his eyes were moist. "I wonder," he said, and his glance strayed around the room, "if anyone in this whole roomful of people has any idea—any idea at all—of what he's hearing? I don't think so." Then I recognized him as the folk singer, Burl Ives, and knew that if no one else realized the beauty of what they had been hearing, he did.

On the morning of the eighth of October, Jeannette Lewis, in New Orleans, did an unprecedented thing. She stopped her routine morning house cleaning abruptly, turned off the vacuum cleaner, and leaned its handle against the dining-room wall. She walked to the back porch and sat on the top step, watching the chickens that clucked about the yard like gossipy old women, her eyes straying to the roof tops and the clear sky. Inside the house the telephone rang for a long time but she did not get up to answer it. Eventually she went inside. That afternoon the telephone rang again and she answered it. It was Lawrence Marrero's wife.

"You must have been out this morning," said Mrs Marrero. "I called and there wasn't any answer."

"I wasn't out," said Jeannette. "I was just sitting on the back porch. It's such a pretty day. I was just sitting there looking at my world."

Just before midnight that night Jeannette went into the kitchen of her home, the bright, airy kitchen with the big refrigerator, and the gleaming stove, looking as new and shiny as they had the day she and her husband bought them. She was searching for something to relieve what she thought was an attack of indigestion. Suddenly she dropped to the floor in a paroxysm of pain. An hour later, in a taxi on the way to the hospital, Jeannette died.

It was two o'clock in the morning in Los Angeles. George Lewis was playing his last set. Nick Gagliano put a person-to-person call in for Joe Watkins, so that he could break the news to George. He did not need to.

"I knew what it was as soon as Joe walked to the phone," George said. "I knew Jeannette had gone."

George was on a plane before daylight. Nick telephoned the next day, from George's house. "He just seems numb," said Nick. "He hasn't said anything at all. His mother's here with him." And I could see him as he must have been, quiet as always in grief, face a lined mask, eyes dead-black and without lustre, trying to accept the unacceptable, his mother close to him, hoping, as she had hoped when his baby had died, to help him to understand.

Later George said to me: "I knew I'd have to keep going, no matter what. I had to take care of Shirley. And I had to take care of my mother too; she was past ninety then and she stayed with us and tried to help. Seemed like I couldn't keep on without Jeannette, then I'd see my Shirley, and my mother, and I knew I had to. I had to be mother and father and everything to Shirley. At first I moved a little cot into her room and slept there so when she woke up in the night crying, like she did, I'd be there to comfort her and talk to her and get her to stop crying and go back to sleep." In his voice were the gentleness and compassion of the man he resembled so much physically, his Grandfather Zeno, that small, crippled, black man who, so many times a night, had crept quietly from his room in a Mandeville cabin almost a century before to pick up a child that had tumbled to the floor from a crowded bed, to tenderly put it back, and then to tuck the quilts around them all.

Five months later the tour which eventually took them to New York, for the first time since the Bunk Johnson engagement, began on the West Coast. It was the tour on which Lawrence was taken ill, and John Lucas engaged, and for four hectic weeks the band toured California, played a brief stand at the Beverly Cavern in Los Angeles and two special engagements at the Hangover in San Francisco, then on to Oxford, Ohio, for "the Rev.," three college concerts, and into New York for two months at Childs Paramount Restaurant.

Gilbert Milstein, writing in the Sunday New York Times on April 10, 1955, said: "George Lewis is a small, thin, infinitely

gentle and greatly talented jazz-playing clarinettist—playing," Milstein continued, "in a large, dim, green cavern at 43rd Street and Broadway." His description, both of George and of the club, was accurate. The Paramount had a capacity of more than 600 people, and each week-end the waiting line stretched up the stairs to the street. During the week, if not filled, it was more nearly filled than any other club in the city.

Again George found that there was not enough strength within him to meet the demands upon him without the aid of alcohol. It was all too evident that he was, without some crutch, close to collapse. And he leaned heavily on that crutch, for besides being a crutch, it was forgetfulness. Had he not dulled his memory, its pain would have been more than he could stand.

Shortly before the end of the engagement arrangements were made—to George's quiet delight—to record for Alfred Lion, the first recording for Alfred since the history-making Climax records. There can never have been a happier recording session than that one, held in a studio in New Jersey built by Alfred's engineer as an annex to his home. The full force of the Lion personality charged the atmosphere like electricity. Alfred, in the control room much of the time, would chuckle and grin through the takes and the playbacks, then suddenly, unable to contain himself any longer, would dart through the door and into the studio, laughing in great bursts of elfin merriment, saying: "Yes! Yes! Is good, George! Yes—I think we make it!" the band laughing with him without really knowing why. Throughout the session his partner, Frank Wolff, roamed through the studio, taking candid camera shots as they played.

These Blue Note records, despite George's ill health, are in this writer's opinion among the most spontaneous, powerful, and stirring ever made by the Lewis musicians. They are also, it is only fair to add, the first records on which George Lewis ever received a penny in royalties. He had been recorded many times. On two or three of these recordings there were royalty contracts, all of them ignored by the record companies, or so tied up with restrictive clauses providing that so many records must be sold before royalties could be paid, that there was little hope of any return.

Louis Armstrong was playing at Basin Street in New York at that time, and several times George and other members of the band had gone over at the completion of a night's work to talk

and reminisce with him. On Monday of the band's final week George received a telegram from Louis: "Am coming down to catch you cats on Wednesday night."

George had for Louis, as much as he has ever had for anyone, something close to hero-worship. Now they were both playing at leading clubs in New York—and Louis was coming to "catch" his band. It was a high point in his career, and George must have asked me ten times that Wednesday if I had made all arrangements for a reserved table for Louis.

George had been eating as close to nothing as a human can survive on throughout the engagement. At six o'clock that Wednesday night he consented to eat a "real meal, please." He ordered scrambled eggs. He said, as he ate not more than a third of the order, that he "felt fine" and at seven he got on the stand. On week nights the band played through the dinner hour, finishing at midnight.

At twenty minutes past seven I noticed that he was missing from the stand, saw him standing at the side of the room, saw a waiter go to him and lead him towards the back of the restaurant, met them, and walked with them to the rear and eased George, now gasping with pain, face distorted, fighting for breath, into a chair. From somewhere—and I have always wondered what it was doing in a New York night club—a canvas Army cot appeared.

I telephoned for a doctor, but did not tell George for I knew it would only upset him further. He was trying to ask me something but I could not hear and bent lower to catch the words. "Is Louis here?" he gasped. When I told him Louis had arrived a few moments before while I was telephoning, he said: "Want to see him."

On our way to George I had told Louis I had called a doctor, but forgot to warn him not to tell George. He stood over the pain-racked little man, big, gentle, smiling.

"Be up in a few minutes and play for you," panted George. "Had these before. It's nothing—go away soon."

Louis's smile broadened but there was pain in his own eyes.

"Stay where you are, man," he said. "Stay where you are like the lady says—till the man comes."

"*What* man?" And I saw the fear, and signalled frantically to Louis who back-tracked as best he could. "Never you mind

what man," he said. "You got nothing to do with it. You just stay there."

Dr Meyer Texon, whom I had called, was there in twenty minutes. His examination was brief, and so were his orders. "Hospital."

"No," gasped George. "No hospital. I—I—want to go home."

I knelt beside him so he could hear better.

"Not right now, George," I said. "Who'll take care of you? You're pretty sick, George."

He looked at me reproachfully. "My mother," he said. "My mother will take care of me. She always has."

It was then Louis took over.

"What are you talking about, man—going home!" said Louis. "Only way you going to get home is by doing what the folks tell you right now. You want to eat them good red beans and rice again, man? You do what the man says."

Perhaps Louis has never understood why I thank him every time I see him for what he did that night. That night when I thanked him he merely said: "Shucks! He's a home-town boy." I have never been able to explain that I was not thanking him so much for what he did; it had been a simple thing, requiring little effort. I was thanking him for the intangibles he represented, standing there sturdy and full of strength and with a smile that I know did as much for the sick man lying on the cot as the emergency injection the doctor gave him. I was thanking him just for being Louis, and that is a hard thing to put in words.

George was taken to Midtown Hospital, a private hospital on the east side, near the river and near the United Nations Building. He was given a private room, and all the busy, quiet, efficient bustle of a hospital floor when there is an emergency admission got under way. An oxygen tank rolled past me as I stood in the corridor. House-doctors strode in and out of the room on rubber-soled shoes. Inside I could catch glimpses of Dr Texon's head bent over the bed, and then a nurse came and told me there was someone in the lobby asking for me.

It was Alfred Lion, white-faced and anxious, laugh lines replaced now by worry lines. We sat there and waited together, and were joined briefly by George Avakian, then of Columbia records, and finally by the doctor.

He would not know until morning, he said. He was not certain now that it was a coronary occlusion, as he had at first believed.

In the morning he told me that there had been no occlusion, but that George had a critical virus pneumonia, with a blood count so low as to be almost unbelievable. This, I commented, was no doubt due to his habit of eating only occasionally. The doctor replied that this was not necessarily so; that nutritional anaemia was rare in the male, and there must be some other cause.

Alfred rushed to the hospital the next day bearing a cheque for a hundred dollars advance royalties, for which he had not been asked. Word of the illness reached the West Coast and letters poured in until the nurses threatened mutiny, but it was an idle threat, for if ever a patient was adopted whole-heartedly and with unstinted affection it was George Lewis, at Midtown Hospital. It was the first time George Lewis had ever known what it was to be accepted in a hospital as a person, and not a Negro. In New Orleans the coloured wards at Charity Hospital would have been open to him; in New York he could have had his choice. "These hospitals, outside of the South," he said to me, "they're just for sick people. I mean just people."

He weighed 96 pounds when he was discharged two weeks later. His blood count was still far below normal, and Dr Texon told him he must do two things—rest for a long time, not less than three, preferably six, months, and place himself in the hands of a competent physician.

The band had gone on to a month's engagement in Boston. George Guesnon, "Creole George," had joined them in New York to play banjo in Lawrence's place, and Lawrence rejoined the band in Boston. He was definitely not well, but there was no holding him at home. Tony Parenti took George's place as clarinettist. He was an old acquaintance of George's, a native New Orleanian of Italian parentage, whose playing approaches the source as closely as that of any white musician now alive, with the exception of Raymond Burke, who seldom leaves New Orleans.

The illness had cost George close to eight hundred dollars, every penny of the reserve he would have had to live on after he returned home, while he rested between engagements. Had the same illness happened today, it would have been at least a third again that amount.

Six weeks after he returned home he was back at work in a New Orleans club, no more fit to take the work—even under ordinary conditions—than a sick kitten is to take on a bulldog in

mortal combat. Yet "my Shirley and my mother" needed him. The burden of the need of others for him was a heavy one to carry physically. Spiritually it was without weight.

eight

On his fifty-sixth birthday George Lewis resembled nothing as much as he did a fly-weight boxer, fighting out of his class, battered and bruised by the heavyweight he had taken on, hearing the count of nine time and again and recognizing it, like a champion, as just one thing—a signal to get to his feet and keep on punching. Any referee would have called off the fight on humanitarian grounds.

Yet on each succeeding engagement his playing increased in power, his tone grew stronger, broader. With gratifying appreciation—and amusing lack of originality—three different critics used the three following phrases in describing the low register of his clarinet: "Wide, dark velvet," "Deep, rich velvet," and "Glowing velvet of the low register."

But there was no lack of hair-splitters. In 1957 a technique-minded listener sat next to me talking to me as one does to strangers in night clubs when one must, by force of circumstance, share with them a common table. "Where," said the listener, "does that man get that incredible tone? Where does it come from? Someone told me the other day he'd never had a music lesson."

I had heard the question so many times. There is an answer, but in most cases that answer would fall on deaf and uncomprehending ears. The question had come from musicians of every school, including the uncompromisingly classical, from critics and from fans, and even—though not as often—from the latter day "musicologists" whose first introduction to the music had been, for the most part, in the swing era, and whose real knowledge of it went back no farther than that.

"What I can't understand," continued my table companion, "is that this man Lewis doesn't breathe right. That isn't the way to breathe when you're blowing a clarinet. *I know*. I took lessons once."

When I recovered, I tried valiantly to keep my feelings out of my voice. To have tried to tell him where George Lewis learned to breathe so that he could hold a note until his audience shouted with excitement, to explain the lightning action of the long fingers that had come to him from Zaier and Urania and Alice, and how he had perfected it, would have been like trying to explain Mozart to a devoted rock 'n' roller.

"That he's breathing at all, young man," I snapped, "is a miracle. Just listen and be glad of it."

George had managed somehow that summer, after his pneumonia, to work at a New Orleans club until his physical condition became so handicapping he could no longer continue. He made a one night gig to Tennessee, travelling by bus all the way there and back, getting little or no sleep, and when he returned there was a nasal haemorrhage of such proportions that it was thought a blood transfusion might be necessary.

Angina pectoris attacks persisted; the swelling of his ankles became something he had to live with and not think about too much. The chronic cardiac cough continued, and the symptoms of anaemia were always present. No doctor who saw him afterwards ever understood why he had never heard that count of ten.

On the West Coast, where he finally arrived for a Los Angeles engagement, his condition improved as it always did. The swelling of the ankles subsided, there were no nose bleeds, and the cough was not as persistent. It was on this trip that Lawrence Marrero had the seizure that marked his last appearance with the band. I rushed him to the emergency hospital in Hollywood on the night of January first, after he had complained of dizziness on the stand. It was a trip not to be forgotten, for I have never seen such terror and fear in a human being as poor Lawrence underwent in that short time as paralysis gradually crept over him, until, when we reached the hospital, it had affected his entire left side.

I can still hear George's stricken whisper, see the numb grief in his face, the flat blackness of his eyes as, an hour later, he stood at the foot of his friend's bed and saw him go into frightening convulsions. "Brudder-in-law's going to die," he whispered. "Brudder-in-law's going to die." Lawrence was taken to the hospital, the paralysis wore off within a few days, but when he was discharged the doctor told George and me that the attack would definitely be followed by others, any one of which

might be fatal. He must not, the doctor said, leave home again or undertake the rigours and nervous strain of touring, or the irregular, long hours all musicians must live under. The attacks, he said, were due to what is called cerebral anoxia, the sudden constriction of arteries leading to the brain and consequent deprivation of oxygen.

Lawrence had many attacks, and frequent ones, after he returned to New Orleans, though he would not admit to them. He was heartbroken not to be with what he called "his" band. His very love and affection for the leader with whom he had been associated for more than thirty years may have led him to do the "hurtin' things" he did as time wore on, and he deluged friends and acquaintances of the band with long letters implying that his friend and leader had abandoned him. Doctors in New Orleans permitted him to return to light, untaxing work, and on a few occasions he played in New Orleans. So long as there was no nervous strain he remained in fair health, but was hospitalized following an attack brought on by nothing more serious than seeing a street fight half a block away during a Mardi Gras celebration. He pleaded near-destitution, yet during those years of long and serious illnesses for George Lewis, the combined family income of Lawrence and his wife must have been more than double that of George.

George has never forgotten, and never ceased to be hurt at, those who criticised him for not bringing Lawrence on his trips after that illness, who refused to believe that it was because he would not risk his friend's life. "I wouldn't have brought Lawrence no matter what folks said about me," said George. "I knew—it didn't take no doctor even to tell me—that Lawrence wouldn't last a month on the road. If anything had happened to Lawrence, I'd have blamed myself. But I hates to be thought a liar."

In the fall of 1956 George's physical condition became extremely serious. He was again working in a New Orleans night club, and the fight he was making now was for more than just strength, it was for physical survival. Nick Gagliano was making plans for a ten-day tour through the deep South, to be followed by a long-term contract at another New Orleans club. On the tour, travel would be by bus, and the chance of George receiving decent medical care in that part of the world, in the event of an emergency, was far from certain.

A three-months engagement was offered on the West Coast, at the Tin Angel, in San Francisco, and I accepted it. I knew the schedule mapped out for George in the South was a suicidal one. Almost daily, letters came from various members of the band begging me to get them back to the West Coast, and those who did not write to me sent messages through those who did.

I learned of George's physical condition through talks with him on the telephone, heard the sickness in his voice, and heard him say that he had not been to a doctor, and "wasn't going to go," because, he continued, "it wouldn't do any good. Plans are all made."

In a panic I telephoned the one person in New Orleans to whom I felt sure he would listen, Mrs Myra Menville. She had been one of the early founders and most active members of the all-white New Orleans Jazz Club, and she had been indefatigable in her efforts to obtain the recognition for Negro musicians that was their due, and for fair play for them. I did not know a musician who was not grateful to her, and who did not have a real affection for her. Once before she had prevailed upon George to go to a doctor, and I felt that she might be able to perform the same miracle this time.

She performed the miracle, and managed to convince George that he must report to the doctor he had seen before, Dr Maurice St Martin, a cardiac specialist. After he had examined George, I called him and was told that George had been ordered to stop work entirely for an indefinite period, and that he was in a serious condition. The ten-day tour was cancelled when his report was given to Nick, and the club engagement postponed.

The band, without George, came to the coast, stopping first to play for their good friend, Marty Hetzel, at Chicago's Hunt Club. Mrs Peggy Tolk-Watkins, owner of the Tin Angel, and a woman of deep understanding and sympathy, agreed to the substitution of Bill Shea for George Lewis for the first three weeks. When he learned that Bill Shea was to take his place, George relaxed considerably. Bill was "his friend." Bill had spent many months in New Orleans, almost living at George's house, travelling with George on gigs and to picnics, and following every parade, and George and Jeannette had come to regard him almost as a son. Bill absorbed from George all that he could of knowledge and skill, and was almost speechless with delight when he learned that he was to take George's place at the Tin Angel. Kid and Jim

remained in New Orleans, with Thomas Jefferson and Robert Thomas taking their places.

Ten days after the band opened at the Tin Angel, George arrived in Los Angeles for a three weeks rest in the Central California city in which I lived. When he arrived, and I watched him walk from the plane to the airport, I thought the gusts of wind that swept it might take him off his feet, he seemed so frail, so weak. I was almost frightened on the hundred mile drive north. His voice was barely audible, and I could sense the exhaustion in every move and word.

Yet he fumed and fussed because he was not with his band, and I lied like the well known trooper and told him that the contract did not call for his appearance for three weeks, and then only on two nights a week until he was stronger. This made him feel a little better, and it was then the psychological change that was to make so much difference in the years to come began to be noticed. He slept from twelve to fifteen hours a day for the first two weeks. He reported to my doctor, who told me that George's heart action was the most exhausted he had ever heard, its muscle showing all the resiliency of a piece of wet blotting paper. He said to me in a puzzled tone: "I don't think, in thirty years of practice, I've ever heard anything quite like it. And, of course, he hasn't enough red blood corpuscles to keep a sparrow alive. The question is not so much one of what is the matter with him, but a real scientific curiosity as to what is keeping him in a vertical position."

One could see the realization dawning slowly in George's mind that rest was not something one did only in one's grave. That a vacation was not a luxury reserved for the other half of the world, and that to do nothing was not necessarily sinful. It was, he said, the first time he had ever taken a vacation; rested for the sake of resting; sat in the sun and let its warmth and strength seep into his bones, with no thought that within a few hours he must work or search for work. Slept with no need to think of tomorrow's labour.

He returned to work gradually, first for two nights a week, then for three, and finally full time. The old troubles returned, and there were several angina attacks. At the end of the year, he returned to New Orleans after a series of them had put him to bed for three days. At George's request, a new contract was drawn up for the band to remain on with Joe Watkins as leader.

Almost immediately Alton Purnell gave notice, and left for Los Angeles where he had always wanted to live, and where he lives today. His place was taken by Don Ewell, the same man who had played with the band on the second New York engagement with Bunk Johnson. The first time I saw him, after he had joined the band, he told me that there had never been and he did not think there ever could be a musical experience more thrilling for a dedicated traditionalist than playing with the men in the Lewis band.

After George had returned home I received a telegram from Berta Woods, jazz writer in Los Angeles, relaying a cable she had received from Manchester, England, asking her to find out if George would consider a tour of England in the spring, playing as guest artist with a British band.

That this had never happened before had always puzzled me. True, I was aware—painfully aware—that not only did the big agencies control almost every major outlet for jazz in this country, but the British-American exchange programme and European tours as well. Yet I knew from the fan mail and press cuttings George received from England that his appearance in that country would be the next best thing to a happy judgment day for the jazz-conscious Britons. The offer came from a young Manchester promoter, Paddy McKiernan.

The problem, of course, was George's health, and the certain knowledge that not to take the trip would come close to breaking his heart. I laid down certain rigid restrictions on playing time, begged McKiernan's cooperation in curtailing social activities, in fact, any activities besides the actual playing, and received his complete agreement. Stuttering with excitement I called George.

George has always had a characteristic manner of receiving good news. There is at first a barely perceptible pause while the quick mind turns the news over, examining it for flaws, not quite trusting its validity. Then, satisfied that it is what it appears to be, the wide, warm smile, and the assent: "I'd *like* that!"

Over the telephone I felt the pause, heard the delighted assent, then a sudden misgiving. "If," said George, "I can play with Ken Colyer."

There was more red-tape-type trouble involved in getting the trip under way than it would be possible to recount in just one book. It was necessary to guarantee, by contract, a similar number of concerts for Ken in this country; and, to make sure

that the contract would be lived up to, necessary for Ken to receive a visa. The State Department, for several weeks, took a dim and discouraging view of Ken's previous unofficial sojourn in the United States. Finally the tour had to be postponed for thirty days, but at last all needed approval was secured.

And so, on April 10, 1957, George Lewis boarded a BOAC plane in New York as a first-class passenger, settled down in the deep comfort of its seats, ate of the many-splendoured meal which it provided, and drank its excellent liquor. Then, yawning contentedly, he settled back to sleep for the remainder of the trip, an over-all thirteen hours in those pre-jet transport days.

"Excited?" he said. "Of course not." And never closed his eyes till the plane set down in Manchester.

As it taxied to a stop a familiar sound could be heard faintly. The stewardess rushed to a window.

"It's a band!" she cried. "A brass band. They must be meeting someone on the plane." Then she caught sight of George, who was managing somehow to look vaguely guilty.

"Why!" she gasped. "It's you! You're—you're George Lewis. I mean *the* George Lewis!" Flustered that she had not connected the name on his ticket with the name she had seen for weeks on the hoardings in her country, she fluttered about like an excited wren.

The plane had stopped. The doors were opening. Far in the distance against the hangars, a crowd of people had gathered. In front of the crowd was a smaller group, close together. Even at that distance the blond beard of Ken Colyer was recognizable.

"It's Ken," breathed George, and as he stepped through the door and stood for a moment on the top step, tears welled to his eyes. The sound of the brasses and the drums of Ken's band rolled across the intervening space, warming the air, chasing the fog. hurting with its gladness, as the boys wailed and shouted with their instruments the grand old hymn—"Gloryland."

nine

WHERE it had once been Mandeville, Ponchatoula, Slidell, Pass St Charles, Gretna, now it was Newcastle, Edinburgh, Glasgow,

Manchester, and the great grey cities of the English midlands, and on in to London. Wherever he went the warmth of the love and appreciation of those who came to see and hear him was a tangible thing, flowing from the audience to the stage at every concert; he could feel it like the glow of a fire.

In Manchester there was the astounding sight of the British audience that packed the Free Trade Hall surging to its feet in spontaneous cheering tribute to the little man who smiled at them all as he smiles at those he calls "my friend," not shyly, but widely, and who, at the same time, saw those thousands dimly through tears he could never seem to hold back.

In England, and later in Europe, an audience to George Lewis was never an impersonal thing, a massed sea of people. It was always the individuals that made it up. Out there, before him, were the youths and girls, the young men and women, who had written him the letters he had found waiting when he came home from the docks not so many years before, aching with tiredness, letters that had travelled over an ocean and across a continent. They were letters written by young people who had saved and sacrificed to buy his records before they were in general distribution in their country, and who, when they had bought the records, heard and responded to the message of his music. And now they were as happy as he was that at last he had been able to come over the sea and play for them and try, somehow, to show his gratitude.

And there were "his boys," the men of the Ken Colyer band, each in his own way a pioneer in his own country in this music, for each of them had played the music of George and his people since their hands were strong enough to handle an instrument. Ian Wheeler, Johnny Bastable, Colin Bowden, Ron Ward, Mac Duncan, Bob Kelly, all of them nervous almost to the point of collapse at their first run-through rehearsal, relaxing at last under the quiet, fatherly affection of the man they had held in such awe, the man who carried what was at times the irksome burden of being a living legend.

"Just go on your own way, boys," he said quietly. "I'll go along with you."

They adored him.

The British traditional jazz public had been treated to a variety of American musicians. Some had left them disillusioned and unhappy. Louis Armstrong's friendliness and warmth, Big Bill

Broonzy's outgoing, uninhibited appreciation, had spoiled them. They had thought all coloured musicians were like Louis and Bill. But they had also been treated to the strange spectacle of a New Orleans Negro musician, then resident in France, shutting himself in his dressing-room after a performance and, after he had rested, announcing with lordly importance that he would "receive the press." Then announcing again: "Now I'll see the musicians. Just the leaders. And one at a time." There had been the New Orleans musician who had been rehearsing with a British band for a European tour who turned to the drummer and said. "Who the hell you trying to be? A small town Baby Dodds?"

The frail, gentle, quiet George Lewis hit them with the impact of a bomb. They told me, many of these fans, that they had thought he would be like that; it was what they had heard of him, when they did manage to get word from some fellow countryman who had met him in the United States, but they could not be sure until they actually saw him. And over and over, in the accents of the Scot, the Lancashireman, the Yorkshireman, the Londoner, I heard the quiet words: "He is more than a great musician. He is a great man."

Backstage at a London concert a couple of such high degree as to be entitled to be identified as Personages invited him to join them after the concert. "I can't," he told me when I conveyed the invitation. "Tell them, please, that I thanks them very much and I'm very sorry, but I promised my boys I'd go someplace with them afterwards."

Ken, standing nearby, overheard him and called me over, grinning from ear to ear behind his beard. "Tell him," said Ken, "by all means to accept the invitation. We've got weeks ahead of us to go places. We can postpone tonight's date to next week."

I told George, but he was not happy about the situation, and at first refused to accept, only agreeing after a long and serious conference with Ken and repeated reassurances that it would be all right. Twice during the evening he turned to me and with a troubled frown said: "I sure hope none of those boys were hurted."

Early in the negotiations I had stipulated that George could not play more than four concerts a week at any time, preferably with a night off between. It was not an easy requirement for a promoter, but McKiernan agreed. Later promoters were to cry

almost tearfully: "But we can't make any money that way!" To which I invariably replied: "Neither can George. But he can keep playing—and stay alive." Other artists in both Great Britain and Europe were sent out on tour schedules that called for, in one instance, 15 concerts in fourteen days; Louis appeared on a tour on which he played twenty-two concerts in eleven days. A little mental arithmetic will show quickly why George Lewis does not have the economic security and the worldly goods that others of his professional stature have been able to acquire.

There was never any question about George's availability for signing autographs, though at first I was fearful of this added strain after a concert. If there was anything he loathed it was musicians who accepted the favours and praise of the public, then withdrew. The only time throughout the trip that I saw George angry was in an English midlands city where a ruling, brought about by an unfortunate incident some months before, forbade any member of the audience to enter the backstage area at any time, or to gather about outside for autographs of visiting artists. In spite of the ruling, the audience—it appeared to be the entire audience—was waiting at the stage door when he at last emerged. The theatre management was ready for them with three sturdy Bobbies, all topping six feet. They escorted George, a small, brown, unhappy figure in their midst, to a waiting cab. Few people have seen him more upset. "They've waited so long," he said. "It's not fair. The folks other places never gave trouble, and they wouldn't have here. I don't like this. I don't like it." And he waved at them disconsolately and blew a kiss or two from the cab windows.

It was in this same city that I also was as upset as I had been anywhere on the trip. An appointment had been made for a reporter from a local paper to interview him before the performance. One of the smaller rooms backstage, with a piano in it, was made available. George sat on the piano bench and I sat quietly in a corner. I had followed the profession of journalism for eighteen years, and I never ceased to be fascinated by the manner in which young British reporters went about their jobs. Never, even in my most youthful and fearless days, would I have had—or my colleagues either— quite the brashness, the temerity, the aggressiveness shown by the supposedly conservative British.

George had an unlighted cigarette in his hand which he

continually twisted round and round in his fingers nervously. He never had the opportunity to light it. From the start it was obvious what the journalist was attempting to do. Each question was more laden with dynamite than the one before. It was all too evident that he was going to go back to his paper with a story loaded with controversy or die in the attempt. His questions were phrased in the manner of the time-honoured trick question: "Have you stopped beating your wife?"—and any answer to any question would have furnished a headline. "Do you think Louis Armstrong is still the best trumpeter? Who has the best band in the United States today? Do you think Kid Ory is too old to play? Tell us about conditions in New Orleans for the Negroes. Do you think modern jazz musicians are as good as the traditional?"

It was not long before I had twisted my legs, in an agony of nerves, so tightly around the legs of the chair in which I sat that they bore the marks for hours. I did not want to interrupt but I could feel a hot tide of anger mounting. "THIS is British fair play?" I wanted to shout. Then, just as I had begun to untwist my legs preparatory to rising to my feet and putting a stop to the torture—and in all probability tossing the young man out bodily, so high was the concentration of adrenalin in my blood stream—I suddenly realized there was no need to do this. That George was handling the situation with all the skill and agility of a championship tennis player. Each vicious, whistling serve was stroked back over the net to his opponent, each tricky return back-handed gently into the reporter's court, just out of reach. I held my breath and my anger began to cool. It cooled entirely and dissolved into almost hysterical laughter at his last, despairing question, and George's answer.

"What bands do you like to listen to best?" he asked.

George answered smilingly, fully aware of the spot he had been on for the past half hour.

"I likes them all," he said gently. "Louis, Turk, Dizzy, Kenton —and when I'm home I always watches Lawrence Welk on Wednesday night."

The journalist fled.

One of the warmest memories that he brought back from that first trip was of the night he played as guest artist with the Chris Barber Band, and the buffet supper the boys "laid on" for him afterwards, and he has never left home since without the clarinet

case the band gave him, the kind he had always wanted, one that would hold two clarinets.

The afternoon of the concert I sat in the auditorium listening to the rehearsal. Beside me sat a good-looking, blond, somewhat attenuated young Englishman with blue eyes and finely modelled features. He gulped rather often, and he blew his nose rather often, and at last he turned to me in embarrassment and said, "I'm sorry, you know. Can't seem to help it. Sitting here like this, hearing that great tone, knowing it's George Lewis. Name's Monty Sunshine."

Monty was Barber's clarinettist and a few years later in Monterey, California, he and George played at the same performance at the Monterey Jazz Festival. Back stage he told us: "Never thought that day in England I'd ever be here. All the time I was out there in front, and knew George was back here, I kept telling myself 'you're in George Lewis's country now, and George is back there listening to you and hearing you.' I tried to play better than I ever had, tried to make every note just so. Wanted to for George, you know."

The night of the English concert Ottilie Patterson, singer with the band and now Mrs Chris Barber, broke down and had to stop and fight for self-control before she could finish singing "Just a Closer Walk with Thee."

"What happened?" I asked her afterwards.

Her eyes were still suspiciously red. "I couldn't help it," she replied. "I was all right at first, and everything was going fine, and I could hear that beautiful clarinet singing along behind me and with me. Then all of a sudden I heard George's voice, very soft, giving the responses 'walking with my Jesus—talking with my Jesus' and—well I guess I'd just had it. I broke up."

Break-up or not, she brought down the house that night.

By the end of the tour, which culminated with three days in France where George played in Paris for Radio Free Europe, and at a concert in Arras, fatigue had begun with nagging fingers to strip the protective covering from the super-taut nervous system that was George Lewis's especial burden. There were three angina attacks, two in France and one in Manchester, and without consulting him I made reservations on the Cunard Line's *Mauretania,* for I felt that the rest and relaxation were essential before he faced the responsibilities at home. He was desperately tired.

He boarded the *Mauretania* in Southampton on May 8, and took to the life of the ship as a first class passenger as though he had been born and grown up to it. The first time I ever saw George Lewis step on a stage and take quiet command not only of his band but of a crowded club full of people I thought, with some astonishment: "Good Heavens, this little man has the dignity of ten thousand emperors." That thought, that first impression, has come back to me hundreds—perhaps thousands—of times since that first night. I have never seen him at a loss, never seen him lose that dignity, whether it was at an all-night hamburger stand in Los Angeles, in the great hotels of Europe, the quiet formality of a British liner, or standing before an audience of seven thousand people, all roaring at once. I remember one circumstance in particular when a fellow passenger on a trip to Europe happened to be a loud-voiced, constantly-talking woman from the South, whose strident tones could be heard from the first-class smoking-room to the rear of the tourist lounge, and who selected as her subject one afternoon, talking to a group of fellow passengers not fifteen feet from George, how much her daddy had respected the "Nigras." He had always taught her, she said in a near roar, that "we need them just as much as they need us."

George rose with quiet, unobtrusive dignity, and walked from the room. Later he said: "She upsets me. I'm afraid everybody's going to think that all the folks in our country are like her."

The first two days on the *Mauretania* were sheer heaven; the quiet; the smoothly running daily schedule of a great ship; the thoughtful, friendly service, and—at last—the regular meals. George had long since succumbed to the habit of breakfast in bed on the road, but only on board ship does he adopt the custom of more conforming humans and eat three regular meals a day.

The afternoon of the second day out he was troubled with a painful leg; by night the pain was intense. That he did not speak to me for several hours after I called the doctor was unimportant; I knew there was something seriously wrong. He had, the doctor said, a bloodclot in the leg. Complete rest in bed for the remainder of the trip and only limited use of the leg for some months thereafter. If he did not remain in bed it might be necessary to confine him to the ship's hospital, I told him mendaciously.

He remained in bed.

"If they'd put me in the ship's hospital," said George, "I'd have fought like a tiger." Adding with due attention to exactitude: "A *little* tiger."

Two days before landing, George had a severe angina attack. I flew for the doctor, met the nursing sister, together we routed him out, and together we ran in single file through the ship's corridors, downstairs and around corners, the doctor first, the nursing sister second, while I brought up the rear. The doctor's words floated back to me as we made one corner without even shifting gears: "This is what I've been afraid of," he said. "Wacky heart. Very wacky heart. These clots move." The doctor's white coat billowed like the sails of a clipper ship in a strong wind, the sister's veil stood out horizontally behind her in the breeze of her going, and, heart pounding with fear, I remember thinking: "If anyone opens an outside door and lets the wind in they'll take off like jets."

After it was all over, and George had been sedated and was sleeping, I lay in my own stateroom on the other side of the ship and thought of Alice Zeno and wondered if once again she knew, as she had known when he was a child, that the son she never called anything but "my boy" even when he was 57, was dangerously ill on the high seas. She did, I learned later.

He left the ship in a wheel-chair, and the next day hobbled through the Pennsylvania Station with a cane. We took the freight elevator to the train level to avoid the stairs, and I could not help thinking as it rumbled slowly downward that in New Orleans all his people travelled in them much of the time; there in that city that held everything that was dear to him they must all take the freight elevator when they played in hotels, use the side entrances to most studios and concert halls, and the back entrance to white homes or country clubs, while white musicians playing the same engagement came through whatever doors they wanted to. Yet I could not wonder, as many do, at his anxiety to return. These things meant nothing compared to the sight of Shirley, the sound of her exultant "It's *Daddy*!"; the loving probing of his mother's fingers as she felt over his ribs in search of a gained or lost pound, the warmth and brightness of the home he had built. He had never been able, economically, to leave there and chance the ups and downs of the music world with a body that might or might not get him through an engagement. There security dwelt in certain form. The roof over his

head was his own, paid for and without mortgage; and in the backyard were turkeys and chickens, albeit only as friends and potential producers of eggs, and not as sources of nutriment.

As for the other aspects of his life there, he had long since detached himself from them spiritually. He had only to take a train or plane or ship to leave them behind, but he knew that in doing so he would leave behind a need for him that mattered more than anything else. Some day, he told himself, some day, when there was no need of him there, but it could not be now.

"Let me show you, ma," he said the night he got home. "They took these pictures when I landed in Manchester with Ken's band there to meet me—and these in London—and—"

She stopped him gently.

"Who are you, son?"

"I'm George Lewis, ma," he said, and smiled for he knew what was coming.

"God's child, son. No different, no better, than anyone else."

"I know that, ma. I know. I never forgets."

ten

As the train from Liverpool was pulling into Euston Station, London, one Friday afternoon in January of 1959, the conductor made his way to the compartments where the George Lewis bandsmen sat in nervous expectancy, and asked them to keep their seats after the train had stopped, and to wait for his return before they got off.

"There's some mix-up in meeting the train," I thought, and said so to the men. They had arrived in Liverpool the day before: George Lewis, Joe Watkins, Kid Howard, Big Jim Robinson, Slow Drag Pavageau, and Joseph Robichaux. George, Kid, and Jim had marched in parades together, ridden in tumbledown jalopies to gigs in the backwoods country of the South, played before packed thousands in big cities in the United States and now, along with the other three men who had shared the latter experiences with them, had just completed a seven day trip on the Cunard liner *Carinthia*. It had been a memorable week.

One of the officers on that trip was Mr Charles Day, who had turned the "Mauretania" upside down to take care of George during his illness, and the staff of the *Carinthia* had been alerted, flowers in George's stateroom when he boarded, and in mine, and the ship became, for the men, a home in which they settled down as though it had been waiting for them all their lives.

Rather tentatively the purser asked me, just before New Year's eve, if I thought the band would mind playing just a bit on that occasion. "We would all fell greatly honoured," he said.

The vote to play was unanimous. There was an "if" stipulated by George. "If," he said, "we can play for the folks in the tourist and if we can play for the crew."

They played for every soul on board, but the performance they talk about the most is New Year's Day night, when they played for the crew. The captain had broken out champagne for them the night before; the crew all but drowned them in beer, and uproarious appreciation. They were to play one hour. They played—to Mr Day's distress and horror—two and one half hours. But he could not stop them, and finally settled down in philosophical and kindly resignation to have, as he had the night before, a ball himself, listening to the George Lewis Band at its uninhibited best.

Now it was a different George Lewis from the sick, exhausted man whose care Mr Day had overseen so kindly and meticulously on the *Mauretania*. A year and a half had passed, and it had been, perhaps, the most important period of George Lewis's life, for it marked the first time he was able to walk with steady, strong steps along the long road that was as "smooth and nice and pretty as anything you'd want to see."

It was nearly a year after his first tour of England before George was able to fulfil his contract calling for an equal number of concerts in the United States for a British musician. The contract had stipulated thirty days. It was three hundred and sixty-five before Ken Colyer stepped from a BOAC plane in Boston, Massachusetts, to join the Lewis band for a three weeks tour of New England colleges with the Rev. Alvin Kershaw—the men's beloved "Rev."

Mr Kershaw was now rector of All Saints Parish in the lovely town of Peterborough, New Hampshire, and the tour was given under the auspices of an interdenominational Christian fellow-

ship group, with branches in the student bodies of the majority of large colleges.

George had played one date since leaving England, the opening performance of the Newport Jazz Festival, on July 4, 1957. It was Louis Armstrong's birthday, the entire evening was in his honour, and this, more than anything else, made George insistent upon taking the trip, regardless of the doctor's orders. While the journey was fruitless from the standpoint of being any professional help to the band (which I had hoped it would be) it had one effect that will never be forgotten. The crowds of young people who attended that opening night of the Newport Jazz Festival had, many of them, come no closer to traditional New Orleans music than the arranged, solo-studded playing of a college Dixieland combo, or a "Clap hands, here comes Charlie!" commercial group. And they had been well conditioned by those who, in these latter days, seem to delight for some obscure reason in the ambiguous label of "musicologist." (One wonders if the next tortuous step will bring us "musiciatrists.") These had done their best through the years to plant firmly in the mind of the young public that to like this music was quite all right, providing one realized that actually it wasn't *really* music, and that one must assess it objectively and intellectually for what they insisted it was worth: "primitive" and non-intellectual.

The crowd at that Festival, forgetting entirely that they were betraying their mentors and brain-washers, expressed their appreciation in wave after wave of thunderous applause. Even George inured by now to receptions like this, was astonished. "Seems like those young folks never heard anything like it before," he told me later. "Like they were hearing something brand new."

In Europe, George overheard one of the best known white American progressive musicians of the cool school, who attended a Lewis concert, say to a reporter: "Yes, indeed. I rather enjoy this sort of thing sometimes. This is 'fun' music."

"Damn!" said George out of the corner of his mouth, in one of the few unfavourable comments I have ever heard him make about another musician. "I sure wish I could get him on a stage with my mens for fifteen minutes. He'd find out what 'fun' music is. He'd be sweatin' before he was up there five minutes."

The reviews of the Lewis performance at the Festival were almost without exception enthusiastic, in many instances extreme-

ly enthusiastic. Even that staunch upholder of modernism, "Metronome," beat the drums for the Lewis band. Whitney Balliett, jazz writer for the New Yorker and one of the very few in the United States today who brings to his writings a keen perception and thorough knowledge of the subject, made the astonishing statement that the presence of the George Lewis Band at Newport that year "saved the Newport Jazz Festival."

The following year when I queried the man responsible for booking attractions for the Festivals about a return engagement in 1958, he changed the subject abruptly and did not even discuss it. Fuming with righteous indignation, I told George what had happened and he looked at me in genuine surprise.

"Why I never did think anything different would happen," he said. Naïveté is not one of George Lewis's outstanding characteristics.

During the period we were on the East Coast I met with Harold Pendleton, when the band played a one-night engagement at the Central Plaza in New York, and plans were made for the National Jazz Federation of England, of which Pendleton was the director, to bring the entire band over for a tour of Great Britain the early part of 1959.

Six weeks after he returned from the Festival, George was stricken with Asiatic 'flu, which quickly went into double lobar pneumonia, and his condition was so critical that his near-brush with death in 1955 seemed merely a heavy cold in comparison. Dr Bettye Powell, whose office in Algiers is near George's home, was called but, as usual, not until he was well within sight of eternity. He was rushed to Flint-Goodrich Hospital, which is today the only private hospital in New Orleans devoted to the care of Negro patients. It is filling a long-felt need, and is struggling to maintain its existence under difficult circumstances. It has an open staff, and is the only hospital to which he could have gone and been assured of remaining under the care of his own physician. Dr Powell fought a valiant battle for his life and he lay for days in an oxygen tent while various specialists whom she called in consultation examined him dubiously. When at last he recovered and reported to her office for a check-up after leaving the hospital, she said: "You're one man I never thought would walk through that door."

There was no possibility, after that illness, of arranging any reciprocal tour with Ken Colyer before Spring. The officials of

the British Musician's Union, once appraised of the true situation, were most cooperative and understanding. Had they not been, the situation could have been a most difficult one.

George had signed a contract with Norman Granz's Verve record company, calling for two long-play records a year for three years. When he travelled to Chicago in the fall of 1958 for one of the sessions, his frailness seemed more marked than it had ever been; he had an indefinable quality about him of detachment from reality; the quietness for which he had always been famous seemed now the quietness of utter weariness. He weighed not more than 100 pounds, if that; the lines in the face seemed to have been carved by a cruelly sharp knife; it was skull-like with deep hollows in the cheeks and temples; the eyes were sunken behind the glasses that now gave him an almost professorial dignity. The shoulders and the thin back were as uncompromisingly straight as they had been when he had walked down St Phillip Street beside his father on their way to Bee the Rider's to get their shoes shined each Sunday morning, but it was the straightness of habit and not of strength. Yet with each year that passed his clarinet seemed to grow more and more compelling. There was more to tell with it now, and much that was happy in its story; and with the rapid decline in physical strength the urge to play became stronger, the playing itself more commanding. He worried constantly that something would happen to prevent the trip to Europe, and I am certain that he would have made the tour even if he had known without doubt that it would be his last, and that staying home might prolong his life.

There was never, no matter how great the inner weariness, how overpowering the fatigue that sapped his mind and heart, any thought of giving up. It does not take a trained economist to realize that the financial picture was a dark one. But even if he had been financially able to give up, there still would have been no thought of it, any more than there was any thought of staying home when he marched in a parade so many years before with Jeannette beside him to pick him up in case he "fell out."

Following the recording in Chicago the band moved down to Cincinnati for several week-ends at the Sinton Hotel. Cincinnati is one of their favourite cities. They were brought there first for a mammoth jazz concert by Barney Rapp, band-leader of the thirties, now an agent as well. Afterwards they played for several

private parties for the George Rosenthals, the same George Rosenthal whose splendid book *Jazzways* was one of the finest pictorial histories of traditional jazz ever published.

Wherever the band plays, their public seems to have a disproportionate number of professional people: doctors, lawyers, professors. In Cincinnati, looking over the guests crowded into the huge ballroom of the Sinton Hotel, and on later dates at the Sheraton-Gibson, I have often thought that if the county medical society had needed a quorum for an emergency meeting it would be necessary to take half the audience.

The opening night of the engagement, in the fall of 1958, the room was packed. Seated directly in front of the stand were the band's special friends, Grauman Marks, and his son, Eddie, Dr and Mrs Henry Lederer, Dr and Mrs Richard Wolf, my own guest, Mrs Jane Riordan, and many others. Dr Lederer, now a member of the faculty of the medical school at Georgetown University in Washington, D.C., was then one of the midwest's most highly respected psychiatrists; Dr Wolf is also a psychiatrist, specializing in the care of children, on the staff of the University of Cincinnati. As midnight neared, requests for "Burgundy Street" came thick and fast, and I wondered idly why George had not played it. At last he announced it, and the usual hush that precedes that number fell over the noisy room. As he played I felt myself stiffening with apprehension. For the first time I heard the notes falter, probably the first time they had faltered since the day he had recorded it, propped up in bed in his home, for Bill Russell. At times the tone which—to quote a San Francisco fan—could "cut through steel" barely reached the corners of the room. And then, the last note played, he laid his horn down and walked to the back of the stand, started to step down, then sat abruptly on its edge, his head in his hands.

I reached behind me and grabbed Dr Wolf by the hand and together we made our way to the stage, Dr Lederer close behind.

George was bent over, gasping, fighting for breath. Just as we got there I saw the beginning of the facial spasm that always accompanied an angina attack. I reached in his pocket for his nitroglycerin tablets and gave him one, and we waited till the worst of the pain had subsided.

The members of the band are always registered guests at the hotel where they are playing in Cincinnati. "We've got to get

him upstairs to his room," said Dr Lederer. "We can carry him between us."

"What do you mean, between us?" said Dr Wolf. "I could carry the little man with one arm."

"Nobody's going to carry George Lewis," gasped George Lewis. "Thank you just the same. I'll be all right in a minute."

Nor did they carry him. It was obvious that the fact that he was being carried from the stand would so upset him that it would be worse for him than walking. But they supported him between them, through the lobby, into the elevator, and up to his room.

When I arrived George was already in bed, his breathing rapid and shallow. Dr Lederer had just picked up the telephone and was calling Dr Robert Stein, a young internist and diagnostician. He was asleep when the phone rang.

"How quickly can you come down and see George Lewis?" Henry Lederer asked.

"Gosh, not till tomorrow night," said Dr Stein sleepily. "I had to cancel my reservation for tonight."

"I don't mean come down and hear him play. I mean come down and see him. He's"—Henry cocked his eyes at the sick man—"well, he's not feeling too well. It's sort of out of my line—"

"Right now!" said Robert Stein.

While we waited, those two eminent specialists nursed George Lewis as tenderly as though he were a sick child. Cold cloths on his head, gentle hands on his pulse, quiet, reassuring, friendly talk, while I sat curled in a frightened, apprehensive tangle in a chair in the corner.

Once Dr Wolf went downstairs to tell his family not to wait for him, and Henry Lederer went into the bathroom for a fresh cold compress. George looked at me and shook his head almost imperceptibly.

"Never had nothing like that before," he whispered. "Not pain at first, just like I was dead."

"You'll be all right, George," I said. "You'll be all right."

But again there was the imperceptible shake of the head, and I saw in his face what I had never seen before, acknowledgement of defeat.

I have always thought of Bob Stein's knock on the door of George's room that night as the first step George really took on

the smooth and pretty road; of that frightening attack as one of the "enormous gestures of God" that masquerade as trouble.

The next day he was admitted to the Jewish Hospital in Cincinnati, embarked on what was probably one of the most thorough diagnostic check-ups in medical history. It was the first time one had ever been done. Again anaemia was present to a dangerous degree, yet George's bag was full of powerful iron pills which he took religiously. There were four days of tests of every conceivable description. Between tests he managed to see a few innings of the World Series on the television set in his room. A bone marrow test was done. A hollow needle was placed in an artery and he was instructed to run up and down a short flight of steps so that the rate of oxygen consumption during exertion could be measured. There were X-rays and electrocardiograms and basal metabolisms and blood analyses, and there were specialists in bewildering numbers. But at the finish there was a clear-cut picture of the internal workings of George Lewis and their various maladjustments and peculiarities, and there was an immediate course of treatment.

Obviously, since his operation in 1936, the anaemia had been one of the chief causes of his troubles. The tired heart muscle, overworked since childhood, could not receive the nourishment it needed; the blood, deficient in red cells, could not perform its job of transporting oxygen as it should, nor could it put up any fight against infections. The lungs, while clear and without infection, were labouring under the handicapping ailment known as emphysema.

It was evident that all the iron he had been taking had been without effect. That he had, in fact, not even been absorbing sufficient iron from his food to keep his blood count close to normal.

Yet no doctor, during that examination or any of the previous ones he had been through outside of New Orleans, was able to report an elevated blood pressure. I told them all repeatedly of the nasal haemorrhages, the warnings he had received in New Orleans about the hypertension from which they said he was suffering.

"What he has had in the past, we can't know," they said. "We do know that there is no high blood pressure at this time. His pressure is well within normal limits."

The night after George's attack I sat at the table with a young

couple who made frequent trips to New Orleans to hear the band when they knew it was playing there, and who had travelled two hundred miles from their home to hear it that particular week-end. I was horrified when they told me: "The last time we were in New Orleans we talked with Mrs ———. She said George Lewis always seemed to have something the matter with him, but actually it was in his head. It didn't seem logical to us, just looking at him. But—like everyone else does, we believe what we wanted to believe, that he was really all right, just enjoying his ailments."

George left the hospital in four days and played the following week-end. Every other day he received massive doses of iron intramuscularly. When I asked him if he wouldn't let me have chairs put on the stand so he could sit down, for he was still weak, he looked at me in anguish. "Even if the boss told me I *had* to sit down, I couldn't. Not for long."

During the week-end he and Dr Stein rendezvoused in a back room between sets and he received another injection, returning to sit gingerly on the edge of a chair at Grauman Marks's table.

Two things were working now, at long last, to put George Lewis on the road to comparative health: his feeling, that night when he collapsed, that he had reached the end of the road; and the magic of young Dr Stein's combined skill and understanding. There was nothing too arduous, nothing too painful, for George to do if "my little doctor" said he must do it. A year later George wrote in a letter to me: "I have to write my little doctor and get a new prescription for Diamox. I really loves him. He seems like my own son, and I thanks God every day for sending him to me."

Two years would elapse, almost to the day, before George Lewis had any further attacks of angina, and those came under extraordinary circumstances of physical strain and grief.

Wherever he went after that, in the United States or overseas, he reported to a doctor—carrying with him instructions from Dr Stein—for routine injections of iron, and a general check-up.

"I've got a whole network of doctors," grins George.

One of the most marked symptoms of improvement was the way he reacted to cold weather. For years he had shivered in temperatures that would seem barely cool to most people, no matter how well insulated he was by "longies" and sweaters and scarves. He did not discard the "longies" or the sweaters and the scarves, but his amazed and wide-eyed band heard him

say to them one penetrating cold winter's night in London: "You fellows *cold*? What's the matter? Can't take it?"

This, then, was the George Lewis who sat quietly in a compartment of a British train in Euston station that January afternoon in 1959, thinking only that there had been some slight mix-up in arrangements, not knowing that within a few minutes he was to step from the train into a scene that would stand out in his memory for the rest of his life as the high point, the focus, of a long and troubled career.

eleven

"THE greatest welcome ever extended a visiting musician," the British press said.

There had been no "mix-up" in arrangements that made it necessary for the conductor to ask the men to remain on board for a few moments, at least not in the commonly accepted sense of that term. There had simply been too many people for an official greeting party to reach trainside, too many people to handle without sending for additional police, too exuberant a crowd to permit the band to alight from the train without guidance and help.

When they did leave their compartment they saw ahead of them, for as far as their eyes could reach, an exultant, laughing, shouting sea of people, yelling welcome. There were brass bands —how many I do not know—and among them shouting its most gleefully, the Ken Colyer band. All of the bands played at once; each of them played something different, and the sounds of their horns and drums rose above the noise of the crowd. Harold Pendleton, who not only arranged the tour but handled every detail of it, was trying valiantly to work out some orderly way to get the men to the cars that were waiting for them outside.

The men stood on the platform, bewildered, unable to speak. "You'll find lots of friends in England," their leader had told them, but they had never dreamed of anything like this. And one of the most amazing features of that tumultuous day was that the welcome had not been organized in any way, but had sprung

from the hearts of those who took part in it. A small notice in the papers, word passed around in the jazz clubs that the band would arrive that day, and the demonstration had snowballed.

Teenagers jitterbugged to the music of the brass bands; far off in the crowd I glimpsed the friendly smile of Jimmy Asman, then it vanished. Pendleton told me: "If you'll stay with George and follow that bobby, he'll take you to the cars, and someone will drive you to the hotel. The rest of us will take care of the men."

It took more than an hour to make our way through the crowd. Now and then there was real fear in George's eyes; he was so small, the crowd so big, and when I saw it I would touch the arm of the bobby who was walking ahead of us, and he would—in the wondrous manner of British bobbies—somehow clear a larger space without hurting anyone's feelings. There was a shout that had a different sound, one of fear, as the roof of a tin shed to which a group of youngsters had climbed for a better view collapsed. The sound of the siren of the ambulance that came to pick up a youth injured in the accident was heard long before we were able to reach the street.

There could be no going back, it was hard enough to move forward, but I kept looking, searching for the men who were following. I saw Slow Drag, looking like a elderly, completely bewildered, but happy pixie, a young girl in long black stockings marching by his side, carrying his bass fiddle, and as I looked another threw herself at him and hugged him as though he were a long-lost father. I saw Jim Robinson, stopped for a moment, tail-gating on the trombone of one of the brass bands. Kid Howard's short rotundity bobbed into view every now and then, and as quickly bobbed out. Joe Watkins waved at me reassuringly, and close to him Joe Robichaux could be seen, smiling broadly. I saw that Harold Pendleton and others had the situation in hand and concentrated on getting George through to the waiting cars. A young boy with a shock of bright red hair and more freckles than are possible on a human face stopped and picked up a cardboard match clip that fell from George's pocket when he took out his handkerchief to wipe his eyes. The boy picked it up, showed it to a friend, grinned happily, and put it in his pocket.

Once in the car, George could not speak. He lit a cigarette and his hands were trembling, his cheeks wet with tears, and he rode in silence to the hotel. It had been the greatest experience of his

life, and one of the most exhausting, emotionally and physically. Just as we stepped from the car he spoke for the first time. "Where are the mens? You sure they're all right?" Assured that they were, he went up the steps of the Imperial Hotel.

The lounge of the Imperial Hotel, in Russell Square, faces the main entrance and is clearly visible as one enters the door. There is a small bit of lobby to traverse before one enters its comfortable, conservative, typically British atmosphere, where big red plush chairs, divans, and dark wood stalwartly hold modernity at bay.

George Lewis will never forget the sight that greeted him as, battered, exhausted, emotionally dazed, he entered the door of the Imperial Hotel for the first time. Sitting on one of the lounge's divans, facing the door like a bearded, wide-smiling, immensely beneficient Buddha—was James Asman, beside him his tiny wife, Dot, her eyes flashing with happiness. Before them was spread one of the loveliest sights the civilized world knows: a proper English tea. Great steaming silver teapots, mounds of hot buttered toast, saucers of jam, plates of sandwiches and little cakes.

"Well, God bless!" murmured George as he walked toward it. "God bless!"

I knew then why Jimmy Asman had vanished from the crowd at the station.

The throngs that welcomed them everywhere they went, the importunate press, the Glasgow *Evening Citizen* that turned its entire front page over to their pictures and the story of their arrival in that city, the hundred and one evidences that, for the British jazz public, the millennium had indeed arrived, all left the men duly impressed and grateful. But the things they talked of afterwards, when they were by themselves, and after they got home, and when they were on the road together again, were the little acts of thoughtfulness, the firm hands of friendship, the homely, unforgotten kindnesses.

The reviews were, in large part, excellent; some, written by Britain's counterparts of America's "musicologists" were snobbish displays of intellectual exhibitionism; a few, obviously written by those sincerely devoted to modernism and what in Britain is called "mainstream" jazz, were written without any evident comprehension or knowledge of the music on which they were commenting; and the general, non-musical press commented at

some length on the great age of the band; "jazz grandads" was a favourite phrase. One of these was in such bad taste that I doubt any American editor would have passed it. The lead, referring to George Lewis, started: "The mouldiest fig this side of decomposition . . ." continuing with a description of George's extreme thinness and general appearance, before discussing the band—which the writer had apparently just heard of.

But there was one group of young Englishmen who learned to its sorrow that the title "grandads" as applied to the George Lewis Band was a misnomer. The members of the Ken Colyer Band, with which they made the tour, found, after three breathless weeks of trying to keep up, that certain members of the Lewis band were far closer to being teenagers than grandads. From the start there was a camaraderie and friendliness between the two groups that made the three weeks speed by like three days.

The opening concert in London was one of two to be given that same evening. Backstage there was chaos such as they had never seen, veterans though they were of backstage hassles. They had spent almost the entire day at a television studio, coming directly from there to the theatre. They had not eaten since breakfast and they were as nervous as it is possible for human beings to be without breaking up completely. George came to me at some point in the tangled proceedings and said with deep concern: "These mens—I never saw them so nervous. And they haven't eaten." His own nerves, his life-long tormentors, showed in the tautness of his face. He was not worried about the performance—he had never since youth been troubled with stage fright—but gravely worried about the men.

I left the theatre to try and find someplace where food to take back to the men could be bought, and, such being London on a Sunday evening, could find no place with so much as a glass of water available, let alone coffee or sandwiches.

When I returned to the theatre I found the Marchioness of Donegall in the hallway inside the stage entrance. She had met George on the previous trip, he had been guest of honour at one of her own weekly jazz club get-togethers at the Gore Hotel, and had sat in with her band which played there. Now she wanted, she said, to meet the men.

"You mean the starving hordes?" I said, and I mentioned their state of malnutrition. Someone came up and asked me something, and when I turned back she had vanished. Three-

quarters of an hour later my nose wrinkled at a familiar smell. For a moment I thought I was home. It was the unmistakeable smell of fresh hamburger sandwiches, with overtones of coffee, and then I saw, trudging along the corridor, Lady Donegall, a large brown-paper bag in her arms, demanding of all and sundry to be taken to the band's dressing-room.

The men ate the sandwiches and drank the coffee with almost hysterical gratitude and delight. Later, on another day when things were calmer, I learned from her that she had run from the theatre, caught a bus and ridden to a spot she knew would be open, purchased the food, and with downright uncanny luck had managed to catch an immediate return bus.

These were the things they talked of later; a proper tea, a fresh hamburger and a cup of coffee when they needed them most, a bottle produced apparently from thin air by a friend in a cold backstage dressing-room, the countless thoughtful acts and courtesies of Harold Pendleton, who accompanied the band throughout its tour; the every-day, friendly things that built a fire in their hearts for Britain that surely will never cool.

The first concert was uncertain; the nervousness was too evident; the knowledge that they were in another country, the memory of the crowd that greeted them and its expectations, the trying-too-hard in a music in which conscious effort is invariably a defect, all added up to tenseness and unsureness. Only George played as he always did, his horn a wide, deep channel from his grateful heart.

The second concert was more relaxed, and by the time they had played Southampton, Leicester, Bristol, the horns and the rhythm were driving, wailing, shouting, swinging, bringing audiences to their feet in city after city, audiences that marched around the aisles in front of the stage, or sat in spell-bound silence, and they wondered daily what the people had been thinking of who had warned them that the British were stolid and phlegmatic.

Before the trip was over every man in the band, including George, but with the exception of Joe Watkins—who conveniently waited till he got home—was stricken with the particularly vicious influenza virus that raged in Britain and Europe that year. Their last concert, a double engagement like their first, was played in London with the Chris Barber Band, and it was played by men whose average temperature, I would guess, was

not less than 102 degrees Fahrenheit. Not one of them, except Watkins, could get through a sentence without a paroxysm of coughing, yet they managed somehow to play with a fire and drive that had to be heard to be credited.

"It must," sniffled Kid Howard miserably between sets when someone complimented them, "be the fever."

On the fifth of February the band left by air for Copenhagen, No one has ever written of Denmark and really done it justice. But George Lewis knew of its people and its charm only by hearsay. He was going now to a completely strange country. In England there had been a common language, and many common customs. And no one from New Orleans feels away from home in France. But this was a strange, cold, northern country, it was part of Scandinavia, of which he knew very little. What would it be like? What would the people be like? Would they welcome him and his "mens" as they had in England? Would they know what the horns and the drums and the rhythm were saying when they stood there on the platforms before them, playing their music? He did not know.

The plane was diverted from Copenhagen because of fog, and grounded in Hamburg. Eventually it was necessary to take an overnight train, a long, uncomfortable journey for men weakened and still half-sick from influenza. The beds in the trains were unbelievably narrow and hard, the rooms tiny, cramped, and cold. Down the corridor, through an open door, a voice croaked: "Man, I'd give all I got for a slug of Old Crow, a hot bath, and my own bed." Before my own door closed I called out a loud "Amen!" and heard an answering laugh.

The train arrived in Copenhagen early in the morning, and the station seemed dreary and dark. The band alighted wearily, feeling cold, unkempt, unwashed, and unshaven. And then Denmark took over. One of the men gasped, "My God! What they got *on*?" George, half-sick and near exhaustion, as close to danger physically as he had been at any time since that night in Cincinnati when he had thought "this is it," smiled in awed and happy unbelief.

Just ahead was a band of bearded Vikings in traditional costume, horned helmets, capes and doublets, leather leggings laced with thongs, wide jewel-studded belts. The Danes show great talent in improvisation in music, and an equal talent in the

improvisation of beards. Each was different. The predominant colour was red.

Instead of the round shields and short heavy swords of the Viking warriors of old they carried instruments: trumpet, trombone, clarinet, drums, banjo. Until one has seen a band of bearded Vikings in traditional costume wailing a blues from the heart of the deep South, going from the blues to a New Orleans march, and from the march to a spiritual without stopping for breath, one has not plumbed the depths of astonishment.

They were the musicians with which the Lewis group was to tour Denmark, and Sweden—Papa Bue's Viking Jazz Band. In Denmark most band leaders seem to be called "Papa," and it was weeks before I found out that Papa Bue's full name was Arne Bue Jensen.

The Danes have a quality of brooding goodness, of elfin mischief, of banked fires just beneath the surface, and towards tiny George Lewis, Papa Bue and his men developed the fierce tenderness and jealous protectiveness of a band of watchdogs told to guard the baby they love. There was Papa, short, square, young, quick-spoken, quick-moving, with bright blue eyes that always seemed to hide an inner sadness; big, blue-eyed, baby-faced Finn Hansen, whose trumpet was so powerful he had to be moved progressively farther away from the microphone during a recording session. There was handsome Jorgen Svarre, the clarinettist, black-bearded and debonair; the banjoist, a little taller, pale, blond, and who said to me: This is the happiest month of my life." I asked him why and his reply was: "Because this month I have my first baby, and this month I play with George Lewis."

There was huge, red-bearded, fey Mogens Seidelin who played bass fiddle with incredible power and dexterity; and there was Ib Lindschow, the drummer, cheeks as hollow as George's, the quietest of them all, looking startlingly like Abraham Lincoln.

The tour was handled by Andy Dyrup and Karl Knudsen of the Storyville Record Company of Denmark, and we were guided through the entire trip by Henry Brieling, at that time connected with the same company. It seemed at times as though there wasn't a home or a heart in all of Denmark that was not open to receive this frail man and his companions who had travelled such a long and difficult road to reach them.

In a city in the southern part of the country, which had taken

most of the day to reach by trains and ferries, the band arrived just as daylight was fading. The hall where they were to play was just two blocks from the station. Just ahead, as they stepped from the train, was a crowd of laughing, singing young people, calling greetings as they converged on the station, bearing great, old-fashioned torches whose flaring flames cast flickering lights and shadows on the snow. When they reached the station they surrounded the band and the men walked with flaming torches behind, before and round them, through the snowy roadway to the hall.

In Sweden the greetings were as warm, though the crowds were more unruly, and, at the Konserthuset in Stockholm, George was trapped for an hour after the performance before it was felt safe to let him out and, surrounded by husky friends, make his way to the waiting car. Just as the car started to leave a young boy thrust a picture through the window, a black and white drawing of an Albert system clarinet, and George started to autograph it hastily. "No, no!" cried the boy. "No! It is for you, Jorge; I make it just for you!" George keeps it still, the work of a teenage boy in far-off Sweden, who made it just for him.

We were not prepared for the warmth of the welcomes in Sweden, the size of the crowds, for we had been solemnly warned not to expect the same receptions as Britain and Denmark had offered. Sweden, the men were told, was strictly a cool country, both as far as weather was concerned, and as far as jazz was concerned. Again, someone seems to have made a mistake, because from the day the band landed in Stockholm, and the crowd on the upper balcony of the airport terminal building started waving flags inscribed "Long Live George Lewis," and young bands played lustily just beyond the customs barrier, and special personnel had to be called on to get the men through to the car, it was very evident that the Swedish youth was as traditionally minded as that of any country in which the band had played.

The band went to Baden-Baden, in West Germany, when the tour was completed. Jim Robinson, when he stepped from the airport terminal building in Stuttgart, made a deep obeisance to something far away in the sky. It was the sun, the blessed sun. They had not seen it for weeks, except for a few times when it feebly struggled through cold mist or fog. It shone now, warm and bright, and as one man the band began shedding scarves and overcoats.

At Baden-Baden they were greeted by Joachim Berendt, who was to present them in a half-hour live television show a week later. Again, someone had misinformed us. Berendt, we had been told, was definitely a modernist, with little use for traditional jazz. If this was true—and, of course, we knew it was not—he hid it well. The band rehearsed for a week for the show, and between shots sat on the studio steps and soaked up the sun like salamanders. The precision, the perfectionism, that mark a German television production were not easy for them. It is not easy to play unrestrainedly and without inhibition the kind of music which they had played all their lives when bars must be counted for the next move, when one's feet are rigidly imprisoned by chalk lines, and when almost every note is a cue for some stage direction. But Berendt was patient; he was gracious and hospitable and genuinely friendly. He took the men on trips through the Black Forest, to country inns for lunch, and showed throughout a thorough appreciation of the music and—"modernist" though he might be—a real knowledge of the musicianship, technique, and skill of the men who played it. In the fall of 1960, in California, Joachim Berendt told me that he is planning a documentary film on the history of jazz, and that the film itself will be the life story of George Lewis.

It was the last stop on the tour for the men, but one incident that occurred the night before they left I shall remember always. It was an argument conducted with considerable force. It concerned the problem of which man should make the presentation to Bill Russell of a splendid leather brief-case they had bought for him. Without Bill Russell's assistance on the American side of the Atlantic several of the men might not have made the trip. He had spent many weeks tracking down birth certificates and baptismal certificates, or individuals who could swear that certain members of the band had been born at all, for the information needed before passports would be issued. George is not alone in his opinion that Bill Russell is a "livin' saint." There is not a man in his band,—in fact, not an old-time Negro musician in New Orleans,—who does not share his feeling. It is Bill Russell, not the Orleanians, who comes to the rescue in illness and destitution; Bill Russell who spends days and weeks and months on behalf of the music of that city, and of its exponents. I never learned who won the argument, and I have never wanted to ask for fear of hurting the ones who lost. I do

know that when the presentation was made, Bill Russell's eyes filled with tears.

The men flew home, except Slow Drag and Joe Watkins, who returned on the *Carinthia,* the same ship on which they had sailed to England, and on this trip Slow Drag was overwhelmed to find at his table one night a large, many-candled birthday cake.

Three weeks remained for George in Germany, playing a series of concerts for the German Jazz Federation with the Papa Bue Band and the Ken Colyer Band. Karl Lyrmann, head of the Federation, handled the tour, and won his way to George's heart immediately, They pub-crawled together—George almost foundering on orange juice and coffee—ate shash-lik together, found time to dine at a dozen of Dusseldorf's wonderful restaurants. When George returned the following year he could not tell which of his adopted foreign cities he loved the most: Manchester, London, Copenhagen, or Dusseldorf.

At George's first concert in the vast Sportspalast in Berlin, an estimated seven thousand five hundred people thronged to hear him. Later he was told that fifteen hundred of those had made their way over on the subway from East Berlin. During the performance I slipped through a door near the stage and saw the auditorium for the first time, and gasped at what I saw. The Sportspalast is huge, and so arranged that the audience is seated in the centre, and on rising tiers on all four sides, with the stage centred in one wall, and more tiers of seats above the stage. If there were empty seats, I could not see them, but I saw young people seated on the ramps that led to the upper balconies.

Police were everywhere, in peaked caps, black jackboots, long greatcoats, and a shiver ran down my spine. There, on that stage, Hitler had declared total war on civilization. From the hall before me the "Heils" had been roared with deafening force, and its seats had once been filled with thousands hypnotized by a frenetic little man who had shouted and ranted and raved, defying a world that had taken little heed until it was too late, and the life we treasure close to destruction. Then the shiver gave way to warmth. Here, tonight, where Adolf Hitler had once screamed defiance and destruction, a young band from Great Britain, and a young band from Denmark, and a 59-year-old American Negro were "making music"—the American's music—and as the waves of applause that greeted George at the end of a number rolled up

to me I felt only thankfulness, and a deep inner prayer that, while the other had passed away, this comradeship, this sharing of a common love and understanding, would never pass away. That each note that was played would be a tiny nail in the pin-toe coffin of hatred and war.

It seemed an unbelievable thing, when I returned to the United States, to pick up a month-old issue of a national magazine, *Coronet,* and read there an article on jazz by a man whose knowledge of its origins must have been gathered from a columnist who, in 1956, referred to George Lewis's "decade as a leader." The article included, among pictures of other musicians, a picture of George when he was working on the docks of New Orleans. It was taken by George Rosenthal, and used in his book "Jazz-ways." It is a picture filled with deep sadness, and shows George in singlet and dock-worker's cap, pushing a hand truck loaded with bags of coffee on the wharf that was "hell on a man's legs." In his face are complete weariness, sorrow, and resignation; its lines are bitter-deep, while the muscles of the shoulders and arms stand out in startling contrast to the near-emaciation of his frame. He was identified in the article merely as one of the early veterans of New Orleans jazz. It was definitely past tense. No one reading the article would dream that he was blowing a clarinet today; would not, in fact, be able to tell whether he was alive or dead.

The day that article appeared on the stands was the day George groped his way from the stage of the Sportspalast, half-blinded by tears, while seventy-five hundred people stood and roared for his return.

Although the Sportspalast is large, there is no backstage area, only a small space behind the curtains at the back of the stage. I stayed there the remainder of the concert that night, and through a crack in the curtains I could see George, slightly in front of the Bue band, his back uncompromisingly straight, and the horn at his lips was saying, as it had so many years ago when he played his first date in a little hall in Mandeville, "Hear me! Hear me! I got a story to tell tonight! I got a song to sing tonight!"

Perhaps because I was as tired as I ever remember being, my mind played tricks on my eyes. Standing beside George I saw the spare, bent figure of a woman in her ninety-sixth year, and I knew that just before he had left home she had laid her graceful black hands on his forehead and said: "Offer it to God, son. He'll help you." I saw the lithe, brown figure of a laughing eight-

year-old girl picking flowers by a stream in Senegal to weave into garlands for her mother—garlands that were never finished. I saw a tiny, gentle, crippled black man, sitting long hours night after night, sewing clothes for his children by the light of an oil lamp. I saw his son, tall, straight, handsome, with long black moustache half-hiding a deformed jaw, standing on the porch of a little cabin in Mandeville for half the night, listening to his boy play in a hall next door. I saw a kindly, Creole-speaking black woman, turning and patting her pralines and *Tante Betsies* on a spotless kitchen table, lining them up on a gleaming tray for her little daughter and son to sell on the streets the next day.

And I saw a thin, nervous, ecstatic little brown boy, wide-eyed with happiness, listening to the music, his thin, long-fingered hands clapping softly—pat-pat pat-pat pat-pat—in double time to the beat as the brasses and the reeds "called the chil'ren in." Through a crack in the curtain in front of me I could see the rhythmic flexing of a man's knee, just as it had flexed so long ago when he was a boy, to the beat of a band on the balcony of Hopes Hall, when to play on that balcony seemed the greatest height a musician could attain.

twelve

EARLY in the morning, in a little house on De Armas Street in Algiers, just across the river from New Orleans, a woman ninety-six years old wakened, long before day. She dressed, and in soft house slippers shuff-shuffed quietly into the kitchen. Once tall and straight, she was bent now and her hands shook with the tremor of age. In the kitchen she made coffee, and sat quietly drinking it, waiting. Just at daybreak she heard her son cough, the quick, involuntary cough of a steady smoker. She poured coffee into a cup she had set out on the table, sweetened it heavily, and took it to him as he lay, only half-awake, in bed. The cup rattled in the saucer in her shaking hand, but her voice was as steady and clear and strong as it had been when she was a young woman; clear and strong and sweetly high, the words clipped, the Creole accent giving it a singing quality.

"Son," she said. "Son, drink your coffee while it's hot. It will help your cough. It's cold this morning. Real cold. This will warm you."

She had done the same thing every morning since she had come to live with her son in 1958, although for a year afterwards she clung to a semblance of independence by keeping the little room on St Phillip Street where she had lived so many years.

On those early mornings her son wanted to sleep. From childhood he had kept late hours, and for many years, since he had given up day work, he had slept late.

"I wanted to sleep so bad," he said. "And I'd get so put out with myself for coughing, but I couldn't help it. It would be just a little cough and I'd only be half-awake but my mother would hear it and right away I'd hear the cup rattling in the saucer, and her walking into the room. But I couldn't say anything to her. Not for the world. It meant so much to her, bringing me that coffee in the morning. I knew I wouldn't be able to go back to sleep but I just figured I'd slip off in the afternoon and go in and get me a nap to make up for it."

After Jeannette's death George had married again, but the marriage had been short-lived. He had felt unable to cope with the problem of being forced to earn a living away from home and the care of a teenaged daughter and an aged mother. As many others have done, and as others will continue to do as long as human nature remains human nature, he had tried to cure loneliness and grief by seeking companionship and someone to share responsibility. His wife was ten years older than he, and while there was no bitterness or hard feelings, the marriage ended abruptly. After that Alice Zeno moved to Algiers.

"My boy needs someone to take care of him," she said, and never realized the positions were reversed.

At night when Shirley was out with friends—she was "going steady" now with a schoolmate Gilbert Watkins, whom she had known since they were both in grammar school—Alice would sit before the television set, fighting sleep. For many years she had gone to bed at sundown, and awakened before daybreak. Adjustment was difficult.

"Ma," her son would say. "Look, Ma, go to bed. Please. I'm all right."

"I'm not sleepy, son. And I'm not going to leave you all alone.

When you get ready to go to bed I'll fix your hot drink, and then I'll go to bed."

"Most of the time I'd tell her okay, okay, I was ready to go to bed. Then she'd shuff-shuff into the kitchen and fix me some hot soup or something and I'd make like I was going to bed. Then when I knew she was asleep I'd go back out and finish watching television till I really got sleepy. I couldn't ever let her think I didn't need the little things she did for me, the things that made her feel she was still taking care of me, still helping."

Alice thanked her God each day those years for the new strength, the new health, her son showed in every move and action. He weighed only 98 pounds, but doctors showed no concern at this. It was better, they said, than having extra pounds for the heart to supply with blood. It was not hard, watching him now, to imagine the cat-quick young man who had ranged the streets of the French Quarter in the jobless days of the thirties, seeking for his music, finding it, playing it. The eyes were still deeply set, the face still lined, skull-like, hollowed, but the lines did not seem so cruelly deep. The air of detachment was gone, the aura of weariness he had carried with him for years, try as he would to disguise it. His back was as arrow-straight as ever under the well-tailored dinner jackets he wore on stage, or the business suits he wore on the street. He smiled more quickly, and laughed more readily, but the years had brought no relaxation of the taut and apprehensive nervous system, and the nerves lay only skin deep, stirring uneasily at the slightest signal from the outer world that something—however minor—was amiss.

He had not touched alcohol in any form since shortly after his Cincinnati illness. He even carried his teetotalism to the extreme of refusing the crêpes suzettes which the head waiters of the various Cunard liners on which he travelled pressed upon him, though he had fond memories of those made specially for him on the *Mauretania.*

"When I quit," says George, "I quit."

Almost a year to the day from the time he returned to New Orleans after the trip to England and Europe with his band, he went back to Europe to travel through Denmark and Scandinavia again with the Papa Bue band; to play in Germany with the Acker Bilk band from England, and to play concerts in Switzerland with Ken Colyer. The Bilk band was the third British traditional band with which he had played, the first whose

leader was a clarinettist. Acker's earliest influence had been the playing of George Lewis. George's European trips were arranged by a London agent, Lyn Dutton, who had guided the Colyer and Barber bands to success, and under whose management the Bilk band was rapidly becoming the top box-office draw in England and the continent. Acker is a country boy, Somerset born and raised. He learned to play clarinet when he was in the army, stationed in Egypt. He was spending some time in the army prison for falling asleep when he should most definitely have been awake, and he asked for a clarinet to pass the time. He practised five hours daily, and says: "I recommend learning the clarinet in gaol. Especially in Egypt." At one time during this trip there was a business discussion with the representative of a German record company about making a single record of George and Acker in a clarinet duet, with only rhythm accompaniment.

"Anything goes with me," said Acker. "Just let me follow that bloody great lead—that's all I ask."

It was on this trip George became known by the affectionate title given him in Denmark. At the end of each performance he always gave a brief "thank you talk," ending it, for the benefit of those who did not understand English, with the one Danish expression he could be sure of pronouncing correctly—"*tuzen tak*."

He closed one concert, after his "thousand thanks," by saying "You been mighty good to me in this wonderful country. It's like home to me now, and I feel like I'm one of you—just a sun-burned Dane."

The Bue boys roared with delight and hugged him, Finn picked him off his feet and swung him in a circle, and the phrase spread until today George is, to his friends in Denmark, their "sun-burned Dane."

The last few concerts of that tour George played with Muggsy Spanier, the French-Irish boy from Chicago with the out-sized cornet and the golden tone, one of those who had made jazz history in the twenties with the "Austin High gang" in Chicago. On the final concert in Essen, Muggsy and George were joined by Milt Mezzrow, who had been with Muggsy during those years. Bilk had returned to England, and Bue was flown in from Denmark. Spanier, Mezzrow, Lewis, a Danish band and a young band from Holland—and four thousand people in the auditorium

shouted their testimony that jazz as-it-was-in-the-beginning was far from dead.

While we were in Copenhagen on that trip I picked up and glanced through a book in that city's biggest department store, a book published in England by a jazz modernist. In it I read that George Lewis's history fascinated many, but that his tone "maddened" many others. The Danes are a tolerant, live-and-let-live people, and no one even stared when I hooted aloud with laughter. There was too much testimony on the record now from critics of all schools for the remark to be taken seriously. There is, of course, always the possibility that some have been "maddened" by frustration, but I do not believe—nor can I find anyone else who does—that the George Lewis tone ever "maddened" anyone. Rather, in my opinion, it is the man himself who has maddened some.

To those of certain modern schools of thought in music, it must seem unfair that a man should bring to himself the acclaim, the appreciation, the love of hundreds of thousands, when he is an unschooled, self-taught musician. Not right that without the aid of big-time agencies, high-pressure press agents, of television and radio exploitation, a tiny, quiet, gentle, little man from New Orleans should capture the ears and hearts of so many; something wrong when writers, latter-day critics, and "musicologists" find themselves ignored by the public they seek to influence; and it must seem grossly unfair that such a large segment of that public should give to a man whose music they deride as "primitive" and "limited" the acclaim that should be going to those whose music their pens define as the end-all and be-all of jazz. And definitely not fair, they must cry within themselves, that the word "jazz," which they bestow so freely on music impossible to play without prior composition and meticulous arrangement, should come to life again for what it is in the person of a little man they would much prefer to forget. And would, most certainly, prefer to have the public forget. He and his like are "conjure men," calling up ghosts, and some of those who once recognized the music for what it is, and later scoffed for the prestige the scoffing could bring them, must recognize that of these ghosts there is one named "intellectual integrity."

To George none of it makes any difference. As they always have, most of the praise and all of the belittling pass over him unheeded. But I can think of three comments that reached deep

into his heart and brought a smile of real happiness to his face.

The first was from an old man, an Alabama Negro who had spent most of his life in New Orleans, and was living, when I met him and his wife, in San Francisco. They called him Cy, and I think his last name was Evans. Had he known George Lewis in New Orleans, I asked? Had he ever heard him play in the early days?

"Shucks," he said. "I know him, leastways to speak to, and I sure heard him play. First time I heard him play was a hot day, and I was out of work, standing under a tree in the shade. Then I heard a parade coming, around the corner from where I was at. And I could hear this clarinet, high and sweet and sad. Then all of a sudden it would take off and there wouldn't be nothing sweet about it all, not at all. It was shouting, and it was wailing. I mean it was talking to the Lord if ever I heard the Lord talked to. Then it would get real soft again, like someone crying. Then the band turned the corner and I could hear it better, but you know something? Danged if I could *see* the guy that was playing it. Then the band got closer and I could see him. Little bit of a kid, he was, seemed like. There he was, not much bigger than that horn he was playing. But by the time they got up to where I was at he had me crying, and he had me shouting, and he was marching just as straight and tall and solemn, this kid was. Just before he took off on his horn real big he'd put his head on one side just a little, and then—I'm telling you—he was really telling 'em about it. I found out later he was George Lewis, when I asked around. Did I ever hear George Lewis play? You listen to an old man, miss, an old man that grew up with the music. When a spindle-shanked kid, playing a horn most as big as he is, can get me to shouting and crying and talking back to him while he's playing—child, that man's a *real* musician."

The second comment also came from one of his own people, one of the darlings of today's avant-gardists, a "way out" musician, Ornette Coleman. The music Coleman plays, and the music Lewis plays, are as far apart as music can get, yet each man recognizes in the other the same dedication. Listening to Coleman, Lewis said: "That man's playing it right. He's playing what he feels. I don't know much about his kind of music, but I know that."

Coleman was with the Modern Jazz Quartet at the 1959 Monterey Jazz Festival, in which Lewis also played. Afterwards,

backstage, he came up to Lewis and said: "Thanks, man. That was beautiful. That was just plain beautiful." In 1960 Coleman led his own group at the Festival, and George was in Monterey resting after an illness. In the lobby of the San Carlos Hotel, where both men were staying, Coleman turned to several other musicians, all of whom were waiting, as he was, for the airport limousine. Lewis had just come up to them.

"Any of you all hear George Lewis last year?" he asked. Some had, and some had not been there. He turned to George. "Sure wish I could have heard you again," he said. Then to the others: "You all missed something beautiful if you didn't hear him. I mean beautiful. When he took off on that clarinet it seemed like that whole big place took fire. You talk about tone!" And he fell back again on the only adjective he seemed to find adequate: "It sure was beautiful."

And the third came from a young English-speaking Danish girl, who stood beside me in the wings of a concert hall in Denmark during the first part of a concert. She did not speak after the music started, and I felt that if I spoke to her she would not hear me.

George played "Burgundy Street Blues" and in the after-hush that followed it she turned to me, and her eyes were moist and wide.

"He plays as the birds sing," she whispered.

thirteen

GEORGE did not return home until early June, a few days before his mother's birthday. Shirley and Gilbert had been married now for some time, and a baby was expected in the fall. They were living at the little house on De Armas Street.

A few weeks after his return I talked with Alice Zeno on the telephone. "My boy looks so well," she said to me. "Sometimes I think he's spoiled, but he was the only one I had." And then the happy words that I cannot forget, high, clear, strong, and somehow lilting: "I never worry about him now. I know now he is all right when he is gone."

Three weeks later another blood clot crippled George, and he was ordered to remain off his feet for two weeks. He was in great pain, and the leg was swollen and tender. Three days after the blood clot occurred Alice Zeno fell as she tried to get out of bed early one morning. She could not get up, and her cries wakened George. The doctor said that in all probability there was a cracked rib, but that rest and quiet, and something to relieve the pain, constituted the best treatment, for in that oppressive heat adhesive strapping would be torture.

But Alice did not rally. Each day she became weaker, and a few days after the fall had a stroke. Just as she had fought off illness and poverty and despair in her youth, and had refused to acknowledge old age as her conqueror, she now held death at the length of her spirit's sword.

George sent Shirley, who was only a matter of weeks from delivery, to stay at her mother-in-law's, for he felt that the day and night strain of her grandmother's illness would be too much for her, but she came to his house each day to help him. Despite the blood clot in his leg, and the doctor's admonishments to remain off his feet, he took over the full burden of Alice's care. Eventually the lack of sleep, the strain of lifting and the constant waiting on her, the worry, brought back the symptoms he had been free of for years. Angina pectoris attacks again tortured him, his heart refused to keep up with the demands he made upon his body, and the old familiar swelling of the ankles returned, as well as the shortness of breath and sick exhaustion. Yet he would not leave her; would not undress at night and go to bed; undressed only to shower and change, and then resume his care of her.

He wrote me one letter that still, in retrospect, cuts like a knife. "I don't think I can go on much longer," he said. "I asks God to help me and give me strength. You ask Him, too, please."

After the stroke the doctor said that Alice could only live another forty-eight hours at the most. She lived ten days, rallying time and again, sometimes recognizing her son, sometimes roaming in her childhood, speaking often in French and Creole.

A kindly neighbour came in to help whenever she could, and one afternoon when she and George were out of Alice's room, they heard her stirring. She had seemed to be in a coma, but when they rushed to the door they found her sitting upright. She spoke clearly, definitely, without a tremor.

"My boy and I," said Alice, "are going on a vacation. We're going away on a long trip, just my boy and I, and I've got to start packing. We're going on a long vacation."

When they managed to get her back on her pillows again, she looked at her son with full recognition, then her eyes filled with tears and she turned her head away, as though at last she realized that the long vacation she had dreamed of taking with her son, when he was a boy and she was a sick, exhausted woman, would never materialize; that when she took the trip that lay ahead of her, she must leave him behind.

She did not speak again, but she continued to fight.

"Early one morning, about four o'clock, I saw she was going," said her son. "She'd fought so hard, she'd been through so much. I knelt down right beside her and I said a prayer, and I took hold of her hand, and then I said: 'You're so tired, ma. Your train's waiting for you to take you home to rest. Take your train, ma, and let it take you home to rest."

She turned her face to him, sighed, and was gone.

Not until three weeks later, when he came to California to rest and recuperate, did I learn how truly serious his own condition had been. At the requiem Mass, that solemn ritual that had sent Zaier from the world, that had commended Urania to the saints she believed in so implicitly, that levels each soul, unnamed, anonymous, to the role of suppliant, he had almost lost consciousness when a vicious attack of angina tore at him mercilessly; yet, with Shirley supporting him, he had gone to the cemetery and stood watching as the body of one of the world's great women was laid in the vault beside that of his wife, Jeannette.

In California, resting constantly, he regained something of his strength; the angina attacks vanished, the swelling of the ankles diminished until it finally disappeared just before he left for a week-end in Cincinnati and a recording date.

There were new faces in the band on that trip. Kid Howard had been very ill for almost two years; Big Jim, past sixty-six, and Slow Drag, past seventy-five, no longer wanted to take road trips; only Joe Watkins and Joe Robichaux belonged to the group who had travelled overseas together. Instead there was Andrew Anderson, a veteran of the Papa Celestin band, on trumpet; Waldren Joseph, Jr., a young, powerful trombonist, with a fiery musical imagination, and Placide Adams on bass.

One of the band's friends said to me, at the close of the first

performance: "George has passed the toughest test for a musician. He's shown that he can bring together under his leadership new faces and talents—and still come up with one of the greatest sounds in traditional jazz."

Grief for his mother was still constant, but the only outward signs were an even deeper quietude, a sort of stoic numbness. He ate scarcely anything; coffee, a sandwich and some orange juice were his quota for twenty-four hours. At last, worried that he would not be able to keep going on such an unrealistic diet, I bought a bottle of high-potency vitamin tablets to supplement it, and gave them to him.

He thanked me, and put them in his pocket, then he turned and said: "I didn't need them. I got some left. There's nothing wrong with me, except I just misses that little old lady, that's all. I misses her so bad." For the first time healing tears rolled down his cheeks.

"Nobody needs me now," he said.

When George Lewis receives a letter today demanding detailed reports about his general health, and an honest recountal of any untoward symptoms—for referral to Dr Stein—a letter much like the following usually comes in reply:

"I wish you could see my little man. You'd love him like I do. Fifteen and a half pounds now and blowing for a new tooth. He knows his grandda most as good as he does his mamma, and every morning he licks my coffee spoon. Yesterday he turned his little fat self over and started to crawl . . ."

Then, after the signature: "P.S. I feel O.K."

Shirley's husband is in the Army, and Shirley and David Michael Watkins, aged ten months, are in full command of the 1961 Lewis household. For those who postulate the existence of some great Plan that rules the life of every human, there is justification in the life of George Lewis, and the kindest provision of that Plan would seem to be that, when the greatest loss he had ever known left him shaken and grief-stricken, a new life should have come along to make it impossible for him to say, as he had after Alice Zeno died: "Nobody needs me now."

In the fall of 1961 George Lewis will return to Europe (he would insist that I add, as he always does, "if God spares") and the warmth and love and appreciation of the thousands who are waiting to hear him again. Security and even prosperity are still around the bend of the smooth and pretty road of his dream,

still out of sight, but it would be impossible to say that George Lewis, who has overcome so much and travelled so far, will not round that bend.

Once again I will hear, in the accents of the Briton, the Dane, the German, the Swede, the words: "He is not only a great musician, he is a great man."

Once again I will hear the question, many times over, as I heard it in New York from Omer Simeon when he sat beside me at a table in the Paramount Restaurant: "*Where* does that tone come from!"

If I had given the answer I might have given to Omer, he would have understood; so would any other jazz man, traditional or modern, who knows that true music comes from the life experiences a man remembers in his heart. The experiences are different, and the story each man has to tell is different, but unless a man's music tells that story in whatever idiom he chooses to relate it, he cannot call his music jazz. That is why I say on behalf of all jazz musicians that there can be no assessment by the intellect alone of the worth of a jazz man's playing. Those who cannot bring to it more than their intellects had best leave it alone, and remain with symphonies and chamber music, big bands and swing, or the counterfeit coin of commercialism. For the meaning of life to any man cannot be defined by the intellect alone.

"Where does George's tone come from?" I might have replied to Omer. "It comes from where, please God, no jazz man's tone will ever come again, but it comes from it in beauty. It comes from the sound in a boy's ears of his mother's crying because she has no money for a communion party for him. It comes from the freezing horror in a child's heart as he runs to his mother's arms, covered with filth thrown at him by a man who did not like the colour of his skin. It comes from the memory of trembling hands and shaking legs as a little boy barred a door in a tiny French Quarter apartment, blood on his head from the rocks of a mob of white boys. It comes from the sound of the horns on the balcony of Hopes Hall, and the strength of the yearning in a boy's heart to tell his story as they were telling theirs. It comes from the grief of a young man, standing on a street corner, watching as his baby's body was placed in a vault in a cheap pine coffin. It comes from the strength within him, that kept him blowing, night after night, half dead with sickness

and exhaustion. It comes from the sound of women weeping at a graveside and in a funeral service. It comes from the shouting, leaping, happy antics of the children in the second line, following the horns, as the children of Hamelin followed the Pied Piper. It comes from the sensitiveness within him, that flinches from a hurt and will not let him hurt another. It comes from many things and it tells of many things, and the greatest of the things of which it tells are the sorrows of his people, the triumphs of his race, and his faith in God. Where else could it come from? Where else?"

I will hear, too, from time to time, from those who do not know the music, the question: "Who is George Lewis?"

It would be simple to answer: "He is a frail, gentle, quiet little man who practises witchery on a clarinet, transmuting into music with clear and beautiful simplicity the joys and sorrows, grief and laughter, of the human heart; the eternal hope and faith and triumph of his people."

It would not be an adequate reply. To it must be added something I have written before: that George Lewis is a man who lives close to the God in Whom he believes; a man who said, without embarrassment and in all sincerity, at the end of an arduous overseas trip on which illness and pain were his intermittent companions: "Sure, I'm tired. But I made it. I guess it's because I never forget what my mother told me when I was just a little boy. 'Offer it to God, son. He'll help you.' Every time I go out on one of these big stages I remembers it, and then I ask God to stay with me and keep me playing my very best for these people who have been so good to me."

And then he added:

"I know He always hears me."

THE END